catch up with the sun

Dedicated to all the Gumby's out there; those that escaped the dog-meat yards, and those that didn't.

# catch up with the sun

### HEIDI DOUGLAS

FINCH PUBLISHING
SYDNEY

Catch Up With the Sun
First published in 2012 in Australia and New Zealand by Finch Publishing Pty Limited, ABN
49 057 285 248, Suite 2207, 4 Daydream Street, Warriewood, NSW, 2102, Australia.

14 13 12   8 7 6 5 4 3 2 1

The National Library of Australia Cataloguing-in-Publication entry:
Douglas, Heidi.
Catch up with the sun / Heidi Douglas.
9781921462368 (pbk.)
Douglas, Heidi--Travel.
Women travelers--Australia--Biography.
Travelers' writings, Australian.
Australia--Description and travel.
910.4082

Edited by Karen Gee
Editorial assistance by Tricia Cortez
Text typeset in Garamond by J&M Typesetting
Cover design by Peter Long
Cover image supplied by Heidi Douglas
Printed by Griffin Press

Follow Heidi's adventures at **www.catchupwiththesun.com.au**.
**Finch titles** can be viewed and purchased at **www.finch.com.au**

# Contents

# The Victorian leg

SA

VIC

NSW

• Balranald    • Hay

• Moulamein

• Deniliquin

⌂ 'Brigadoon'

• Echuca

2 inches of rain

Mt Terrible
— snow

Piglet
went lame

Marysville    Mt Howitt

MELBOURNE

Healesville

GEELONG

• Dargo

Sale

Total fire ban
with northerly
winds

Bass Strait

# The New South Wales leg

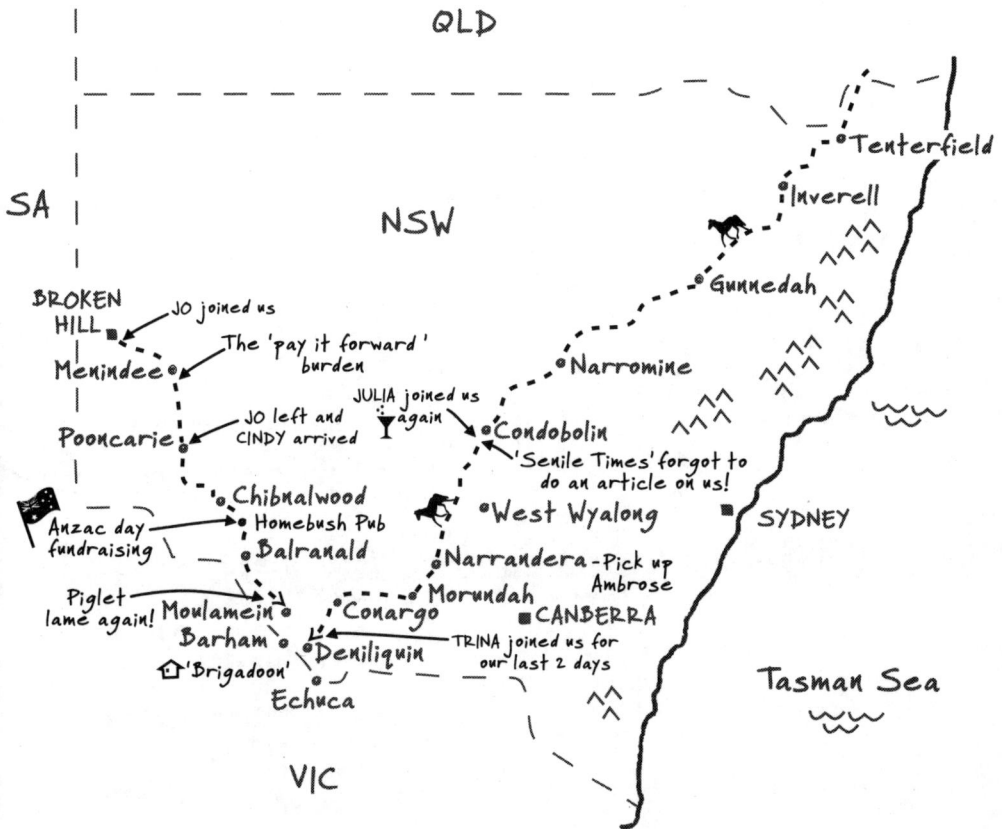

QLD

SA

NSW

BROKEN HILL

JO joined us

The 'pay it forward' burden

Menindee

JULIA joined us again

JO left and CINDY arrived

Pooncarie

Condobolin

'Senile Times' forgot to do an article on us!

Narromine

Gunnedah

Inverell

Tenterfield

Chibnalwood

Anzac day fundraising

Homebush Pub

Dalranald

West Wyalong

SYDNEY

Piglet lame again!

Moulamein

Conargo

Narrandera - Pick up Ambrose

Morundah

Barham

Deniliquin

CANBERRA

TRINA joined us for our last 2 days

'Brigadoon'

Echuca

Tasman Sea

VIC

# The Queensland leg

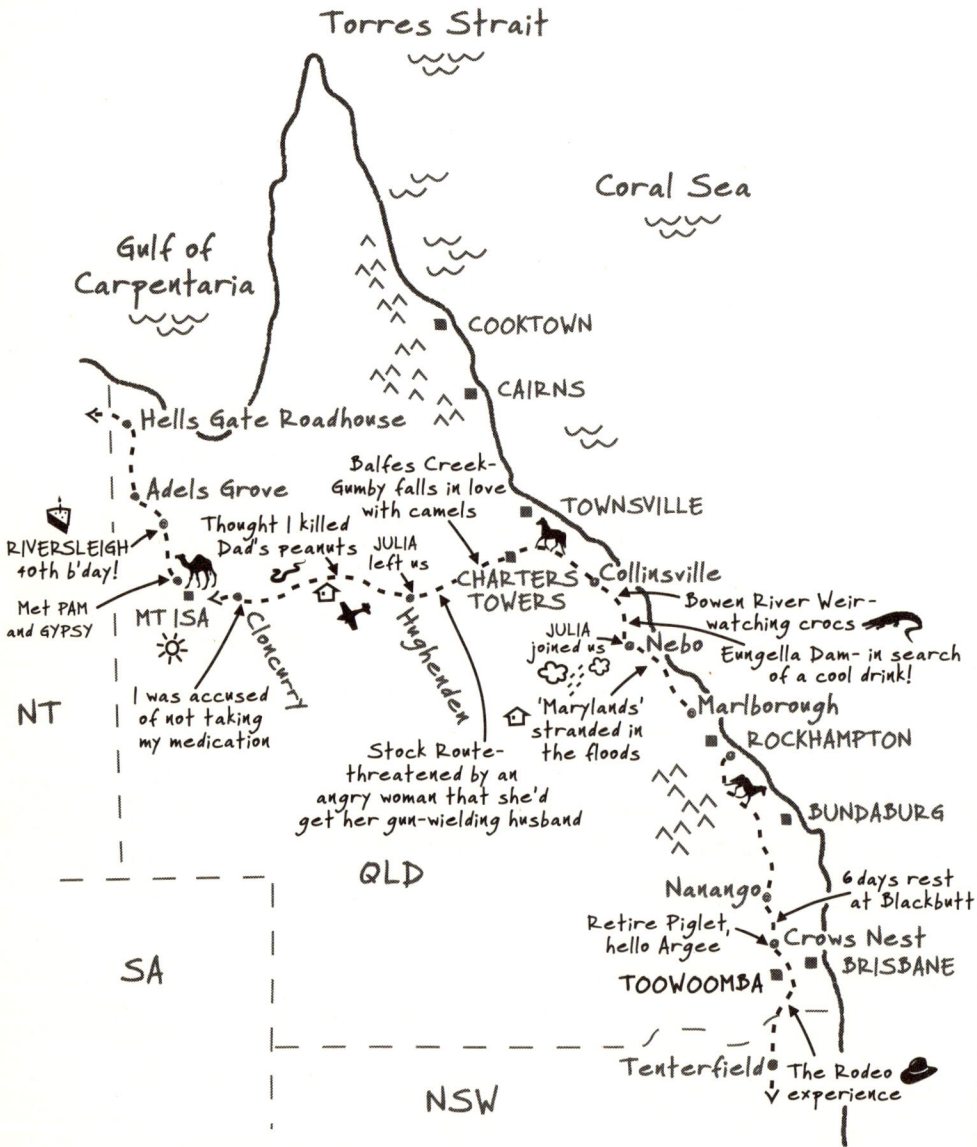

Torres Strait

Coral Sea

Gulf of Carpentaria

COOKTOWN

CAIRNS

Hells Gate Roadhouse

Balfes Creek-
Gumby falls in love
with camels

TOWNSVILLE

Adels Grove

RIVERSLEIGH
40th b'day!

Thought I killed
Dad's peanuts

JULIA
left us

CHARTERS
TOWERS

Collinsville

Met PAM
and GYPSY

MT ISA

Cloncurry

Hughenden

JULIA
joined us

Nebo

Bowen River Weir-
watching crocs

Eungella Dam- in search
of a cool drink!

I was accused
of not taking
my medication

'Maryland'
stranded in
the floods

Marlborough

ROCKHAMPTON

NT

Stock Route-
threatened by an
angry woman that she'd
get her gun-wielding husband

BUNDABURG

QLD

Nanango

6 days rest
at Blackbutt

SA

Retire Piglet,
hello Argee

Crows Nest

BRISBANE

TOOWOOMBA

Tenterfield

The Rodeo
experience

NSW

# The Northern Territory leg

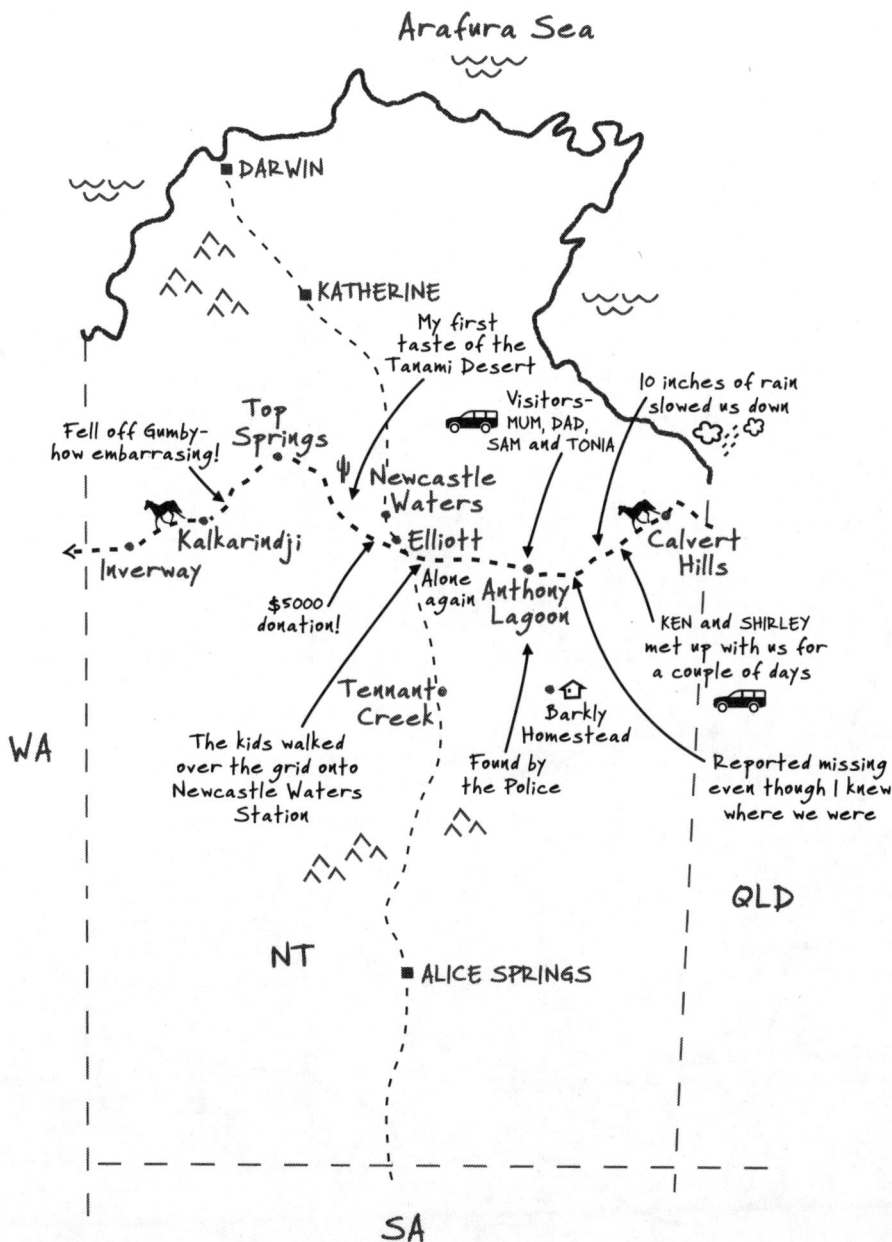

Arafura Sea

DARWIN

KATHERINE

My first taste of the Tanami Desert

10 inches of rain slowed us down

Visitors— MUM, DAD, SAM and TONIA

Fell off Gumby— how embarrasing!

Top Springs

Newcastle Waters

Kalkarindji

Inverway

Elliott

Calvert Hills

$5000 donation!

Alone again

Anthony Lagoon

KEN and SHIRLEY met up with us for a couple of days

Tennant Creek

Barkly Homestead

The kids walked over the grid onto Newcastle Waters Station

Found by the Police

Reported missing even though I knew where we were

WA

NT

ALICE SPRINGS

QLD

SA

# The Western Australia leg

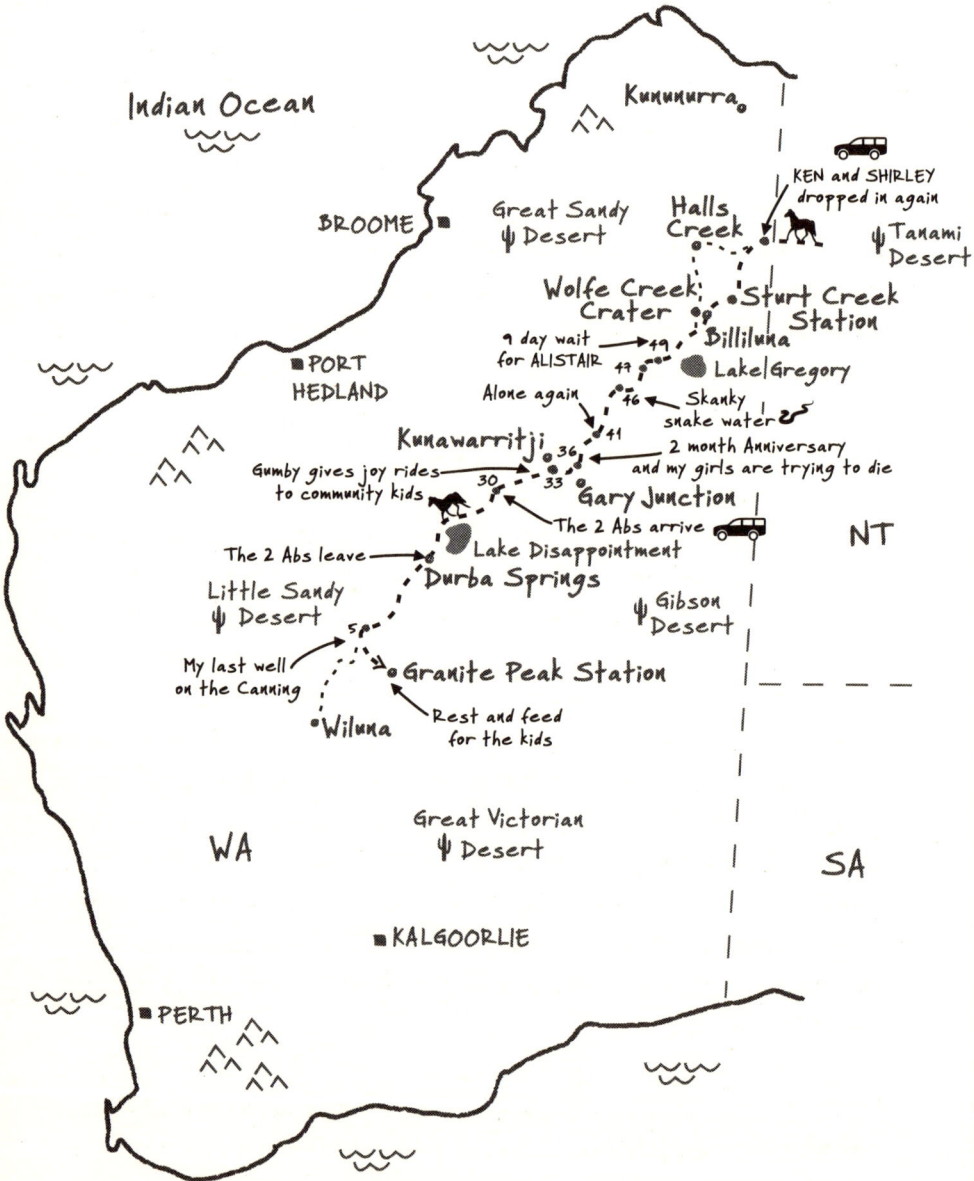

Indian Ocean

Kununurra

BROOME

Great Sandy ψ Desert

Halls Creek

KEN and SHIRLEY dropped in again

ψ Tanami Desert

Wolfe Creek Crater

Sturt Creek Station

PORT HEDLAND

9 day wait for ALISTAIR → 49

Bililuna

47

Lake Gregory

Alone again

46

Skanky snake water

41

Kunawarritji

36

2 month Anniversary and my girls are trying to die

Gumby gives joy rides to community kids

30

33

Gary Junction

The 2 Abs arrive

The 2 Abs leave

Lake Disappointment

NT

Durba Springs

Little Sandy ψ Desert

Gibson ψ Desert

5?

My last well on the Canning

Granite Peak Station

Rest and feed for the kids

Wiluna

WA

Great Victorian ψ Desert

SA

KALGOORLIE

PERTH

# Prologue

I flew to Sydney yesterday for a function. I had a 22.8-kilogram swag that was very awkward to carry, a 17-kilogram wheel-on hand luggage bag and an overstuffed laptop bag. I was pushing the envelope as far as Qantas was concerned, but to their credit I only got greasy looks. I pulled up at the hotel (that had been booked and paid for by the people holding the function) and juggled my gear out of the taxi. Stumbling through the front entrance, getting caught by my bulky swag on the door, I noted a doorman (well, a man in hotel uniform standing idly at the door) staring blankly at me and my comic efforts. At the front desk I explained my room had been booked and paid for in advance and showed the desk clerk my papers.

'Where's the receipt?' she snapped. What does she mean? This is the receipt. It's all the paperwork I was given, and it had information about payment. What else could she want?

'The receipt?' No, sorry, saying it louder doesn't clear it up for me. That must only work for people in wheelchairs and non-English speaking people.

'I need the *receipt!*' I can see that, but you're not getting blood out of a stone lady, I ain't got no receipt. 'Humph. Well I will need to sight the receipt. I *suppose* I can give you the key but you'll need to produce a *receipt.*'

With that all sorted I proceeded up a flight of ten stairs towards the elevator, partly dragging my awkward swag, laptop bag choking me around the neck and wheelie bag flipping on its back like a cast turtle. By this stage I had three hotel staff staring at me with mild amusement. Finally my water bottle broke through a plastic bag and hit the deck. One of the staff stepped forward, picked up the water bottle and handed it to me with a magnanimous look, took two steps back and continued to watch my struggle up the stairs. God, I hate city living!

I remember the time I travelled west through central Queensland and camped with some stray cattle at a bore on the stock route. The owner of the property met me as she was doing her bore run. I had just set up camp and was settling down to my journal entry, contemplating yet another exciting packet pasta-and-sauce concoction, when she offered to take me back to the homestead for a steak. And it wasn't even my birthday! So I jumped in with her, she finished the bore run (about 50 kilometres) then drove me to her house (about 100 kilometres); she fed me steak and vegies (the best meal in the world as far as I was concerned) and drove me back to my camp (about 100 kilometres), dropped me off and drove back to the homestead (another 100 kilometres). She never even thought twice about the extra 200 kilometres she had driven just to feed me – a stranger – a steak. You don't find that sort of hospitality in the city.

On the road, people stopped and gave me cold Coke, fruit, condensed milk, cold beer, fresh red claw (yabby things), cappuccino sachets and more. Once a man passed me and left me two mangoes. He asked if I liked them and I said I had never eaten mango and would give them a try. The next morning he stopped by again on his way home, in all of a guilt-ridden panic, apologising profusely for not telling me the special way of cutting them up. He then left me two more mangoes to practise on. Pity I'm not that keen on mangoes, as it turns out. The big lesson for that trip was: the further into the outback, the more generous the people. Honestly, they would give you the thongs off their feet.

So where to start? How do I explain what the hell I did and why the hell I did it? Why did I decide to ride a horse around Australia? I remember one day, when I was 38, doing a few maths calculations in my head (I love doing maths calculations in my head – very therapeutic) and I realised I would turn 40 in less than two years. That couldn't be right – I hadn't completed the bucket list yet and I had that 'back-up' bucket list to work on too. I had worked in agriculture on all sorts of properties; I had lived and travelled all over Australia; I was a commercial pilot and a pilot in the Royal Australian Air Force; I was a veterinary surgeon and a veterinary chiropractic and acupuncture practitioner; and I had ridden horses through the Victorian Alps. But there was one main thing on the primary list I hadn't yet done – and that was the minor adventure of riding a horse, with pack horses, around Australia. That shouldn't take much to sort out, surely!

I had never done any packing before, not even seen it. Come to think of it I hadn't really camped much either (unless you count rolling out the swag in the dust at a drunken B and S ball in my youth). I have been asked many times, 'What made you want to ride a horse around Australia?' The honest answer really is: I don't know. I came up with the idea when I was about thirteen and at boarding school. I hated boarding school passionately: the city living; the huge number of students; the Melbourne weather; being away from the open countryside; and the high proportion of vacuous upper-class girls who didn't seem to have a clue about the country they lived in (sorry, my issues). The rebellious side in me thought the best way to really get to know this great country was to ride a horse around it, with pack horses, a swag and a Kelpie.

Admittedly I hadn't really thought out the finer details but I just had this knowledge that, one day, I would do it.

So, back to being 38 years old. I set myself a target: start the trip before I turned 40.

# –1

# The lead-up

Preparation for my ride was huge. The more I prepared and organised, the more I found I had to do. The costs were huge too. I didn't really allow myself to think about all the organisation and money it would take because I knew it would be too overwhelming; I just took one step at a time.

First things first. I had to learn about packing – or, more specifically, pack-horsing. I knew a bit about horses; I'd ridden them all my life mustering stock, playing polocrosse and tent pegging and, being a vet chiro, my business was mostly horses. But, like all horse sports each discipline required different knowledge, different equipment and even different horses. I knew of a fellow polocrosse player, Trevor, who did a lot of packing so I set out to introduce myself and wring him dry of all that he knew. Trevor was great. He lent me a saddle to study, discussed all the pros and cons of different styles of saddles and horses, and told me about all the gear I would and wouldn't need.

I used to make and sell leather tack to help get through uni so this experience, along with studying and practising saddle fitting and horse chiropractic, helped me design and make my own pack saddles, pack bags and gear. There are plenty of different designs out there but my horses were going to be working hard for me and I wanted to make sure their gear fit well and wasn't going to rub and hurt. I had to find someone who would cast the arches, get a woodworker to carve the panels a particular shape, and persuade a very patient next-door neighbour to sew canvas packs and buckets to my specific (and fussy) needs. Sourcing all the leather, wood, 1-inch felt, strapping, buckles, clips, ropes, lamb's wool, etc. I needed was a long and expensive process. I then had to sew, stud, glue, bolt, rivet and buckle it all together, producing five pack saddles, with associated gear, that were hopefully strong, unbreakable and comfortable for the horses.

Sourcing horses was an experience in itself. You would think you'd need large 'clumpers' such as Clydesdales (the big chunky cart horses) that are strong enough to do all the work; however at Trevor's insistence I resisted the urge (thank goodness) to get such horses and instead went for small and sturdy 'good doers'. Smaller horses, about fourteen hands high (the size of a pony), can carry similar weights to Clydesdales on a day-in day-out basis and need far less feed in the process. So I was on the lookout for short and fat. I put the word out to friends and chiro clients that I was looking for cheap (or free) horses and got a huge response. I think it appealed to people to have a conversation over dinner with friends that started nonchalantly with, 'Oh, whatever happened to that horse we had? That's right, he walked around Australia carrying a pack saddle.' I was given all sorts of horses, ranging from a fat, needy standardbred named Tank to an old, lame, infertile thoroughbred mare (called Caro), to a fully sound, grand prix dressage horse (Hero) and a brilliant Australian stock horse called Muddy that played a mean game of polocrosse and was even better at bucking. I also got my hands on a highly strung endurance Arab (called Elphine, whom I later named Piglet). At one stage I had about twenty horses.

I started training the horses to pack and then, based on how they worked, culled them down: Muddy too dangerous; Caro too old and lame; Trinity too unsound; Switch too unpredictable; Turtle too skinny; and Hero, too much of a girl's blouse, even though he did move beautifully (he was going to be the one to carry the eggs and the crystal ware!). There were many others with many different issues that all went by the wayside. In the end I had my core team: Piglet the grey Arab, Tank the chestnut standardbred and Quinnie the brown Australian stock horse. Quinnie was the only horse I bought (for a pretty decent sum ... but she was worth it). She was a perfect size and shape. She was quiet and had hard work under her belt. She had done camp-drafting, showing, polocrosse and even completed the Quilty endurance ride. She was my pride and joy and I looked forward to riding her, on my last day, through the gates at home.

There were so many other things to organise. I bought about $2000 worth of topographical maps and grouped them in piles for each leg of the trip. When I neared the end of one leg, my parents would post me the next lot of maps. I had to work out my route and get permission from land-holders, councils, the Department of Primary Industries (DPI), communities and police. I had to find out about quarantine borders such as the tick line in Queensland and the Northern Territory and work out how I was going to traverse them. I had to get my firearms licence, buy an appropriate rifle (in case I had to euthanase an injured horse, or maybe even defend my horses against a wild bull camel in rut), and develop a strategy so I could legally carry it. I wanted to take a dog for company and security. Otter, my poor old Rottweiler, was basically arthritis on legs. I needed a kelpie. I acquired a bitch pup called Flynn and trained her with the intention of her being about eighteen months old when we left. Like many of my brilliant plans it was a disaster. Poor little Flynn died suddenly one Sunday morning. One minute she was a bit wobbly and the next I was in the vet clinic I worked at with a brilliant vet nurse, Jo. Flynn died – I'm not sure why – despite our efforts. I was devastated.

After pulling myself together, I had to reassess the situation. I wanted to travel with a dog but I couldn't get a pup as I was leaving in six months and it wouldn't be old enough to handle the trip, or so I thought. That's where Furphy came in. Piglet's owner rang me and offered me an eighteen-month-old red Kelpie. Apparently, Furphy had been showing as much promise as a working dog as a blind Chihuahua. So Furphy came with me, fully grown and just busting to please.

I needed a lot of equipment. I got an EPERB (an emergency beacon), a satellite phone for emergency communications, a BlackBerry to send emails, a GPS to help navigate and measure distance travelled, an iPod to counter boredom, rechargeable batteries for torches and a solar panel and dry-cell battery to run everything else.

I had to be prepared for all terrain and all weather in all sorts of environments. I needed a first-aid pack that could treat humans, horses and dogs. I needed waterproofing for those wet days. I needed farrier's gear to look after the horses' feet. I needed wire strainers for when I came to grids with no gates and would have to cut the fences to get through. I needed an electric fence so I didn't lose the horses at night. I needed fly veils so the flies didn't drive the horses insane in the more humid areas. I needed repair tools and spares for all my equipment. I needed gear for the snow of Victoria, the tropics of Queensland, the highlands of New South Wales and the deserts of Western Australia. I needed absolutely everything! How was I going to fit all that onto two little pack horses?

If I was going to do something so unusual and crazy as this trip it seemed a logical step, and too good an opportunity to miss, for me to raise money for charity. There was never any question as to what kind of charity. I would raise money for homeless kids. I really wanted to take a couple of kids with me for a month at a time to help give them confidence and self-assurance, and to show them that there are some great and amazing things about the world. After consultation with Youth Off the Streets, a charity run by Father Chris Riley that helps disadvantaged young people make positive changes in their lives, I realised I couldn't do that safely and effectively by myself. So I resigned myself to simply raising money for them. I decided if the meagre amount of money I could raise helped one kid make better and more informed choices in their life, then it was worth it.

Since I am as good with computers as I am with synchronised swimming, I had to find someone to set up a website for me; I didn't really care whether I had one except it would provide an avenue for fund-raising for Youth Off the Streets. A good friend of mine, Tia, lived in Scotland and was going out with a computer-savvy guy, Scott, whom I had met when they came to Australia for a visit. So he set up a website titled Walkabout Hoofprints and emailed me to check it and tell him of any changes I wanted. All I would need to do while I was on the road would be to send him my entries and photos and he would post them on the site. A really nice guy.

I had to consider the possible dangers I might face during the trip. I had people telling me snakes were my biggest threat, others saying spiders were, and I was even told scorpions were a reason not to go. People cited the Peter Falconio story, Ivan Milat and even the movie *Wolf Creek* as reasons why I should pull the pin on my plans. I knew, though, that my biggest dangers were bushfires, especially in the south, and saltwater crocodiles in the north. Being from the south, I find crocodiles very daunting. I don't understand them, I have no experience with them and I don't like the way they cheat. Any predator that can go on land or in water, fresh and salt, is cheating in my books.

Most people who found out what I was doing either told me that they were going to do the same thing but hadn't yet because … or told me flat out that I was going to die. My family were all a bit stunned at first, then went through various stages of denial, incredulity, avoidance and finally full support with a keen interest.

I didn't know anyone who had done anything like this. With lots of things planned but still more issues in limbo, I decided to consult the experts to check just how insane I was. So I contacted Andrew Harper. He runs camel expeditions through central Australia with the Outback Camel Company and in 1999 he walked with three camels from the west coast to the east coast of Australia along the Tropic of Capricorn. He was the man to see and he lived in Deniliquin, my home town.

Andrew's reaction was brilliant. When I told him what I wanted to do he said, 'That's a great idea,' just as casually as if I had told him I was going to put money in the parking meter. He didn't seem to think I was crazy. He seemed to think it could be done and, even better, he indicated there was no reason to think *I* couldn't do it. Just what I needed – a shot in the arm from someone who thought I was normal and had reasonable plans, rather than a crazy chick with suicidal tendencies. We looked at maps, talked about water, tracks, weather and terrain. At one stage I remember saying to him, 'You think I'm crazy taking horses; you think I should take camels instead, don't you?' He conceded camels would make things easier but he was very diplomatic; as far as Andrew was concerned, nothing was impossible. But I wanted to take horses. It was always horses. I had never pictured riding a camel around Australia, and the thirteen-year-old in me demanded it be a horse. Besides, I have no idea about camels. I couldn't possibly learn 'camelmanship' before my ride.

By the end of the afternoon, however, I had somehow arranged a trip to the Simpson Desert to work with Andrew's camels for two weeks. Travelling with camels as pack animals would certainly reduce my stresses about the dryer country. Horses are water hogs compared to camels which can carry a few hundred litres on their back. Using camels would mean I could travel for days between water holes. Andrew also offered to lend me two of his working camels and pack saddles for however long I needed them, to walk through the Northern Territory, Western Australia and South Australia. He would drop the camels off in about May 2007 near Mt Isa where I would continue with just the one riding horse. This was an offer I couldn't refuse. The generosity of a total stranger! This was just the start of my experience with outback Australians willing to help, even when it cost them their own time and expenses and gave them nothing in return.

As you may be starting to appreciate, the pre-ride work was huge. I was continually discovering more things I had to do and work out, as well as mulling over the same old questions I thought I had answered. How far could I walk in a day? How many rest days would I need? What time of year would I be travelling through which areas? The task was humungous. Where to start? Every time I sorted out something I got a fleeting sense of achievement, but when I ticked the box on 'The Big Board' I had put up, I just added more jobs. For eighteen months I worked on the 'to do' list on 'The Big Board'. It was never-ending. I am exhausted just reminiscing!

So, enough of this. All I can say now is, hang onto your spurs and enjoy the ride.

# 0

## The false start

On the first day of October 2006 I rode out of Healesville, Victoria, to begin my big exploration. I had chosen Healesville as my starting point as it is there that the Bicentennial National Trail, a 5330-kilometre route which heads all the way up the east coast, begins. Before that day, I had walked into a bed and breakfast in Healesville called The Stables, introduced myself to the owners, Rae and David Rogers, and blurted out my usual introductory speech:

'Hi, I'm Heidi Douglas. I'm going to ride a horse around Australia raising money for homeless kids.' You know it's not a bad introduction – you never would have heard it before anyway! Rae and David were great. They let me camp on their property for a few days before I left as it was right at the start of the trail. The Stables bed and breakfast was beautiful and peaceful and had lovely gardens (which I was paranoid about making messy).

My friends Mick and Laura Jarmaine had driven to Brigadoon, my family's property west of Deniliquin, New South Wales, picked up the horses and brought them to The Stables in their horse truck. When we opened the truck to let them out we saw Piglet had gone down, her head held up in the air by the tight lead rope. And that's when a great cracking thunderstorm suddenly hit us. Was this some sort of portent? What a start to the trip! We managed to unload the horses in between disconcertingly close flashes of lightning, huge crashes of thunder, and hail the size of golf balls (okay, maybe marbles). Lucerne hay went flying everywhere through Rae and David's beautifully clean garden and Piglet was sore and cut up. This was the first of countless times I would ask myself, 'What the hell am I doing?'

By the time I set off from The Stables, Piglet was fine and I had cleaned up all the offending hay from around the garden. The day I left there was a crowd of family and friends bigger than you'd find at the under 13s Riverina district footy grand final. The pressure was on!

Mark Birrer, a horse breaker and friend from home, came with me for the first few days. He brought along a friend of his, Geoff. 'Thanks for letting me come along,' was the first thing Geoff said to me. 'It'll be the holiday of a lifetime.'

Oh my God, he thinks it's going to be a holiday! He's in for a rude shock.

We had to get all the gear onto the two pack horses. I still remember that morning, staring at Mark and Geoff's swags wondering how the hell we were going to fit them on. Each swag had a 2-inch foam mattress in it that didn't lend itself to being rolled up tight. Finally, after putting them on and off Tank for half an hour I announced

'That's it! The mattresses have to go.'

'Great idea,' said the ever-energetic and positive Mark, and he proceeded to pull his swag apart. But poor old Geoff's face dropped. I think this was the first of many disappointments during his 'holiday of a lifetime'.

That night I sat down to start my journal, a habit I would keep up for the next couple of years.

### Day 1, 1 October 2006: The first camp of many

Leaving Healesville I felt a little bit like Lady Di; at one stage there were no less than five cameras behind a hedge taking photos. Mark and Geoff left with me, with three riding horses and two pack (Quinnie, Tank, Piglet, Turtle and Geoff's horse). We didn't get packed up till 11 am and that was not until after I threw both their huge mattresses out of their swags (don't think Geoff was very happy).

Today seemed a long, hard day; had to stop a fair bit to settle the packs etc. At one stage we commented on a stupid sign that said 'P9' and kept going, to later find out that it was our camp and had water. So we just camped on the side of the road.

S 37° 37' 56", E 145° 31' 52".   2957 ft   24.0 km
Total: 24.0 km

**Low point:** Not finding the proper camp – good start Heidi!
**High point:** Finally have left, hooray!

### Day 4, 4 October 2006: Keppel's Hut camp

Huge day today with really vague directions. We were looking forward to Keppel's Hut with watered horse yards but found the yards inadequate and the feed scarce. Poor horses; hard work up rough country and now it's cold and raining. They are hungry, exhausted and tucked up. Geoff had bought a brand new saddle for the trip, but the gullet touches the spinous processes in the wither without the girth done up (in other words 'ouch big time!'). Poor horse is really doing the hard yards. His back end is also really struggling with old sacral issues being stressed on these hills. That's one tough horse.

The tracks are really stony and rough and playing hell on the horses' feet. We are rotating the easy boots but there aren't enough to go around. Piglet's feet are tough, so is she. It's good to have a hut since it's raining. I think some sort of god is smiling upon me.

S 37° 27' 38", E 145° 51' 06".    4363 ft    35.7 km
Total: 80.1 km

**Low point:** Hungry horses, poor feed.
**High point:** Shelter from the rain. I know Geoff's high point is that there are some mattresses in the hut. He mentioned, though, something about how his looks as if a dog's had a litter of pups on it ... maybe the mattress is his low point. He's still using it, though.

### Day 6, 6 October 2006: Big River camp

Today was a shocker. The horses went well but very windy, cold and stormy. It rained most of the day. The guys thought it was about 4°C which I was surprised about but I think my new Swandry jumper earnt every last cent of its $140 cost. Sure I was cold, but not 4°C cold. The rain was a bit sleety and we decided it wasn't far off snowing. The rain has settled tonight and we have a roof of a hut (no walls) to sleep under.

*I find it hard because I have made or acquired so many things for this trip and organised so much that I feel a bit anal around Geoff. But shit! If he puts those hobbles wrongly around the horses' necks one more time I am bound to lose them for good! Of course I want it done my way; this stuff has to last me two years not just a week.*

*S 37° 22' 36", E 146° 02' 51".    3122 ft    37.8 km*
*Total: 136.2 km*

**Low point:** *The weather, but not everything is wet yet!*
**High point:** *Mark is a great laugh — keeping me going.*

The first day I was on my own after Mark and Geoff left me was a hard one. I planned to go up Mount Terrible and back down again to Kensington. I don't think they quite got the name of the mountain right; more apt would be Mount Bloody Hard Yakka or even Mount Maybe Try and Go Around Instead. The Bicentennial National Trail is a documented route that starts at Healesville and covers over 5000 kilometres up to Cooktown in northern Queensland. It was developed in the early 1980s for bushwalking, horse riding and cycling. It is great because you get printed guides telling you about water, grass and shelter availability along the trail. The guides also give directions on following the route, and there are yellow and red triangles intermittently nailed to trees to help guide you. Every effort is made to update the guide books but it is a fully voluntary enterprise and has limited funds. As a consequence there can be a few yellow triangles missing or road changes that are not mentioned.

These things took a bit of getting used to and I was failing tragically the day I scaled Mount Terrible. I totally missed a turn-off and ended up travelling an extra 5 kilometres before I was back on track. Five kilometres out in the 'other' world is nothing – a quick trip in the car – but for me and the horses it meant over an hour or more of unnecessary hard yakka. We really didn't need that! The mountain was so steep and rocky that the horses were refusing to be led up while I was on another horse, Tank. Some patches I had to ride up first, then tie up Tank, walk down and pick up one pack horse, walk her up and tie her up then go back and pick up the last pack horse. I was riding Tank for the first time that day. Tank was a chestnut (I don't like chestnuts) standardbred (not a fan of standardbreds either) mare. But she was great, an absolute comedian. She would spend the whole day playing practical jokes on Piglet. The days when I rode Piglet, and packed Tank, Piglet would have these strange little Tourette syndrome episodes of shaking her head, ears back and swishing her tail. I would turn around to see Tank and Quinnie, head down walking quietly behind me. What was wrong with this Arab? Then one day the sun was behind me and Piglet had one of her episodes. What I saw in the shadows was Tank harassing Piglet, pulling faces and threatening to bite her. When I whipped around there was Tank, quietly walking, minding her own business. I was onto her! What a sneaker! From then on, every time she did it I would tell her off, usually while trying to stifle a laugh.

The trail guide said there was probably no water at the hut on the top of Mount Terrible but, thank God (or whoever), there was. We were exhausted. After settling the camp for the kids (which could take an hour or so) and rolling out my swag, I lit a fire outside the hut and proceeded to cook my delicious pasta-and-sauce packet concoction. I really was too exhausted to do it but knew from the day before that if I didn't eat properly it would just make me more and more tired. So dried packet pasta and sauce on an open fire it was; alfredo with a bit of cheese and a light sprinkle of cayenne pepper. The pepper container was brand new and as I waved it gently over the pot a clump the size of a golf ball, along with the lid, fell and landed unceremoniously in my meal. Ahhh! Spoon! I frantically fished it out but plenty had already dispersed through the meal.

I was too tired to cook up another batch, couldn't afford the food wastage and really needed to eat. So I continued stirring the pasta, occasionally fishing out dangerous red lumps, and then found white ash was falling into my meal. My God, maybe I could sprinkle a bit of horse manure in as well, to get the full five food groups. But no, it wasn't ash, it was snow. Was that better? Looking across at the cold, weary horses I realised I would rather have eaten ash.

So, on my first night on my own I sat at the top of Mount Terrible under a light dusting of snow, looking across to the other glowing snow-covered peaks, eating a very hot alfredo pasta. I was exhausted, I was cold, my tongue was burning and my bum was sore. Could this get any better?

**Handy hint no. 1:** Each day, when you think it can't get harder or tougher or rougher or steeper or rockier or wetter or hotter … it can and it will.

The day after it snowed it was about 35 degrees. There was a hot, gusty northerly and it had that ominous feeling of bushfires. I managed to lose my guide book in a gust of wind and had to call the volunteer advisors for this section of the BNT. Kevin was great. He helped me with directions and gave me bushfire updates.

**Handy hint no. 2:** Carry two copies of your maps and directions just in case there's a hot, gusty northerly.

### Day 13, 13 October 2006: McAllister River camp

*Wasn't so bad today, considering the horses are quite sore. Quin is lame in the right knee because she tripped carrying the pack and landed hard straight on her knees on a rock. Yesterday she had trouble going downhill and today has pulled up sore in the hammies.*

*It was about 35°C again … and to think it snowed two nights ago! South of here is all about bushfires. Kevin said there are none in this area and will notify me if any start. I just need to keep checking my sat phone. It was a short day (four hours' travel) but the horses are tired and sore. I will have to keep riding Piglet because she is too much of a pain to pack and lead. I am so over her idiosyncrasies! Because of two Total Fire Ban days I am struggling a bit with food. I have been eating tuna sandwiches using a shocking loaf of bread I made a few days ago. It's so bad I can't even call it cooking! It's time to get ingenious. The only things I have left to eat are flour, uncooked pasta and sauce and raw rice. So I cooked dinner on my camp stove, perched on a rock in the middle of the McAllister River. Surely having a 10 m fire break of flowing water is safe enough. And I get a bonus — have a tub while cooking! But it wasn't entirely successful. Somehow I managed to burn the rice even though it was still uncooked. I need a bit more practise on my new stove.*

*Last night I went to bed without socks on. Bliss. My feet have been slowly withering away with suffocation. I have discovered wearing socks 24/7 leads to rotting feet, which then leads to feet that don't like to walk. Piglet has a swelling over her wither.*

*S 37° 27' 10", E 146° 33' 04".   1407 ft   23.3 km Total: 228.9 km*

**Low point:** *Sore horses and the threat of bushfires.*
**High point:** *The track was great and not too hard on the horses.*

It had started raining that night and didn't stop till mid-afternoon the next day. So much for bushfire danger. I then had to contend with the next hurdles: slippery tracks and my entire camp soaked right through. Luckily we found a great camp with plenty of feed and water, and got a fire going that, somehow, dried out everything including my swag.

> **Handy hint no. 3:** Half a box of Jiffy firelighters and an entire weekend newspaper can start a fire with any wet wood … eventually!

So, as only Victoria can serve up, my first four days on my own consisted of snow, hot northerlies with associated bushfire threat and at least 2 inches of rain. Welcome to the world of packing!

I discovered all sorts of things in this country. Huts, for instance, sound great for a rest, but are not so good to camp at. Yes they provide shelter (or most of them do) but they are still zarking freezing (yes, I am a *Hitchhiker's Guide to the Galaxy* fan). And they seem to be put in the wrong locations altogether. Up the very top of the mountains on the open plateaus where it can only ever be bloody cold and bloody windy. Also, the wildlife is fascinating: 95 per cent of it is pigs – there are wild pigs everywhere. All along the tracks you see poo perched strategically on top of little rocks. I decided this was wombat poo and probably some sort of territorial statement.

Furphy was fascinated by it and once I caught him doing his own poo on a little rock. Strange dog. The Victorian Alpine region is huge. It is wild and beautiful, friendly and threatening, and full of life and death. It is always changing its mind about weather, terrain, and plant and animal life. I loved this country. I was just hoping me and the kids could rise to meet its challenges and come out sane and alive on the other side.

### Day 15, 15 October 2006: Howitt Hut

*Spoke to Dad quickly on the CDMA today before it cut out. I feel bad because I know they worry heaps. If I tell them how tired I am and the doubts I have, they will definitely try to stop me.*

*What the hell am I doing? Is this just an exercise in torturing horses? If so, I think I am doing a sterling job! The poor horses are always sore, hungry and exhausted. They have chafe marks on them caused by hobbles at night and easy boots by day. Tank has rapidly developed a work ethic and is now my 'rock'. She is my night horse. Tie her anywhere and she will stay. The other day she was hungry and angry, so all night she followed Piglet around harassing her, in their hobbles. Neither of them needed the extra exercise! At 1 am I tied Tank up to a tree and she stood beautifully all night.*

*Quin is also a brick. As long as she has the easy boots on she is there. Today I let her follow loose (she normally tail ties to Tank) which she did obediently. I left her bell on so if I stopped hearing the bell it meant I had to check her. She is sore and tired and has lost more weight than I would like. I hope they can all put on a bit of weight with a few days off in Dargo.*

*Piglet was a bit stiff and slow this morning for the first 50 metres but soon became pushy as ever. Hopefully she will pull up okay in the morning.*

*S 37° 22' 19", E 146° 39' 24"   5682 ft   22.4 km*
*Total: 291.2 km*

**Low point:** *Losing condition on the horses. These mountains are in a huge drought and there is such little feed. The place would go up in a fire far too easily — it's a bit unsettling.*
**High point:** *I didn't swear or get angry before noon.*

I camped at Mount Howitt for a few days. The first morning I woke up to find Piglet non-weight bearing and lame in the left hind. I threw everything at her: chiro, acupuncture, non-steroidal anti-inflammitories, homeopathy. She wasn't going to get better in a hurry and I had big decisions to make.

### Day 17, 17 October 2006: Howitt Hut, rest day

*Today is the most depressing day so far. The fact that Piglet is still 'four-and-a-half out of five' lame on her left hind is a brain blower. I realise the southern part of the BNT is the hardest and roughest so am doing it the wrong way around. This country is really killing the horses. Quin has lost weight and I am wondering what the hell I am doing! I have to be in Townsville by April and I have already busted a horse. How much further is the rough stuff before it starts to get a bit manageable? I'm not sure any of us will survive! What the zarking fardwarks am I doing? Piglet doesn't seem to have improved. I am not giving up on this ride but I have to try and work out a solution. I have a few requirements:*

- *I ride around Australia.*
- *The horses and I survive.*
- *We make Townsville by April 2007.*

*If Piglet doesn't improve soon the only way I can see to achieve these goals is to truck the horses halfway up the trail, north of Sydney, and restart from there. I rang Sue and told her my dilemma. Later I spoke to her again and she had sorted it. A horse truck can pick me up about 30 km from here and take me to Dargo to rest and regroup. She has found a replacement horse (soft and very unfit) if I want him. She is a great friend. She has already dropped stuff off at Dargo for me: easy boots and horse feed.*

*New Approach to the ride: Take my time, no hurry, enjoy the
scenery and, on average, ride two days, rest one, ride three days
and rest one again. Maybe even do touristy things and, when I
can, take advantage of available help and accommodation. This
is not a race; it is a way of life. I am going to have to change my
way of approaching things from 'get things done' to 'let's cruise'.
Plans must be 'ever fluid'. The only thing I can really plan for is the
continual need to change my plans ... we will see!*

*S 37° 22' 19", E 146° 39' 24"    5682 ft    O.O km
Total: 291.2 km*

*Low point: The realisation that I need to change a few plans if
I want to achieve my goals. Be flexible Heidi, be flexible.
High point: What a good friend Sue is.*

Sue Chittenden, a good friend from Gippsland from whom I bought Quin,
was rapidly becoming my 'mission control' and had found a replacement
horse, Derek. Poor old Derek. He was pulled out of a paddock after years of
no work, had his feet done, teeth done, chiro done and was wormed. He had
a crash course in the crupper and britchin (both used to stop the saddle
moving too far forward on the horse), pack saddle, bells, hobbles, tail ties,
electric fences and was put on a truck to north of Sydney with my other two
horses, Quinnie and Tank. Because I had lost time with Piglet going lame
and with training Derek, and the fact that Derek was very unfit, I was
trucking the kids further north to make up for lost time. I would just finish
my ride there, rather than Healesville. I headed home to Brigadoon for a
couple of days, after the horses were put on the truck, then planned to travel
north to meet them when they arrived. So, start with a clean slate. I had
learnt the hard but necessary lesson that all good plans may go down the
toilet so I needed to be flexible. This wasn't exactly my forte. My comfort
zone only includes the expected and planned.

'Hello, Heidi speaking.' It was Jason, the truck driver.
'How are the horses going?' Jason told me they had made it to Sydney

but Derek was not quite himself. (I would love a dollar for every time someone has told me their animal is 'not quite himself'; I have to resist the urge to inquire that if he is not himself then who the hell is he? I don't think many people would appreciate the joke, especially when their beloved pet is 'not himself'.) Jason had called the vet to be on the safe side and said he would call me when he knew more.

I know the stress of trucking can bring on diseases that may not have otherwise taken hold of the horse. One of the biggest problems is shipping fever, although what Jason described didn't sound like that. Horses are very prone to colic, too. It really is a generic term that basically means 'belly ache' and can be caused by lots of things, even stress. So, Derek was sick. I thanked God (or whoever) it was Derek and not Tank or Quinnie. Tank was a real comedian and Quinnie was such a great worker. I felt bad about Derek but the others had worked so hard for me already in the three weeks in the Victorian Alps they didn't deserve colic. An hour later I get a phone call from the vet, an efficient, university-based veterinarian who knew everything in the books but nothing in the real world.

'Hello, is that Heidi? Your horse has colitis X so we can euthanase him or take him to hospital for $5000 to $10000. Which would you like?' Who is this degree infested robot? It still amazes me that the only thing you need to graduate as a vet is an IQ. Most are very good and caring but some academics slip through the cracks. Recovering from the complete lack of bedside manner, I admitted to the vet I couldn't afford treatment and I would get the truck driver to organise the knackery (just as humane as the vet). Maybe she could give poor old Derek some hard core pain relief to help him till the knackery truck arrives? Maybe even some Finadyne? 'I can't dispense him Finadyne, because it will mask the clinical signs.' Surely that was the idea! Did it matter if his clinical signs of excruciating pain are taken away if he was going to be euthanased anyway? Apparently, yes. So she left Derek in severe pain, Jason distressed, and me ... just a little bit angry and apologising profusely to Jason for my veterinary colleague. As she left, Jason noted Quinnie and Tank were looking dull. Could this nightmare get any worse?

Within two hours Jason had called another vet, Gary; very professional, very knowledgeable, very caring and actually interested. Jason was obviously happier with Gary. He was concerned about all the other horses on the truck and needed advice. By the time I spoke to Gary, salmonella infection had been diagnosed in all three horses. He thought he may be able to manage Derek's pain so he was spared being euthanased. Salmonella is a bacterial infection of the gut. It can infect many different species with varying affects and prognoses. Horses tend to get it from ingesting food or water that have been contaminated by things such as dead birds or reptiles. Salmonella in a horse has a very poor prognosis. Even if they do survive their recovery is often limited and they may become carriers themselves, infecting others. Horses get a colic with severe pain and projectile diarrhoea. It is awful to watch. Gary thought they probably would have got infected from contaminated water when they were yarded during a rest stop along the way to Sydney. Although Derek wasn't looking so bad, Gary said Tank was in too much pain and needed to be euthanased.

Tank. Poor Tank. She had never hurt anyone. She was such a comedian. Always playing the practical joke while travelling along, always stirring Piglet for some reason. She had worked harder for me than I ever deserved, and now she was leaping in the air and throwing herself on the cement ground, trying to somehow alleviate the incredible pain of salmonella. I told Jason, 'Yes, please euthanase her.'

What have I done to them? I wondered. What have I caused? She didn't deserve to die. She deserved even less to suffer such indescribable pain, and I had seen it before: the owner refuses to make the 'hard decision' at the cost of the horse suffering one of the most distressing and painful conditions, and then finally dying. It's odd, you know. Many times when I have euthanased animals I have been asked by distraught owners, 'How can you do this? This must be the hardest part of your job.' It's actually not. I feel privileged and relieved that I can free this animal of its pain. No-one (in their right mind, anyway) likes to kill an animal for no apparent reason. But every time I euthanase a suffering animal that cannot be cured or managed relatively pain free, I am helping them. I tell owners they are responsible for their animals and with that responsibility may come the difficult decision to end their suffering. It is not a burden, it is a privilege. I don't know how people in human health cope when they have patients in pain which can't be relieved.

I digress. Tank was gone. No more of her practical jokes, harassing of the ever painful Piglet, or commentary on the hard work I was inflicting on them. She hadn't deserved it and I was the reason why she was on the truck. It was my fault and my responsibility.

Late that night my father announced he was going to drive me to Sydney to see the horses, to be there. It took great control to refuse his offer and delay until the morning. I was exhausted, as uncontrolled grief can cause, and it was late. The ten-hour drive may well have ended with both of us in a car wreck. 'They are just horses,' I had to keep saying to myself.

First thing in the morning we set off for Sydney. About 10 kilometres down the road I received a phone call from an exhausted Gary. Derek and Quinnie were trying to kill themselves by thrashing around, and it was time. Even though there was no choice, it was still difficult.

'Okay, send me the bill. Thanks Gary.'

Now Quinnie was dead. By this stage I was numb. How was I going to tell Sue? Quin used to be Sue's horse, until she sold her to me. In your life you get the one horse that stands out from all the rest and Quin was that horse for Sue. How was I going to tell her? This was the cherry on the guilt icing. I had killed her horse.

Where to go to now? What to do? Why me? This situation did not fit into my plans. I had spent the last two years doing nothing but preparing for this ride. I had handed over my business – all my clients – to a friend and colleague who could do right by them. I had prepared all this gear, spent all this money, closed bank accounts, signed over power of attorney, sold my car, got my family on board … I was standing on the edge of a cliff and had been about to walk a ridge from one mountainous peak to the other, when suddenly the earth came out from under my feet and there was no way forward; I couldn't even contemplate a way back.

My devastation was multifaceted and complete. It was my fault they were on that truck. I had killed my horses. My horses, who had worked so hard for me. I had no job, no business, no career. I had no direction. I didn't even have a car! Where to go? If I got new horses did I have a right to put them through the same thing? Could I pick myself up and start a new business? I had already handed over all my clients. I hid in the cottage I lived in on the family farm and cried harder than I could have ever imagined. The guilt was the hardest. I remembered something my aunty had said when she went into aged care, not too long after her husband died: 'Stop the world, I want to get off.' I wasn't suicidal; I just couldn't see a future. Tank and Quinnie had died. With them they took the last two years of my life and, apparently, the next two years. Where to go ... I didn't know. All I was left with was a $2500 truck bill, a $4500 vet bill, three dead horses and the heavy weight of guilt.

That night I wrote in my diary:

> I have no horses, no big ride, no money, no ute, no job ... and what I have been building up to for two years has been ripped out from under me. I am stunned. God really does hate me. These horses I was responsible for, for dragging into this stupid madness, are now dead because of me. What have I done?
>
> Everybody's reaction has been surprising. This is my thing, my baby, but it seems to have affected everybody. Mum doesn't know what to do, so she is just trying to feed me to obesity. Dad keeps repeating, 'Don't worry about the money; just decide what is best to do.' I know my sisters have all been quite upset, even crying at work. What makes me think I had a right to do that to them ...

After a few days, Dad came down to see me.

'You know Hi,' he began, 'we support whatever decision you make. You can decide whatever you want, but you are *not* going to stop now. You are going to keep on going with this ride and finish it. You'll just have to get more horses and change your plans. You can do anything you want now, but you *are* going to keep going.' One may wonder how that made sense, but what it did do was give me permission to consider the possibility of starting my ride again.

I still felt devastated at what I had done to Tank and Quinnie, but the heavy blanket of guilt was slowly lifting.

# 1

## Hard lessons

Reading back through my journal entries was very painful. But I needed to, to try to work out where I went wrong, and to learn from my mistakes. I didn't want any more horses to die. I didn't think I could survive it a second time. When I reached the page titled 'New Approach to the Ride' I realised that what I had written there needed to be my new guide. I had been tackling my ride as if I was going for gold in the Olympics. I needed to take the surfie's attitude: cruise along, deal with surprises as they come and enjoy each day. It was always going to be bloody hard yakka but I had to learn not to plough on ahead so hard that I didn't look up, relax and go with the flow.

Once I had decided I was going to start again, the weight of organising such a huge task returned. How had I done it before? It felt like planning Woodstock all over again (this time maybe with more portable toilets and showers).

So when I had scraped myself up off the floor I had to find more horses. I had spent over eighteen months collecting and rejecting horses to finally arrive at the Piglet/Tank/Quin trio. I no longer had the luxury of time. For six weeks I toured the state, travelling to all the 'dog meat' auctions: Echuca, Pakenham, Colac etc. Mark helped me enormously by 'test driving' horses that came my way. He also helped me get back on the horse, so to speak, giving me the confidence to accept that my horses' deaths weren't my fault and it wasn't going to happen again. Thanks Mark.

I found Willow at the Echuca sales, a fat little thirteen-year-old liver chestnut mare with very sore feet. It's a sad fact that many horses at the dog meat sales are being sold for just that: dog meat. A lot of them have been neglected or forgotten in the back paddock for various reasons. Maybe they were too much for the owner to handle. Maybe they were lame or sore. Maybe they bucked or were dangerous, or maybe the owner just got bored and distracted by life in general. In short, you can be lucky at these sales and get an absolute gem – or unlucky and get the horse that is going to trash your confidence, injure you or both.

Willow was quiet but very forward moving, so a bit nerve-racking for beginner kids. She was very sore with long and cracked hooves (laminitis) and chiropractic restrictions in the neck. She needed a bit of work but I was up to the challenge.

Cruise (what a boring, nothing name … he was so *not* a Cruise) hadn't made it to the sales yet. I'd heard through a friend that there was a horse for sale in Leopold, south of Geelong. The owner had to sell because she was agisting on someone else's property and was told, due to the drought, she would have to get rid of one of her horses. (I found it fascinating that, of her three horses, she kept her two and sold her eight-year-old daughter's pony!) I went out to see the horse at the place where he was kept. It was quite windy, which many horses don't like, and a big sheet of plastic in his paddock was flapping about wildly. He was standing in the middle of the paddock flicking his head up every time the plastic flapped. He was tense and somehow a bit lonely looking. He fitted my criteria though – short and fat – and I was desperate.

'I'll take him,' I said. Cruise's owner told me the dog meat sales were the next day so if I didn't bring back a float and pick him up before then, he would be gone. So, wondering what on earth I was doing, I drove home to Brigadoon to pick up my float and then back again (just an eight-hour round trip). We loaded Cruise in the float that evening and I handed his owner the money. Her parting words to me were, 'Oh, and I think he's a rig.'

A rig! What the? 'Rig' is a name for a horse with one retained testicle. In general, you geld (or castrate) male horses unless you want them to breed, otherwise they can be quite a handful. If the horse has one testicle that isn't yet descended then you only take one out and wait for the other to drop. Fishing around inside the horse's abdomen looking for a stray ball that can be any shape or size is generally time-consuming, fruitless, expensive and dangerous to the horse. Much better to leave it and hope it drops. If it doesn't, people often sell the horse on without disclosing this information and buyers can get caught out. Rigs can be worse than stallions. They can be even more aggressive, harder to handle, impregnate mares, and be a general pain to keep. If you wanted a stallion you would have gone out and got a real one! Wearily, I drove out of the agistment centre regretting my decision already. Little did I know it would turn out to be the best $250 I had ever spent. I put Cruise in the round yard for the night, or what was left of the night, and went back out in the morning with some trepidation. He was a stocky, flea-bitten grey with his head held high ready for the lion around the corner. He was covered in sand and, I realised, looking at the ground, he had rolled extensively through the night. Did he have colic? Oh God, I drove twelve hours and spent $250 for a scared rig with colic. God really wasn't happy with me.

I kept an eye on him in the round yard for the day; he had no other clinical signs. I was a bit baffled till I finally worked out he just loved to roll in sand. He was not happy about being caught, however, and was quite nervous of me. I started by hunting him around the round yard, making him stop and start and turn when I asked him. I think it took about four minutes before he stopped to face me, lowered his head, half closed his eyes and gave a great big sigh. That was it. From then on I had the quietest, calmest dag of a horse that has ever existed. I had my Gumby and I never saw any sign of that Cruise again. I have realised Gum just wanted someone else to take control of his world. He is not a leader, he doesn't know how to make a decision and is very happy to do what you want, as then he feels safe.

That afternoon Dad wanted to shoot a few rabbits that had got completely out of control around the house and sheds. He came over and asked if Gumby would be happy with it and I thought it would be a great test. I was rapidly becoming Gumby's number one fan.

*Bang!*

Gum was looking away at the time and didn't even turn his head (it fleetingly went through my mind that he may be deaf!). But within seconds I had Furphy, a born coward, and Otter, my old arthritic Rottweiler who had somehow jumped a fence, cringing up against my legs … petrified. That made Gumby turn. He pinned his ears back and hunted the poor dogs out of the round yard. I had discovered the first of his two vices. That's okay, I thought; I could live with an aversion to dogs.

Bart has his own story, much of which I am sure I don't know. Only Bart knows what he has been through and I suspect it hasn't been pretty. I bought

Beau – another vacuous, fluffy, nothing name that didn't suit) from the Echuca sales. Mark was with me and Beau seemed to pass the initial handling challenges to which you are limited in those saleyard pens. He was a chestnut Welsh cob with chunky legs and feathers, a frizzy, taffy mane and tail with long white socks and a white blaze – a very striking pony. But I wasn't looking for pretty, I was looking for short and fat, and those legs and solid back looked as though they could carry a grand piano up Mount Terrible! I finally won the bid for him against a local trail-riding school, the meat guys having dropped out early, and so paid about $500 for him. Later, a man approached me and introduced himself as the husband of Beau's previous owner. He told me Beau was a bolter, a pretty good one, and his wife couldn't ride him any more. She did trail riding and Beau would double-barrel any horse behind him. He also said the owner before his wife was a girl who had also lost her riding confidence. Poor old Beau was a victim of his good looks: chosen by women because he was pretty, even though he was totally inappropriate for those riders. What had I bought now? As the nice man turned away, after telling us many bolting stories, Mark said with a big grin, 'We'll see about that!'

I bought Beau two days before Christmas and had already formulated plans to leave for Queensland, with the horses in a float convoy, on 3 January. Time was pretty tight so Mark took Beau to get him trained up until the day before we left. Meanwhile I was giving Gumby and Willow a crash course in pack saddles, britchin, cruppers, tail tying, bells, hobbles and electric fences. I wormed them, did their feet, fitted their boots and gave them a chiro treatment. Mark had some success with Beau and decided he could make the grade but he was, as we'd been warned, a true bolter. Some horses take off and you can pull them up down the track, but some horses are bolters. A switch flicks in their brain and not even a 200-metre cliff is going to stop them. Beau was also petrified of his own bum and anything behind it. He didn't mind the crupper (which horses can struggle with) or the pack bags but really struggled with the britchin. So Beau, only going to be a pack horse, would be tied on at the very back of the string. He was a happier horse, and even a bit mischievous, when I got him back from Mark so I re-named him Bart; a much cheekier name.

In December, Piglet's owner, Jen Moncur, very kindly and courageously offered Piglet back to me because she was 100 per cent better. I couldn't believe her faith in me after what had happened to the others. I eventually agreed because Jen genuinely wanted me to take her. So, I had finally got together my second plant (that's what the drovers in the good old days called their team): Gumby, Willow, Bart, Piglet and Furphy. After running into trouble last time, I thought that if I took four horses I could have a spare and each horse would get a rest from carrying every four days.

On 3 January 2007, we set off from Brigadoon for Bundaberg, Queensland, from where I would rejoin the nearby BNT and start the ride again. There was my father; my brother-in law, Dick Shirley; a family friend, Ken Horkings; and me in two utes with floats in tow. That was a trip in itself! We allowed three days to reach Bundaberg. Fewer days would have been a bit tough on the horses travelling for so long in the float each day, and any more ... well, I don't think the horses would have been too happy to load on the fourth morning.

None of the men had ever had much to do with horses except Dad, when he was a kid, and I think he'd rather keep those days behind him. So, I was chief 'wrangler'. Ken had done a lot of camping through the Top End so he was camp controller. Dick was responsible for 'refuelling' in the form of diesel and alcohol and Dad was navigator. The trip went pretty well, despite us having to stop only 200 kilometres in and get a bit of welding done on one of the floats. Bart, Gumby and Willow were very good considering how they had been thrown in at the deep end.

We reached our destination in the early afternoon of the third day. Peter Goudie lived just out of Bundaberg. He was a total stranger to me, though I had met his father, Phil, once, and it was Phil who offered Peter's place as a starting point for the ride. The generosity of strangers again. We planned to camp for a few days at Peter's place, sort out all the gear, rest the horses and then float them to the BNT camp on the Kolan River, and leave from there.

I had forgotten what Queensland was like. The first night we saw a ute-load of next-door neighbours drive across the paddock towards us then proceed to invade our camp and drink copious amounts of Bundy Rum. Great people, but we were knackered and wanted to get into our swags in good time. The trouble was, everyone was sitting in amongst our rolled out and set up swags and we couldn't sneak off. The Bundy flowed and Dad, Dick and Ken were doing all they could to stay awake. The highlight of the night was the demonstration of a 'Bundy Bomb'. Needless to say I am not going to publish an instructional on it, but it involved diesel, petrol, Bundaberg Rum and fire. Did these people want to die? I was relieved that at the long-awaited end of the night there were no trips to hospital, and we finally crawled into our swags. For the rest of the nights there it was a similar story: just as we were about to get into the swags the dreaded ute lights would come over the hill and spew out a number of oblivious drinkers carting their eskies.

Soon it came time to leave. The Kolan River was bone dry. It seems the entire country was in drought. After two days on the phone I established we could leave from Marlborough, further north, and have a better chance of finding water. Dad and Ken had gone home so 'Big John', one of the constantly visiting next-door neighbours, offered to take two horses in his float. At least I would get some good use out of that damned ute I had learnt to hide from. We arrived at Marlborough on 11 January. It was bloody hot and bloody dry; no other way to describe it. Actually, we were all a bit stunned by what a dry hole it was; even Big John, the relative local.

We needed to research the water situation. My sister, Trina, who had flown up to meet us and would join me for the first four days of the ride, accosted some poor local woman, Dot, in her nightie, watering her front garden. Dot and her husband Keith were a great old couple who spent the whole time laughing and stirring each other. Their relationship was just beautiful – the kind that makes you think maybe marriage isn't that bad after all. Keith rang up everybody he knew and got local information about water heading north, which was great because it made Trina and Dick feel a lot happier. Me too, I must admit.

So ... more generosity from total strangers. I was certainly clocking up the favours. This whole trip was turning into one big 'pay it forward' exercise. Many times I promised myself that from now on I would make sure I offered total strangers help if they looked like they needed it.

# 2

# Bravery, or the lack of it

It took till 11 am to fully pack up at Marlborough. For some strange reason I hadn't put on my hat till then and I burnt my nose to a complete crisp. I didn't think it would ever stop glowing! So, we left: Trina on Gumby, me on Piglet, and the redheads, Bart and Willow, carrying the packs. Initially we followed railway lines. The rail traffic was surprisingly heavy, but it only took half a day for the kids to stop noticing the trains. The horses worked quite well once we sorted out that Gumby couldn't walk in front (he's an avid follower) and that Bart had to be at the back because of his 'bum issues'. We rode 20 kilometres, which was a big first day but we had to make it to water. We set up camp at Kooltandra railway siding, totally exhausted and sunstruck.

That day was the first of only two days on my whole trip where I had to look after myself before the horses. We stopped and unsaddled the horses, tied them to a tree and lay down in the shade for an hour before we set up a paddock for them to graze. I don't think they minded too much – they were just happy to have the weight off their backs and be resting. But I still felt ashamed. The dam was not much more than a mud puddle; Keith's informant had said it was a good water source! That night was spent with all seven of us soundly sleeping, despite the regular trains flying past literally 10 metres away.

The four days Trina rode with me ticked along quite well. The BNT guide said there was a great pub at Ogmore, the next town we would reach, so all day we talked about ice-cold Coke, beer and a shower. But yet again I was to get a hard lesson in changing plans: we got there to discover the pub had closed down and people were living in the building. We were so close to just walking in anyway and demanding a beer! That's when Steve, a local, came along and offered us both his bathroom and fridge.

We spent a lot of time following the railway lines. The horses became so 'train trained' I'm sure we could have pulled off the perfect train heist, just like they do in the westerns. It was very hot and dry, around 40 degrees. We were drinking about 4 litres each a day but only producing a cup full of urine (not that I measured it). The rest was lost as sweat; at this rate I was going to need some serious electrolytes.

After a couple of days we started to get into nicer country; still dry but not 'godforsaken', which is how I would describe what we had left behind. We camped one night by Granite Creek. Actually, we camped about 700 metres from the creek. I had spoken to the station owner who advised, 'Just don't go swimming in the creek.' What! I fired a rapid sequence of panicked questions at him, my irrational fear of saltwater crocodiles bubbling up to the surface. He just laughed and said he had never lost any stock but wouldn't go swimming there in a hurry. Hence the 700-metre safety distance. Yes, I am a coward. I think Trina thought my cowardice was a bit amusing. I didn't care. Some people are afraid of cats! Surely I am allowed a little bit of irrational 'salty fear'.

We were following the BNT published guides but it wasn't easy in some places, especially since they'd been written for southbound travellers and I had to invert all the information. At one stage we saw up to three guiding triangles at once and then all of a sudden nothing but very confusing and contradictory directions. We managed to navigate our way around 'the pondage' even though neither of us knew what the hell a 'pondage' was, and nothing we saw could possibly be described as such. In the end we made a beeline for the trusty old railway line, and managed to find camp.

Trina rode with me for only four days but it was invaluable. I don't know how I would have started up again without her. Physically it was hard work and I needed her to help get the green horses into a system – but I needed her support even more for my mental status. Was I just going to trash these horses, as I had in the Victorian Alps? The terrain was a lot friendlier but the two boys, Bart and Gumby, obviously didn't know what hard work was and the days were very long and hot. Then, on our fourth night, Dick, Trina's husband and Harry, my nephew, came to our camp (yes, beside a railway line again). They cooked up a big barbecue feast and then left with my float, my ute and my sister. I was all alone, again. How the hell was I going to do this?

That first night on my own I received a very sad sounding message on my phone from Sue, at 'Mission Control', asking me to call her as soon as I could. What she had to say was devastating and almost beyond comprehension.

### Day 24, 15 January: Wumalgi siding

*Dick and Harry turned up with a brilliant steak and salad BBQ then took everything, including Trina, and left. So, now I am on my own.*

*I spoke to Sue on the phone (I have reception if I stand on my tiptoes in the middle of the railway line). She told me that, 36 hours ago, Scott (the boyfriend of our Scottish friend, Tia) died suddenly and unexpectedly while asleep in Tia's arms. I am shattered for her. I don't know what happened. Sue doesn't know. I think he was about 30. See, it's moments like this that I don't understand how there could possibly be a god. How incredibly unfair. I am at a loss. I can't ring Tia from here in very dodgy range, on the other side of the world. It's not a conversation you can have with the overseas lag and bad reception. Besides, I'm not up to it. Sue is trying to ring her. I am sitting here in the middle of the train tracks, somewhere in Queensland ... I am at a helpless loss. I can't write any more. I can only cry. Suddenly the death of my horses seems so inconsequential.*

*S 22° 29' 36", E 149° 33' 46"   40 ft   15.0 km*
*Total: 380.2 km*

**Low point:** *Sue's phone call.*
**High point:** *There can't be one ... not today.*

I wanted to go to the funeral, but short of abandoning the horses and dog by the side of the railway line and flying to Scotland, it couldn't be done. I wanted to be there for Tia and am still sorry I wasn't. Tia and Scott had decided to get married but hadn't told anyone. I think Tia announced it at the funeral. They were too young and too in love. It was all wrong. I felt like a very bad friend, not being there for her. She has many friends and family, all in Scotland, but I still feel I failed her. I kept on going, just a little heavier in my heart.

### Day 25, 16 January: Waverly Creek

*I left in a bit of a flap this morning — the first morning on my own. Trying to handle four horses was a bit stressful. Before I had gone a kilometre I found myself in a paddock of about 20 horses. I was riding Piglet, leading Gumby, with Willow tail tied to him and then Bart tied to Willow. Well, Willow decided she liked the other horses so broke free from Gumby's tail and was off, screaming 'wait for me' in horse language. Poor old Bart was in tow, trying to do the right thing and stay attached to Willow, but she didn't have a pack on and Bart did! Willow was cantering (not very fast, as she seems to be a very slow horse) and so was Bart. Piglet started to lose the plot and Gumby decided it was all too hard and stressful so closed his eyes and planted the anchors. Finally I managed to get Piglet under some sort of control, tie Gumby to a tree and catch the others. I am quite proud of my packing: ten minutes of cantering and I didn't lose a thing; the pack saddle didn't even slip to one side. I was also pretty pleased with Bart as he didn't lose the plot and he didn't break the tail tie (which has a weak point of rubber for such occasions) till he got exhausted and just couldn't keep up. I wasn't so happy with zarking Willow!*

*If I wasn't so concerned about my pack I would have been laughing and filming it! Willow pumping her little legs trying to keep up with the big horses, Bart cantering behind clanging, banging and flapping as he went and causing the big horses to gallop for their lives.*

*Well, I laugh now, in the safety of the camp, horses unhurt, gear still intact ...*

*S 22° 26' 21", E 149° 28' 35"   119 ft   16.5 km*
*Total: 396.7 km*

**Low point:** *Willow's breakaway.*
**High point:** *Bart's pack hadn't moved! I must be doing something right.*

So I managed to survive the first day on my own with four horses. Maybe I could do this! I finally worked up the courage to write an email to friends. I hadn't written one since I left the Vic Alps.

---

Hi guys,

Sorry I haven't written for such a long time … yes heaps has happened but probably not what you were expecting … or maybe you were!

My new kids are settling in. As much as I miss Tank and Quinnie I have to admit these horses deserve nearly as much credit for their entertainment ability as well as their work ethic.

They are all individuals with heaps of character.

*Piglet:*

Piglet is a grey Arab mare that was very kindly lent to me by Jen Moncur. She is a very hard worker but gets impatient with the others when they walk too slow or are being slack. She is my main riding horse as she is easy to manoeuvre and likes to be in front and set the pace. Her biggest flaw is that she would love to be head horse but is third in line. As a consequence when she is in a foul mood (which is not uncommon) she takes it out on Gumby (the bottom of the pack). One day they were in hobbles and I saw Bart put Piglet in her place. So Piglet went straight up to Gumby and as Gumby was leaping forward and away she was cantering backwards in her hobbles throwing in a double-barrel kick with every stride and getting him every time. I suppose at least she is athletic. Now if she is in a foul mood I night line her as she can do too much damage to poor old Gumby.

*Gumby:*

I bought Gumby in November for a mere $250 down in Geelong. He was about to go to the meat yards as the owner couldn't sell him. He is a Connemara x Quarter horse and is very flexible with his neck and body. You can be riding him and all of a sudden, somehow, his head is just about on your lap looking for a pat!! He is a big fatty boombah and is very quiet. I think he has had kids on him a lot that didn't take control so he is much happier with a positive rider … he would much prefer to follow the crowd rather than have to make the decisions. I am discovering Gumby has never been made to work hard so we have had to have a few discussions about how standing still and refusing to move is not the preferred option. He is getting the hang of it. He doesn't lead well and would prefer to be dragged but I am afraid that is a bit hard on both Piglet and I!

*Bart:*

I bought Bart at the Echuca sales. He has a lot of great attributes and a couple of paranoias that he really struggles with. For some reason he is really scared of his back end! He had no problem taking the pack, wasn't too bad taking the crupper but was petrified of the britchin (which goes around their back end to stop the pack moving forward). He also freaks if something walks up behind him. He loves to follow and has a short, fluffy tail like a foal so can't tie anyone to his tail anyway. He loves to walk behind a horse tied to their tail as long as nothing else is behind him. He is a surprisingly hard worker (I thought he may be a little precious) and very well behaved.

*Willow:*

I bought Willow at the same place as Bart. She was being dogged too. She has obviously been a kids' pony because she is dead quiet, a hard worker and has absolutely no mouth. She is quite tight in the front and I have been doing chiro on her neck to free her up. She is very quiet but sometimes is a bit too independent.

Apart from the heat the country is great. The amount of feed for the horses is better than in Vic and so far they are holding their condition. I have two fears at the moment: 1. I am dreading the wet season to come pouring in as it should have started before Christmas but hasn't; it feels ominous. 2. Saltwater crocodiles – salties give me the heebie jeebies.

Tonight I am camping by an empty creek and a bore with a trough – have you ever seen a grown woman swim in a cattle trough? If not, check out Google Earth; I'm sure it got me. At least there are no salties in there! Finally, I just have to say thanks to heaps of people – some I haven't even mentioned yet but they know who they are. When my horses died I was stunned at the offers of support I got from so many people. Some offered their horses. Others offered their precious time to help truck my horses up north, and I had one great Australian offer of a chook raffle to help pay my vet bills! I think that last offer seemed to say it all.

So basically I am still on this ridiculous trek … I seem to be such a slow learner!

HiD

---

It was fast approaching late January and there hadn't been a break in the season yet. This wet season was becoming a late one, if it was going to arrive at all. I came to one camp where there was a small paddock I could put the horses in. It was very dry and rough but at least the horses could have a night without their hobbles on. Also, it meant I didn't have to put up the electric fence. I was growing to hate the electric fence. It was a lot of work, time consuming and a pain to pack up. Pity it was so essential; there was no way I was prepared to get up every morning and track the horses for 5 kilometres or more, bring them back to camp and then start packing up. Yes, I hated the electric fence but I couldn't live without it.

So, at this camp it was great not having to set it up. I soon discovered the horses were pleased to have me camp in their paddock and while one distracted me by trying to drag away my hoochie with his teeth the others were raiding the pack bag I called 'the kitchen'. It was at this camp that Gumby discovered the joys of two-minute noodles. He stole the packet and galloped off, hobble free. While I was dealing with the others slowly destroying my camp, he was chewing through the packet to open it. By the time I reached him he had finished eating the crunchy noodles and had started on the flavour sachet. So yes, I had to get out that damned electric fence anyway and put it around my camp to keep the horses out!

> **Handy hint no. 4:** Don't set up camp in the same paddock as your horses, especially if you have a 'Bart' or a 'Gumby'.

It was also at this camp that I managed to skilfully soak my entire swag and bedding in one point of rain.

> **Handy hint no. 5:** Don't set up your swag in a depression in the ground, especially when you put a large waterproof hoochie under it. The hoochie just serves to catch the rain and guide it to the bottom of the depression, and by the time you wake in the morning you are wishing your swag was a boat.

Despite these few hiccups I was starting to think that maybe I could do this. The horses were holding condition quite well – no rubs or sores to speak of – and their feet were travelling okay. I was still sane, or so I thought, and we seemed to be putting a few miles under our girth (as we say 'get a few miles under our belt'… riding horses you get a few miles under your girth). We were consistently doing about 20 kilometres a day, and the horses were only getting stronger. Then the wet arrived.

On 22 January I woke up to the sound of heavy rain that seemed to hum a tune of persistence. Luckily, the day before I had been met by the owner of Marylands Station, Iain Day. On his insistence I stayed in their single-man quarters for the night, so I woke up listening to the delightful sound of rain hitting the tin roof. Ahhh, I was dry; what luxury! Judy, Iain's mother, came around and said I could stay longer because the rain was going to get worse before it got better.

## Day 34, 25 January: Marylands

Judy is an interesting woman. She has lived on the place all her life and works harder than most men I know. She is in her late 60s and her husband died last year of cancer. I initially thought she hated me but I have decided she is just really shy. Iain told me they have been informed that a coal mining company is going to acquire the valley 'for the good of the community' and build a dam. Marylands is on the edge and they haven't been told if the houses will be flooded. The Days have no choice in the matter at all. I feel for Judy as the property/house is everything to her. She has lived here all her life, her husband died here and although her house may not be a palace, it's her house and, I suspect, the one she always planned on dying in. How is a coal mining company 'for the good of the community' anyway?

The volume of water that has fallen over the last few days is just huge. I'm sooo glad I am here at Marylands, in shelter. All the creeks have flooded and the road is completely impassable. Judy is feeding my horses sorghum hay, which they are slowly getting used to, but they are not too happy about standing around in all this rain. I bet my next issue is going to be foot abscesses but there is not much I can do — there is nowhere dry for them to stand! Judy told me the next camp in the BNT guide, Murray Creek, can flood very wide. When I asked Judy how far she would camp from the creek in case water came down she said, 'about a mile'. Is she taking the piss out of me? Does she have a sneaky sense of humour I haven't cottoned onto yet? A mile? Thank God (or whoever) I'm safe here. I don't have enough phone range to talk but can send texts and emails. I sent Tia another email. I am thinking about her heaps.

I'm starting to get a bit of cabin fever. Gotta get movin'. We went to the next-door neighbours today to help lift a $20 000 pump (brand new) out of the flood water. I was amazed at seeing what has happened. A huge body of water has powered through all those creeks and gullies I rode through just a few days ago. It's a bit like a bushfire: you think, 'Okay, I can picture its ability *for destruction' but until you actually see it, you can't. You can't imagine the level of power of all that water and you also can't imagine your own complete lack of power against it.*

*S 22° 07' 09", E 149° 11' 57"   567 ft   0 km*
*Total: 1055.7 km*

**Low point:** *Cabin fever setting in.*
**High point:** *I have a roof over my head – very luxurious.*

There was around 10 inches of rain in the end. We stayed for five days and, as I feared, left with Piglet nursing a foot abscess. So she was the 'spare horse' for the next few days (she didn't carry a saddle). I gave her some anti-inflammatories so she could bear weight on the poulticed foot, and it didn't take long for the abscess to burst. Even before it burst, and she was still quite sore, she was rushing ahead of Gumby, who I was riding. Gum was quite happy with that because the disadvantage of being ridden, as far as he was concerned, was that he had to be out in front ... still a very scary prospect.

It didn't take long for a green pick of grass to appear and now I was dealing with a whole new situation. There was plenty of food and water for the kids but the going was wet, slippery and boggy, and the choice of camp site ... well, let's just say I still had Judy's words ringing in my head: 'at least a mile away'.

I found I was hopeless at reading the weather. Having grown up in southern New South Wales, I had intuitively learnt that weather and I was now having to interpret a whole different 'language'. A southeasterly was no longer freezing, a northerly was no longer hot and dry, and the weather seemed to come from any direction! I found it very disorientating.

### Day 36, 27 January: Tierawoomba Creek
*I camped next to a feed trough with a little gal-iron roof and ran my hoochie off it. Rain looked a chance. The station owner drove up in a Land Cruiser and said I shouldn't try to cross Funnell Creek; I needed to go around via the road and cross the bridge. I thanked him for his help then he looked my camp up and down*

*and said, 'It might rain ...' I thanked him again for his concern and said I would be okay. Well ... it poured down; water rushed down the hill and straight through my camp. I put my irrigator's genes to the test but failed dismally. I managed to shovel trenches and banks so my camp filled with water and created a dam! I had to shovel out a bank to drain it. Sorry Dad ... I'm not much of an irrigator's daughter. In the end I carted all the gear up the hill and started again. This camp is much better. After that, all I wanted was a swim in the creek, like I did last night, but ... the creek is dry! How has that happened? I was completely drenched from the rain, hot, sticky and knackered. Oh well, if God (or whoever) gives you lemons, make lemon meringue pie. I stripped off in the middle of the open, whipped out the bar of soap and had a shower in the pouring rain. So, in the end this camp is a good one.*

*S 21° 51' 32", E 149° 09' 53"    577 ft    22.6 km*
*Total: 500.9 km*

**Low point:** *The display of my total lack of irrigating ability.*
**High point:** *When I finally 'gave up' and had a 'shower'. Wow. I've reached the 500 km mark and am still going!*

Taking the station owner's advice, I crossed Funnell Creek via the bridge. We camped at a roadside rest area right on the creek. Absolute luxury ... a rubbish bin! Soon, a couple of cars with boats and families pulled in for a five-minute break and we started chatting. I had heard all their questions before, but patiently answered them again.

'Where are you heading to?' Around Australia.

'Wow, that's a long way isn't it?' Yes, it is.

'Why are you doing this?' I'm not sure really, just always wanted to.

'Are you on your own?' Yep.

'Are you going to write a book?' Well, no, I don't think anyone would be interested.

'You must be so brave!' No ... This takes a lot of things but not bravery! Why brave?

I then steered the conversation into a U-turn: What is happening out in the world? Apparently Paris was caught driving with a suspended licence. This type of person is beyond my comprehension. She is rich for God's sake; *get a frickin' taxi!*

The fishermen left as fast as they had arrived, leaving me standing there, holding a plastic bag containing some redclaw crayfish they had caught that day and some plastic bottles of ice to keep them cold. They misinterpreted the excitement on my face when I saw the bag, and insisted on adding another yabby. I didn't want the yabbies. I don't like them. I don't like any fish (except tinned tuna as it's more like lamb than seafood). It all tastes the same. What I did really want were the bottles of ice. That night I settled down to the obligatory pasta and sauce with cheese and surprise peas, sucking on my luxurious ice, contemplating my apparent bravery.

The very next day gave me even more reason to think about bravery. We were following a railway line when we came across a few workmen fixing the tracks. They must have thought we were a very odd sight: four horses, a dog and a woman wandering around in the middle of nowhere. The first one I came across was a big burly looking fella with a long, angry beard and skin as black as the night. Even though I was sitting on Piglet I felt small and inconsequential. When he started talking I realised he had the softest, friendliest voice and the gentlest brown eyes I had ever seen. I distinctly remember him saying I was crazy doing what I was doing on my own, and that there was no way he would do it.

'There are too many scary people out there,' he said. I had to laugh. Here was this guy, who looked like the type everyone else would be afraid of, telling me he was afraid of the crazy, dangerous people out there; he could probably have fought off Arnie Schwarzenegger with one arm tied behind his back. Bravery is an interesting word. You are not brave if you are doing something you're not scared of, even if it is dangerous and you should be scared of it! On the other hand, if you are phobic about felines it is very brave to pat a cat. No, I'm not brave – stupid maybe, but certainly not brave.

After the rain came I developed a pretty decent headache which only seemed to settle when I was soaking in a creek. I was drinking more than

5 litres a day and hardly producing any urine. I felt a bit sorry for my kidneys but was struggling to drink such huge volumes of water. I had run out of my powdered Gatorade and was starting to get cramps in my toes and calves. It was still just as hot as before the rain, but the humidity was really knocking me about. I felt quite exhausted all day, then would lie in my swag at night in a pool of hot sweat. Unable to sleep, I had to resist the urge to unzip my swag to encourage more air in. I had heard of too many occasions where snakes like to bunk in with you in your swag. I am not scared of snakes but I'm not stupid. Well, that could be argued I suppose.

From daylight to dusk I was wet with sweat. It just wouldn't evaporate. Sweat would continuously drip down my back and face, which drove me to distraction. The horses weren't getting any fitter; in fact, they had gone downhill. I had to drag them along and they were taking any opportunity to stop. The day I pulled into Nebo was the hardest day we'd had so far. I was at the end of my tether, nursing this continuous headache, and was about to strangle Gumby and Bart with my bare hands. The day started out with a bout of diarrhoea which is always fun when you're camping, and went downhill from there. It involved crossing a bridge with a blind turn at the end into death-seeking traffic; no water at the published camp in the guide so we had to go on; Gumby getting cramps in the back end halfway through the day; and pulling the pack off Bart and putting it on Piglet because he became suddenly physiologically distressed. These guys needed a rest … and so did I, but we had to keep going till we got to water. In the end we walked all the way to Nebo – 42.3 kilometres, which was by far our biggest day yet. Of course the showgrounds, where we would camp, were on the other side of town. We walked along the Nebo Creek banks to get through town. The creek was a dry, sandy bed with huge old eucalypts in the middle. Quite beautiful, and I remember thinking I should come back and take a photo of it once I had settled the horses.

After the horses were all watered, fed, washed down, hooves picked out, medicated, brushed and yarded, I could spoil myself. I walked down to the pub and skulled three cold cans of Coke, which really nailed my headache. Is there a disease called 'deficiency of Coke'? With my head no longer pounding I started on one of the best cold bottles of champagne I have ever had. I woke the next morning to my familiar pounding headache back again (I don't know why!) and the sound of heavy rain on the show pavilion roof overhead. The timing was perfect. I spent most of the morning snuggled in my swag, dry as a chip.

It was that day that I recognised my developing fear of rain (sorry Dad and all the other primary producers out there). It was totally illogical. I wasn't scared of water, being wet or even standing in a puddle. I was just paranoid about rain while I was out there – about all my gear getting soaked right through and not having any shelter. I wasn't going to get very cold, the rain is only water, not acid, and everything would dry out, so it didn't seem to make sense. But on that day, as much as I tried to logically think myself out of it, I still didn't want to leave the shelter of Nebo showgrounds. Talk about brave!

I had reached Nebo at a bit of a low point, physically and mentally. It rained persistently for the week and I wasn't going anywhere till it stopped. In fact, I was struggling to find the head space to even contemplate setting off again. I was too tired, too sore, too brain fried, too low and too dry. Could I go on? What if I stopped here? It would be another big, fat failure in my life. I have been told repetitively by a trusted family friend that I have never finished anything in my life. Logic says this is not entirely true, but this comment always pops up in the back of my mind when I am making decisions about the direction my life is taking. Could I face it back out there?

The longer it rained, the more difficulty I had picturing myself continuing on. I had just done over 500 kilometres.

So I used a technique that I am very skilled at: avoidance. I buried myself in all the jobs that needed doing and tried not to think of 'beyond Nebo' until a solution knocked on my doorstep. I know it sounds strange, but my days off could get pretty busy. I would get pellets for the horses if I was in town, do chiro, trim feet, repair gear, catch up on my journal, send emails, wash clothes and gear, do shopping, sort the camp and re-pack, treat any injuries, make phone calls, post used maps home and the dreaded: plan the next stage of my trip.

My phone rang. 'Hello, Heidi speaking,' It was Peter Goudie's sister, Julia. I had met her once for about 2.2 minutes. She was also a friend of Mark's but I wouldn't have recognised her if she held me up at gunpoint.

'So Julia, you're going to Mount Isa to find a bit of work in the mines, then after that you'd like to hitch along with me for a while?' Do I hear a solution knocking on my door?

'Actually, Julia, do you reckon you could skip the Mount Isa thing and come straight here?'

# 3

# I'll have an 'L' for laugh, thanks Glen

Julia basically got off the phone and jumped straight in her little old car, Fizzy. By the time I called Dad at Brigadoon, to tell him Julia would be stopping in to pick up a couple of things on her way past, she was zooming down the driveway. That was only a 40-minute drive … she doesn't hang around!

Over the following week, Nebo endured 10 inches of rain and Nebo Creek ran for the first time in seven years. I never did get that photo of the dry, sandy creek bed. I spent a lot of my time sitting in the pub planning my maps, writing in my journal and draining the one-pub town of its only champagne, Killawarra, left over from an unsuccessful wedding celebration. From my seat I watched drunken miners who didn't have to work in the rain shoot past on large inner tubes on the very fast-flowing Nebo Creek. I couldn't believe no-one died! There was some cyclone somewhere in the north, causing a large part of eastern Queensland to flood and we were certainly feeling the effects.

Julia only took two-and-a-half days to get to Nebo, which must be some sort of record in a 1987 Ford Laser when half the state is flooded. I quickly introduced the horses to her and we set off to the pub to drain the town of the last couple of bottles of Killawarra. I was soon to learn Julia had a ripping sense of humour. She also had mad skills for imitating people, with a special fascination for the *Wheel of Fortune*; 'I'll have an "H" for hysterical, thanks Glen'. Later I Googled *Wheel of Fortune* and apparently there was no host answering to the name of Glen; there had been Larry, Tony and John but no Glen. It didn't matter. I had no idea whether Julia was up to this sort of work – not many people are – but one thing was for certain: if we were going to die, we were going to do it laughing. Next day we went down to the flooded bridge to see if we could cross it. The water was about 0.8 metres on the flood indicators. We could have probably got the horses across but Furphy would have been swept away like a leaf on the wind. We'd try again the next day. We were only too happy to nurse our sore heads back to our swags.

Julia didn't have a clue how long she was going to ride with me so we had to find somewhere to leave Fizzy. I got chatting to Val, the showground toilets cleaner and in true country style she offered to keep Julia's car at her place, taking her own car out of her garage and replacing it with little Fizzy.

When we finally left Nebo, the floodwater at the bridge was down to 0.6 metres. Even so, the horses had to work reasonably hard not to get swept off their feet as it was quite fast flowing. We carried Furphy across on the horse … much to Gumby's disgust!

Julia was the hardest worker I had ever seen. I kept waiting for her to say, 'Bugger this, I'm outa here.' But the harder the work and conditions became, the harder she worked. She surpassed me and at times left me feeling lazy and inadequate.

When I was on my own I had rapidly discovered that life was much easier using my little camp stove rather than lighting the fire at night. I was always too tired, too hot, too wet, or all of the above. The stove was great to cook on but it didn't give that much-needed morale boost that a good campfire can. Julia took it upon herself to supply a fire every night. It was great. The first night was a huge challenge, with wet wood and soggy, muddy ground, but she managed it. The rice was a little crunchy from such a 'cold' fire but it sure lifted us.

A few days north of Nebo we made it to Eungella Dam. The day we got to the dam we had Val's voice ringing in our ears: 'They have a chalet up on Eungella Dam where you can buy grog.' We hung out for this, deciding what we were going to drink first, how long we were going to stay etc. Julia was very keen but when we got there we were disappointed. It was just a huge camping area on a very low dam that was infested with blue-green algae. The only structure was a very sophisticated recycling long drop … no chalet!

There was a house about a kilometre away so Julia went over to stake it out. I had complete faith: if there was alcohol within 10 kilometres, Julia was going to find it. She finally got back to camp and said she had accosted a poor fellow who said he had run out of beer the night before. At the time I thought it was a likely story; he was holding out on us! But later I discovered Julia was so persuasive she would have been able to talk weapons of mass destruction out of Saddam Hussein.

She had a plan, though. The guy had told her that there was, in fact, a chalet, but it was on the other side of the dam and about 20 kilometres away via road. Julia must have been very thirsty, because the next morning she set off at 9 am and arrived back at 2 pm after of hitching some of the way with several 'upstanding members of the community' but walking most of the distance in her Chinese safety boots (as she affectionately called her thongs). She returned with a dripping plastic bag with 'ice' written on it, a warm bottle of champagne, a warm six-pack of beer and wild stories about Ivan, one of the guys who had given her a lift. We spent the afternoon sitting in the shallows of the blue-green dam, sipping away our warm but much appreciated ale and chomping on freshly cooked bread. I'll have a 'W' for warm grog, thanks Glen.

After that, the days really heated up. The temperature was in the high 30s but the killer was the humidity. There was plenty of water and feed for the horses, though – always got to remind yourself of the good points. I was very glad of the electrolytes for the horses, which Mark had sent up with Julia. I would mix up the powder in a little bowl and syringe it into the horses' mouths. They loved it so much they used to fight over it and Bart and Gumby would grab the syringe in their teeth, refusing to let it go so they could suck every last skerrick out of it. If I put the bowl down Bart would grab it in his teeth and bound off in his hobbles so he could lick it clean without the other horses fighting over it. My cramps, too, had settled as I had restocked on powdered Gatorade. Once we all had our salts on board I realised we were getting quite fit. The thing that had held us up on the way into Nebo was electrolytes, not lack of fitness!

**Handy hint no. 6:** Don't forget the electrolytes, for everyone.

With all the rain we now had the problem of high rivers and, would you believe, 'quicksand' as the locals called it. It wasn't quicksand in the classic western sense – where you would sink to your death unless John Wayne or Lassie (or preferably both) were there to pull you out with a handy nearby log – but it was treacherous. Occasionally, while walking on seemingly innocent sand, a horse would sink suddenly up to its belly; the pack horse would have both pack bags touching the ground. They would be able to get out by lunging forward but it took great effort and as the day went on it got harder and harder, and I was always concerned about injuring the horses. Luckily we were stopped a couple of times by station owners who advised us of the bad spots we needed to avoid.

One day we met a couple of local 'rocket scientists'; we couldn't remember their names so we named them ourselves – Justin (it started with J, anyway) and Hernia Boy. They had travelled out of town for sand as they were going to do some cementing and were very proud of their half-barrow load on their trailer. According to them, they had done a full day's work; that's townies for you. Hernia Boy was young and impressionable and wore a wide and unattractive belt that Julia and I could only imagine was used to prevent a hernia, with all that tough shovelling they had done! We had chatted briefly to them in passing, always using the get-out-of-jail-free card of 'we can't stop because it's hard for the pack horses to stand around without moving'. When we rode away Julia announced 'I'll have an "S" for superheroes, thanks Glen'. The Bowen River had had a huge amount of flooding. This particular day we were walking about a kilometre from the river, through long but flattened grass; the Bowen had flooded that far out. From where we were we could see huge eucalypt trees on the side of the river that had been pushed over by the force of the water and were struggling to survive the disruption. We set up camp about 700 metres from the edge. We had heard that there were salties in the area but everyone said that the rapid flowing water meant the crocs would make themselves scarce. That day was a near miss that we didn't even recognise until in hindsight. I learnt a big lesson: you can never be too careful.

### Day 52, 12 February: Bowen River

*Because of the detours we had to make we are no longer on our maps … that's what you call living on the edge! The only real concern is that we can't see where creeks are to plan on a camp to water the horses. We pulled over a 4WD just to confirm a few things (now that we are mapless) and met Mick. Great guy – very intelligent dozer driver. He gave us all sorts of info as well as a cold* can of Coke. He was going out to do a dozing job on a property and said he will bring us more cold Coke tomorrow morning — looxury!

We are camped about 700 m from Bowen River Weir. We walked the horses down for a drink and I stood in fast-flowing water past my knees for what seemed like an hour (probably 10 minutes) holding the horses who all refused, point blank, to have a drink. Even Furphy didn't want to have a swim. I tried to explain to them that this was all they had to drink but they really didn't like that fast-flowing water. In the end I lost patience, told them they could all die of thirst for all I cared and walked them back to camp.

On the way back we came across our superheroes again, who said after a hard day's work shovelling half a barrow of sand they were going to have a swim. By the time we reached our camp the superheroes were driving up behind us. Hernia Boy, eyes wide, was stammering something incomprehensible so Justin translated. He informed us they weren't going for a swim because they saw the biggest croc they had ever seen. Apparently, they followed our tracks down to the river and saw a croc, eyes just poking out of the fast-flowing water about 5 m from where I had entered the river. Justin was visibly shaken, and Hernia Boy completely speechless, so we (I mean, Julia) managed to charm a couple of cold beers out of them then we sent them on their way. I strongly suspect the horses knew better than me. Wouldn't be a first and I'm sure won't be a last.

Today is my one month anniversary. I asked Julia if she is going to throw me a surprise party but I don't think she is. How inconsiderate!

S 20° 45' 08", E 147° 56' 07"   525 ft   34.6 km
Total: 736.1 km

**Low point:** What an idiot. I was loitering around in croc-infested waters.
**High point:** Meeting Mick with Coke.

When we rode into town we noticed the standard country town welcome sign said 'Welcome to Collinsville, a town you will always return to' and commented on how it sounded a little creepy. After a while we started to think the people were all too nice and decided it was like one of those scary American movies where you go to leave the friendly southern town but then it gets all weird and things start happening, so you can't leave. Before you know, it your spark plugs (or horses) have mysteriously disappeared and if you listen really carefully you can hear that *Deliverance* banjo music coming up behind you.

In Collinsville we were overwhelmed by generous people helping us out everywhere. On the way into town we asked Brian for directions to the showgrounds where we could camp, and within a short time he had given us to the key to the Lions Club to stay in as long as we liked, shod Willow (refusing payment), welded our broken cow bells and introduced us to half the town. We caught up on the usual shopping, washing, repairs, emails and phone calls and became regulars to the Top Pub – they had champagne. We loved Collinsville and the people and were reluctant to leave. Julia was catching up on all the gossip in the trashy women's magazines at the laundromat, desperate to know how Jen was coping without Brad.

On 17 February I wrote to friends:

---

Hi guys,

Well, we made it to Collinsville in pretty good time. I shall tell you about a typical day so you have an idea of what I am up to. One thing people *always* ask is 'Do you have a sore butt?' This is the least of my worries and I shall try to explain why …
I wake up before sunrise at 5 am, dress and spend the next 30 minutes packing up the swag, hoochie and pack bags. The pack bags need to be weighed and adjusted to weigh the same so they are even on the horse. They are changing weight with every camp because of changing levels of food and water so this has to be done every day.

I then spend the next hour or so with the horses. I brush them down to check for any sore spots, pick out their feet and put easy boots on the ones that need it (this may take a while!). I pull up the electric fence and the poles and pack them away with the gear (the horses are now usually grazing with hobbles and no fence).

It takes about 45 minutes to saddle. As I bring each horse in I take off the hobbles and put them around their neck, watch how they walk and turn their cow bell off. I saddle the riding horse first and leave it tied up. I then bring in the two pack horses and saddle them at the same time so one pack horse isn't standing around with a pack on waiting too long. It is hard for them to just stand still with the pack on, especially first thing in the morning; how comfortable is it for you to stand still when you have a heavy back pack on? Much easier to be walking. They have the pack saddle and all the associated harness on, then a pack bag either side, then maybe a swag and camp oven or the shovel, electric fence posts, saw, axe, etc. The canvas buckets are perched right up on top of one horse and the solar panel is draped over the other pack horse. I give the horses a drink if available. Now I am ready to leave … normally takes about two-and-a-half hours from wake up to ride out.

We travel at about 5 km an hour but when you take into account stopping for 5-minute rests/eating/drinks/gates and rough country sections it ends up being about 4 kilometres an hour. The distance we travel depends mostly on weather and water. We camp beside water so the horses can have some just before sunset and then in the morning. Even though the pack may weigh less than a rider it is harder to carry because it is a dead weight and the horse has to do all the work balancing it. Even the ridden horse has a harder day than you would expect … it is quite hard for a ridden horse while the rider is leading one or two others, because your hands aren't quite as good on his mouth and your weight is shifting around to accommodate the led horses. When you stop at a gate, for example, the pack horse just leans on you or your ridden horse, and often your legs are trapped and you can't move the tired pack horse off you. So rider and ridden horse end up bruised all over from the packs.

During the ride I multi-task a little. I eat brekky/lunch (nuts and dried fruit) and then I clean my teeth (toothbrush and paste in the saddle bags) all from the back of the horse. Gumby often tries to share my brekky whether I am riding or packing him. Gumby can actually turn his head right around and steal cashews out of my hands while still walking in a straight line (or straight for Gumby anyway!).

When I find camp I hobble the horses and unsaddle the pack horses first and then the ridden one. The horses get a wet rub down, their feet checked, electrolyte drench, which they love, and massage/brush. They then graze as I set up the electric fence. After the horses are settled I set up camp and then rest. I find the heat really knocks all of us around. I cook dinner, water the horses, write in my journal, fill up tomorrow's water bottles and stagger to bed.

When put down in print it looks easy, but I swear it isn't. Even before the sun rises, as you are doing stuff around the camp sweat is just dripping off you. So that is my typical day, if there is one. Just throw in 10 inches of rain or detours due to flooding or worrying about fires or dealing with huge trains or catching runaway horses, or following maps that are wrong or blah blah blah. Well, that's my life I s'pose ...

HiD

---

We had to work out a route to keep travelling, deciding whether to head north and then west or more west and then north. It all depended on the rivers and the Burdekin Dam, which was currently overflowing at the weir. Rivers were flooding all over the place and Murphy's Law says whichever way you go, the rivers will rise even further and you will get stuck. I chased up the postman, who gave us a fair idea of what was going on out there. So, we bit the bullet and set off, all the while looking behind us waiting for some South American accented gunman with a single tooth in his head and a coon hound at his side. But the banjo music was faint and we managed to escape undetected.

That day was an interesting one. It started out a bit slower than anticipated; we were a bit seedy. The horses did it hard, all loaded up with supplies (29 kilograms per pack bag alone) and walking through slippery mud. Julia announced she was going to give Bart a day off from packing and she would ride him the next day. I told her I would keep my camera at the ready; I didn't think a couple of months packing would have cured his bolting issues. By that stage Bart had earned the name Barty Butt Cheeks because every time anyone came up behind him he would clench his butt cheeks so tight that he got wrinkles over his rump. Poor little Barty. He also answered to Bart Bart the Upstart, Barge Arse Bart and Bart Simpson (which was the original reason he got the name).

Halfway through the day we met Jen who drove out to meet us, leaving us with biscuits she made especially for us. By the time we made it to the station homestead she had next-door neighbours over, a barbecue fired up, beer on ice and quarters set up for us. I went to bed in reasonable time but Julia fired on.

The next morning I sorted out the horses so we just had to saddle them and then tried to wake Julia at 8 am (we had only 11 km to travel). I don't think she'd had much sleep and I thought there was no way I was going to get her out of bed. I had resigned myself to staying another day but she insisted she was fine and, even more surprisingly, she would still ride Bart! So, we saddled up and set off. That day Julia and Bart travelled about 50 kilometres while the rest of us did only 11. The day consisted of us walking quietly along then Julia and Bart suddenly bolting off over the horizon, butt cheeks clenched (on both of them, I think), with Julia swaying on top. A few minutes later Bart would gallop back to us, Julia still there, and settle next to us again; this pattern would then be repeated every five minutes or so. Julia insisted on leading a pack horse (you could never accuse her of not doing her share of the work) so Gumby got very used to continuing to walk along, dragging his lead rope and waiting for Bart to come back around to pick him up again.

That night we stayed with a local, Wal. The week before, a willy-willy had taken his house away (or most of it) and he was camping in his four-horse gooseneck float. When I grow up I want a four-horse gooseneck and Land Cruiser trayback to tow it. I could go to polocrosse weekends, towing my kids and my house all in one luxury stretch horse float.. Jealousy aside, Wal was great. He fed us a huge amount of food from a barbecue he'd converted from a beer barrel, watered us with XXXX and took us for a drive around the district. This leg of the trip was turning out to be very luxurious (and alcoholic!). The next day Wal rang his next-door neighbours to let them know we were coming, then he drove all our gear to their place and we rode without packs. It was great to blow away the cobwebs and do a bit of trotting (although I think Julia and Bart had blown away the cobwebs the day before) and we could tell the horses really enjoyed it too. We got a bit cocky from trotting the horses and were so excited at how much shorter the day was that we tried trotting again, but with the packs on. Surprisingly, the pack horses were happy to jog along and they didn't get too tired. However, the next day they had sore patches all over them and they were extra slow. Oh well, we weren't tempted to do that again.

It was great living 24/7 with the horses. I got to know them really well, and they had such entertaining characters. Bart, for example, was never going to get over his bum issues. Even after months on the road, if he had a day off. saddling him the following day involved a slow introduction to the britchin again. I felt quite sorry for him because he wasn't trying to shirk work or get away with anything – he was genuinely petrified. He also used to talk in his sleep. He'd stand there, sound asleep, and do a few little neighs. The others would look over at him with wary looks on their faces. I used to imagine he was saying offensive things and would wonder if the other horses knew not to take it personally. None of them ever went and woke him up. I suppose they thought they could just tease him about it later. Gumby used to 'sleep walk' but luckily only when he was lying down. He would lie on his side and swing his legs back and forth in a canter, sometimes neighing as well. I fancied he was dreaming about galloping along the windswept Irish peninsulas, wild and free, like his ancestors … maybe not.

Bart and Gumby had also turned into teenage boys, egging each other on as to who could be the most revolting. Bart would win hands down but Gumby still tried. They had developed a habit of stretching out to urinate, far more than any self-respecting gelding would, and proceed to shamelessly fart and groan for what seemed like an eternity. Very classy! They loved to perform this attention-gaining act simultaneously, in formation, while in front of strangers. Julia and I would often give the odd talk here and there at the schools that we passed on our way and we will never forget the talk we gave Homestead Primary School. I am sure the teacher would not have been able to stop those kids giggling for the rest of the day!

The more Bart and Gumby goofed around the more Willow and Piglet took themselves seriously. Piglet used to be always pushing to walk harder and faster and be out in front. I remember one day we were walking through a stand of ringbarked trees. We had to pick our way through them as they were fairly close together and this meant Piglet had to drop back behind me and Gumby. She was 'Not happy, Jan'. Well, she reached a point where she had had enough; she was going to get in front even if it meant leaving her pack behind, hooked on a tree. She saw a gap and surged forward. One of the pack bags hit a dead tree about 25 centimetres in diameter but she wasn't going to lose this opportunity. She pushed through, breaking the tree off at the ground and causing it to fall right alongside her, just flicking her ear. She didn't even break stride.

'I'll have an "E" for environmentally friendly, thanks Glen,' I heard behind me.

Willow was a real snake in the grass. We would basically forget about her. She would trundle along, no hassle, no problem, then – totally out of the blue – she would sit down on the ground or break her tail tie and shoot off over the horizon. She was always keen to see station horses but seemed to have a bit of an identity crisis: she couldn't distinguish between horses or cattle, often calling out longingly to bemused Brahmans, disappointed they didn't neigh back. Willow's feet were a big problem. Years of 'foot abuse' had left her with weak and badly shaped hooves. Bare footing was a perfect solution for her but that was going to take time, and we were rapidly getting sick of putting on and taking off all four easy boots for her, let alone the cleaning and maintenance of them.

And then there was Furphy. What can I say about Furphy? He was a tragic, sadly obedient to the letter and always busting to please. He spent his entire time planted just behind my heels when I was off the horse, which drove me to absolute distraction. I lost count of the number of times I trod on him when I stepped backwards. Every person I came across said I was so harsh on him because he was 'just trying to please'. But … he was sending me to the asylum quicker than a 1940s nervous breakdown. He would eat, breath and sleep apologetically. A friend later nailed it when she looked at him and said: 'He is just a pathetic creature, there's no other way to describe him.' It didn't take long for Julia to announce one night, by the fire:

'Yep, he is one strange dog, that one.' We used to discuss whether or not he was enjoying himself. In the end we decided he had to be because: 1) he was a Kelpie and 2) he was having a 100-kilometre run every day. What better life could a Kelpie have? I knew the argument was sound but every time I looked at the pathetic, apologetic ball of red fur I wasn't convinced. Secretly, I don't think Julia was either. But anyway, we let him follow along, apologising all the way.

Furphy seemed to be on a fairly short, imaginary bungy cord. As we trundled along the track he would trot 20 metres ahead, then trot back to us, then 20 metres ahead again. This would go on all day. One day we were travelling along and he trotted past us to cover our left flank, and he got no more than a metre off the road when he casually turned 180 degrees and trotted back to our right. What we saw only a few metres to our left, in the corner of our eye, was one very angry looking red male kangaroo, rising up to over 6 feet tall, putting his 'hands on his hips' as only a pissed off roo can do. We had no choice but to keep walking at the same pace so as not to threaten him. There is not much uglier than a big, angry, male kangaroo! The horses didn't seem to fathom the gravity of the situation and walked calmly on. It was a classic Furphy moment where if there was danger he would pretend he couldn't see it, so it mustn't be there.

This incident reminded me of the time I had my own 'one on one' encounter with a pissed off roo. I still marvel that I came out of it without a scar, but am disappointed at the lack of witnesses. I was jillarooing on a station in central western Queensland when I was about 20, having the time of my young life. I was sent out for the day, on a motorbike, to do the water run. This involved checking all tank levels, troughs and pipes for leaking and any contamination of the water with dead animals, and it took longer than daylight to dusk. I was checking a tank that was reinforced with dirt pushed up all around it, right to the top. The advantage of this was there was less stress on the structure of the tank but it also encouraged animals to walk up the side and drink fresh water directly from the tank rather than the trough. When the tank level dropped the animals would still drink there, stretching further and further down to the dropping water level. Occasionally an animal would reach a little too far and fall in to the tank, which was usually about 5 feet deep. On this day I found a little joey in the tank, swimming around the edge. The tank was surrounded by a thick, dense band of small boobialla trees, making it impossible to approach the edge except via the narrow stock track in. I could hear the joey's laboured breathing and see his little head just above the water. I already knew that you should *never* underestimate a roo in water; they are great swimmers and often lure a potential predator into the water to drown them. But this was a little joey, with such a little head! So as he passed by me, I reached in and grabbed his front feet to pull him out. Even though the feet were so tiny, the claws were huge! I let him go, so he swam another lap, and took off my shirt and wrapped it around my hands as some sort of token protection. I grabbed his paws as they passed again and started pulling.

Well, he was like a magic trick. The more I pulled the bigger he got! Finally I let go as I realised I was staring straight into the eyes of one pissed off, fully grown roo. But it was too late. He made the last lunge out of the tank and stood there, nose to nose with me. I had thick saplings behind and in front of me, a tank full of water with no escape route to the right of me and one very pissed off 6-foot red buck roo to my left! He was so close I could smell his breath.

What do you do in such a situation? I decided that I would let him make the first move (or maybe I was just frozen to the spot in fear … who would know). So he sat up tall, looking me in the eye, then turned to his right and assessed the escape route to the open paddock, then returned to eyeballing me and then back to the open. After what seemed an eternity he fixed on my eyes, rocked forward (into what could only be followed by a rock back to shred me with his talons) but then stopped. He spotted my shirt lying on the ground between us. He picked it up in his teeth and proceeded to 'punch its lights out'. At this stage I was quietly pressing up against the boobialla saplings, trying in vain to penetrate them. After a time he stopped, assessing me with my shirt still dangling from his teeth. He looked at me, then out to the right at freedom, then back to me. I had visions of my mother collecting newspaper clippings with headings such as 'Twenty-year-old woman found shredded, wearing nothing but shorts and bra on outback station: Police treating as suspicious death'. After an eternity, he turned away, shirt in his teeth, and bounded off to 60 000 acres of freedom. 'Phew' was fairly quickly followed up with, 'I have to ride a motorbike 60 kilometres home, half naked, over two major highways … ' I followed the roo for about 4 kilometres before he relinquished my clothes and disappeared.

> **Handy hint no. 7:** Roos are like icebergs; what you see above the water is no indication of how big they are below the water.

So, back to the kids. They were a constant source of entertainment to us. When I was on my own I stressed more about how the animals were coping and if I was asking too much of them. Whenever I turned to Julia and asked if she thought the kids were handling it all okay, or if she thought I was working them too hard or if they would have preferred to go to the dog meat factory instead, she would always answer with, 'Nup, they are having the holiday of a lifetime.' Poor old Geoff, he will never live that down!

When you travel along so slowly, your mind starts wandering outside the normal bounds. We started speculating about our kids as to what they would be like if they were people. We decided that Piglet would be the bitch who'd tread on anyone to forward her career, not aware that other people hated working with her. If she was in a movie she would be played by Sigourney Weaver, good looking but driven. Gumby would be the office clown, always up for a joke. His work would be fairly sloppy but no-one would have the heart to sack him, especially since he was so good for office morale. He would be played by Jim Carrey. Bart was the office shagger: late for work every day and sleeping with a different girl every night, but he'd get away with it due to good looks and charm. He'd be surprisingly good at his work, even though he wouldn't appear to apply himself fully. He'd have his own strange issues but most people would ignore them, arguing that they didn't affect them. Bart would be played by Hugh Grant, of course. Willow would be the PA who'd had the same job for 32 years and had 27 weeks of holidays owing. She'd know the company inside out, never gossip and would be very efficient. Willow would be played by Maggie Smith. Furphy would be the postal worker sacked for inappropriate behaviour, who would return to his place of work with dynamite strapped under his jacket. He'd never manage to kill anyone, instead just singing a few hairs on his chest. He would be played by Steve Carell. So, yes, we had too much time on our hands.

We managed to navigate our way through flooded country for what seemed like months. The insects were driving us all crazy, giving us rashes and welts all over. The poor horses copped a lot on their bellies from the sandflies. We tried putting all sorts of insect repellent on them but I wasn't convinced of its effectiveness.

We approached Dandelion Station with a mix of curiosity and dread. Although we had been told we could stay here as long as we needed (which could possibly be weeks if the river was up) we were a little anxious. All the neighbours we talked to about the station either got very vague and changed the subject or denied far too forcefully that they knew the people who lived there. I had spoken to Hazel, the station owner's wife, a few times over the phone and she had said we were very welcome – but she sounded a little vague and scatty. As we got closer I started to imagine that she had dementia and had no real idea of what she was saying at all. Could I trust the river level reports she had been giving me? Was her son, who worked on the property, going to be an axe-wielding maniac who had not even been informed of our pending arrival? We hadn't seen anybody for ages and I didn't fancy my chances of escaping from the 'crazy hillbillies' in the night on a galloping Gumby. Maybe I could have taken Bart for the escape; he may not have steering or brakes, but he could move!

# 4

# I'll have a 'P', thanks Glen

When we arrived at Dandelion Station our questions were still not answered. We met Hazel, an older woman, who said we could stay 'over there' as she waved her arm in a general easterly direction. She invited us to tea and said she had a roast on, especially for us. It was 2.30 in the afternoon and she already had the roast on! It was either huge to start with or she was going to serve us a shrivelled up walnut!

We settled ourselves in a donga (that's a Queensland word for demountable living quarters) that was in an easterly direction but soon found out the hard way that there was no water to even flush the toilet. We hunted around the overgrown, falling down houses and dongas to find one out of the five toilets worked, but only if we turned on an outside tap – but that also involved an outside broken pipe shooting water through a smashed window into another house. We were starting to get the feeling that the family weren't big on handyman skills.

We went across to the main house for tea and were introduced to John, Hazel's son. He grunted a greeting and went straight to the fridge to help himself to a beer. Now, Julia and I never expected the great hospitality we had been receiving so far, but we did find it amusing to see that John had no qualms about helping himself to a beer in front of us, without even offering us a drink. He grunted to his mother that she should have put the roast on at 7.30 in the morning and to my horror she replied that she had. What! I only brought one set of teeth with me! Julia and I exchanged glances and then Julia said with a winning smile for all to hear, 'I'll have a "T", thanks Glen'. Of course it went straight over their heads and yes, she was right. It was the toughest meat I have ever attempted to eat – and I went to boarding school for six years. Honestly, I would have preferred to have eaten my RM boots, spurs and all. In the end I gave up, snuck out to get a sharper knife to cut the meat into tiny pieces and then swallowed them whole. After the meal, Julia and I volunteered to do the dishes. We had removed our shoes to enter the house, mainly because our hosts were also barefoot, but were regretting it immediately. I'm not convinced they even knew what a broom was, let alone how to use one. We walked around, getting all sorts of unidentifiable sticky things stuck between our toes. We did the dishes (the tap worked – wacko!) but soon realised we had to start by washing the dish rack itself. It had old fat dripping off the underside, as though it had lived directly above the stove for the last 20 years. Julia was washing and spent most of her time dry retching. I was sorting dishes (couldn't locate a tea towel that had been washed in this millennium and didn't snap when folded) and finding dirty ones and passing them on. I found a frying pan with a lid on the stove top and assumed it had been used for our meal. Under the lid was a whole new colony of hairy fungus that I'm sure hadn't been classified yet. I sympathised with Julia's lack of interest in the taxonomy of the living organisms and so took over the dishes; her dry retching was really interfering with her work.

The house was just like the rest of the property: a shit tip. There is no other way of describing it. It reeked of neglect and lack of motivation, with a faint odour of cruelty to animals. Innumerable dogs, half of them tied to posts without shelter and the other half loose, were continually blueing with each other. They were all skinny as rabbits in a drought and came in every shape, size, age and colour, with no evidence of a single desexing operation. Hazel told us John loved his animals and had had pet camels, emus, pigs and kangaroos. John told us he'd lost the station equipment used to geld horses years ago and consequently the place was covered in stallions and colts. What's going on there? They mustered by motorbike and didn't even use the horses! John did not appear to wear boots. He must have had feet of steel because he did everything barefoot. He insisted we could swim easily across the river and was a bit perplexed as to why we weren't going to do the same. He said it was too deep for the horses to keep their feet on the ground but they could still swim. I don't think he quite understood the difficulty a horse would have swimming fully loaded with packs in fast-flowing, saltwater crocodile-infested water that had submerged barbed-wire fences lining the bridge they were somehow supposed to follow.

### Day 64, 24 February: Dandelion Station, rest day
*This place is interesting to say the least ... not really our type of people. As Julia says, 'They're as rough as hessian undies.'*

They own several properties all around the place and Hazel calls it 'the Family Empire'. She has been talking lots about getting the 'empire' tied up in family trusts so no 'in-laws' can get their grubby hands on it. As it turns out the 'Empire' originated with her inheritance, not her husband's, and she is trying to work it so he has minimal claim to it (that was our interpretation anyway). She revealed to us her husband, Bob, has been shagging a female worker from another of their properties. She said she will stay with him 'for the good of the Empire'. What? Does she think she is a Kidman? Or maybe even a Skywalker! The whole thing is a bit sus and we think there is something major she is not telling us. We assumed Bob was on another property at the moment but we found out he is on holidays in Thailand. According to Hazel he loves it there and goes regularly. Hmm.

Anyway, Julia and I are a bit dumb struck. Half the place didn't have water when we got here and there was only one working toilet (and shower) for everyone and it was in a house that none of us were living in! The kitchen is so grotty whenever you wash up you have to mince a large live insect of some description down the plug. Doing the dishes last night we found a frying pan with a lid on the stove and looked to see if it needed cleaning. Boy, did we regret that! God knows what was in there originally, but we theorised it had been fed to the guys who used to live in the abandoned house and that maybe we should keep an eye out for evidence of a shallow grave.

There are hundreds of horses here and the whole property is one big paddock: 310 000 square miles and not a single functional fence beyond the house. The river is 3.2 metres and going down so that is promising — hope to be able to go on Monday.

Gumby is developing a skin infection over the crupper and britchin area. Doing chiro on Willow as she was really struggling yesterday — this work is not ideal for her bad neck. She also has lots of lumps over her ventral abdomen. The sandflies are driving the horses crazy but wiping on that toxic stuff we bought helps a bit.

*S Who knows where, E Who cares.*
*O.O km (not far enough!)*

**Low point:** *Getting caught out by Hazel watching a DVD, like naughty children doing a break-and-enter.*
**High point:** *Three chapters of Saddlebum – we couldn't stop laughing.*

I used to read by torch at night in the swag. Back at Nebo I'd told Julia she should grab herself a good book to read at night.

'Na, no good, can't read. Got bung eyes,' she replied. However, she bought a couple of 'books' anyway and announced I was going to read them to her at night. Surely she could read … she had two degrees for God's sake. I thought she was joking, but apparently not. She was pretty much blind as a bat and insisted I read to her.

Julia's initial choice of books was pretty dodgy – and it went downhill after that. At Dandelion Station we were reading one of those western 'books' that are a bit like a comic but with words. I think they are the male equivalent of Mills and Boon. They are very short and have small words and simple themes. The storylines have hard men, hard riding and hard guns. The only female characters are bar whores, Mexican cooks and wholesome school teachers. The perfect book for a bloke! Julia had chosen *Saddlebum* for us to read, announcing it was appropriate as we were a couple of saddlebums ourselves. I must admit I had underestimated the book's ability to entertain; however, I don't think the author intended for *Saddlebum* to be a comedy. I would read by torch light and if I thought Julia was asleep I would stop, but she would wake up and insist she was listening and make me continue. In the end, to test her cognitive status, I would read the book but change some of the words or add a few of my own. For example, the book would read: 'The tough cow hand admired the pretty school teacher in her fine dress as she rang the bell for lunch.' Then I would add, 'A pang of jealousy struck him as he realised the dress was silk and he longed to feel it against his skin. He wanted to try it on himself, by the privacy of his own campfire.' She used to wake up so confused and grumpy and make me reread it. I thought it was funny, anyway.

I wrote to friends about the family at Dandelion Station but I think they thought I was just writing a 'funny piece' rather than a documentary:

---

… They don't like all the other land owners around (who we thought were great) and say they are hoity toity! These people are nice at heart but not really our cup of tea so we won't be too sad once the river gets low enough to cross. To sum it up, it's the kind of place where you cover the toilet seat with toilet paper before seating yourself, all the while regretting coming in the first place and swearing next time you'll take the shovel for a walk. It's the kind of place that makes you wonder when you were last vaccinated for tetanus. It's the kind of place where you wear thongs in the shower. It's the kind of place where the pegs make your clothes dirty again. It's the kind of place where you pour water down the sink and it all lands on your feet. It's the kind of place where you don't want to put anything on the fridge shelf as it looks to have a life of its own. It even seems to be the kind of place where the horses are hesitant about eating the grass!

All in all, nice people and we appreciate their hospitality but just a little bit scary. We are pretty keen to move on a.s.a.p even if it does mean a quick swim with the horses, the salties and the submerged barbed-wire fence.

HiD

---

Bob (the husband) arrived at Dandelion Station after a few days. Nothing could have prepared us. He was slimy and sleazy and sweaty and pale and pasty. He sat on a chair on the veranda, wearing nothing but tight footy shorts, his big belly hanging over the top of them, his pale, pasty face and rosy cheeks indicating high blood pressure, rubbing his sweaty, bloated belly and chest and all the while talking baby talk to the poodle. 'Did you miss your daddy? Is Daddy going to give you some lovin'? Daddy missed your lovin'. Daddy going to give you some lovin' tonight.' I developed a sudden urge to have a shower after meeting him.

It was interesting watching the reactions of the others to Bob: John became even more silent than usual but carried a palpable cloud of pure anger and hatred around him; and Hazel went quiet and unsure of herself, waited on Bob hand and foot and reminded me of a beaten woman. Julia and I both came to the same conclusion about Bob before we even got an opportunity to talk privately. The very angry son, the strange behaviour of Hazel and her inconsistent story of his so-called affairs, the frequent trips to Thailand and the skin-crawling feeling when we met him. As we walked away I heard Julia quietly say, 'I'll have a "P", thanks Glen.'

The banjo was playing louder and louder and we decided to get out fast, desperately hoping the river was going to drop rapidly so we could cross it. We would still have the problem of about 50 kilometres of stallions to fight through (Piglet and Willow are pretty good lookin' chicks!) but that would be better than another meal watching Bob rubbing his sweaty chest and giving the poodle his 'lovin''.

We got hold of Wal (who was by now hundreds of kilometres away) and he said he would come and visit us and bring a few beers.

'Thank God,' Julia announced. 'I'm dry as a stud bull's balls at the end of breeding season.'

As we were battling the bigger problems of escaping the clutches of the hideous, poodle-loving-visiting–Thailand Bob in outback floods, apparently the stock market had crashed and things were getting ugly. I'm glad I didn't know about it as I would have worried excessively about my huge portfolio of 112 AMP shares.

### Day 67, 27 February: Dandelion Station, rest day ... again

Well, Julia is a bit hung over. Wal came over last night with his four-horse gooseneck, beer, rum, Coke and champagne. Actually it was spumante (or, more aptly spelt, spew-mante) but I didn't have the heart to tell him the difference, he was so proud of himself – I drank it in silence under sufferance. He also brought meat and his infamous barbie made out of an old keg. Why is it that guys think a balanced diet of the five food groups is chops, steak, sausages, bacon and beer? We didn't mind; at least he didn't bring horsemeat, which is what we suspect we have been eating for the *last few days. We had a feast. I went to bed at about 11 pm but Julia and Wal stayed up till 3 am. Between them they knocked off 25 cans of rum plus the beer! Thus the hangover. But I must admit I have had a bit of a headache all day; a spew-mante headache.*

*The water has been at 2.4 metres for two days ... it's not going anywhere. Wal offered to get us out with his four-horse gooseneck and drive around the flood and drop us off on the other side. We are desperate beyond being polite, so we launched on his offer. That's not really cheating, is it? So we spent the rest of the day drinking and saying wilder and wilder things about Bob, plotting our escape.*

*S Still don't care, E Get me out of here!*
*0.0 (still!) km*
*Total: Not far enough*

**Low point:** *Being greeted this morning by Hazel and her 'front bum' (as Julia calls it) with her fly down.*
**High point:** *When Hazel finally did up her zip!*

When we set off the next day I reflected on how lucky I was that Julia was with me. I think I would have lost my sanity completely without her and tried to swim the river, with or without the horses. Also, I don't think anyone would have believed me. Hell, I don't think I would have believed me after a while! It was a whole different world and thank God (or whoever) we managed to leave it behind.

# 5

# I'll have an 'A' for alone again, thanks Glen

As it turned out Wal spent four days with us. He was so generous. He ended up driving us to Charters Towers and leaving us at the showgrounds. He refused to drop us off any earlier because every time we stopped the sandflies were so bad we were breathing them in. It was the peak of the humidity for the wet season and the insects were having a party. I was feeling very guilty about all this 'cheating'. It was all right if he drove us round to the other side of the flooded river (which would have been as far as driving us to Charters was) but leaving us at Charters felt like cheating. I hate taking the easy way out and was feeling very guilty – maybe I should have been Catholic! I kept telling Wal and Julia I wanted to get in the back and sit on Gumby as we drove along, so I could say I rode that part of the trip, but they didn't take me seriously. And if I didn't think it would have been such stupidly unnecessary hard work for Gum, I would have!

We camped at Charters for a couple of days so I could plan the next leg. No longer were we following the published route of the Bicentennial National Trail; I had to do all the homework myself. I worked out the stock route path, spoke to the Department of Primary Industries (DPI), and rang land-holders for permission to travel through their land. Well, actually, I didn't officially need permission, because the stock routes go through their land but are still owned by the shire, so as long as I didn't stray off my path I wouldn't be trespassing. However, it was courteous to ring and ask permission and tell them when I would be there. The conversations always had that familiar ring to them. 'Hi,' I'd begin, 'my name is Heidi Douglas and I am riding a horse around Australia raising money for Youth Off the Streets and am ringing up to see if it's okay to travel on the stock route through your property.'

'Where are you heading to?' West through Queensland.

'Wow, that's a long way isn't it?' Depends how far I get.

'Why are you doing this?' It's this or work.

'Are you on your own?' I have a friend tagging along for a bit.

'Are you going to write a book?' How can I? I can't even read!

'You must be so brave!' Not this little black duck.

I had to also start considering the 'tick line'. This was a line drawn on the map that demarcated tick-free versus possibly tick-infested areas. Cattle ticks have plagued cattle production for over a century. The ticks themselves may cause loss of condition and even death, but they also can transmit a protozoan parasite that causes tick fever. No matter how you look at it, ticks are bad for production and export. A line was drawn so that any cattle (or other animals, such as horses or camels, that could possibly carry the tick) need to be inspected, sprayed and quarantined when travelling from a 'dirty' area to a 'clean' area. The difficulty was, we were basically travelling along the tick line. I had to choose a path that crossed it minimally so I didn't have to keep spraying my horses. The tick line actually passes straight through the middle of many towns, so often people would have to spray their horses every time they went to pony club, for example. Anyway, I discussed it with the DPI and we worked out a path to follow.

The caretaker of the showgrounds was a great guy and he wheeled out a fridge from the padlocked kitchen area so we could use it. We were very appreciative and filled it with cold drinks. The weather was really humid; I think a cyclone off the coast was affecting us. The first day we went into a dodgy pub to buy ice and the scary looking publican (who had weird 'poppy' eyes) said in one breath, 'Are you two backpackers? Where are you going? Where are you staying? What are you doing? Do you want a job?' We politely declined and walked out briskly. When we reached the safety of the street Julia said, 'I'll have an "I" for Ivan, thanks Glen.'

### Day 73, 5 March: Charters Towers, rest day

*Today we bought a revolting puzzle from the op shop and are doing it in the cool cement shelter at the showgrounds. It is a bit slow going because there seem to be many missing pieces and Julia is not pulling her weight. She is distracted by the gossip magazines she acquired from the laundromat. Apparently, Jen didn't want kids but Brad was desperate for them. Also, the big news: Paris was caught doing 70 miles per hour in a 35 zone, without her headlights on in the dark with an already suspended licence! Surely she could afford a limousine from one side of the country to the other! What is it with these brainless, vacuous, rich bimbos who could do better things with their money and time than going out and getting photographed without wearing undies? What about all the kids out there who don't have a roof over their heads, let alone the means to afford to abandon their undies at random. Get off your soap box, Heidi.*

*This morning we went wild and had brekky at Red Rooster. It was just us, three other girls and the kid behind the counter. The streets were bare as only an outback country town on a Sunday morning can be. Next thing, the three girls get up and leave then drive past the window, one of them flashing a brown eye! Women doing a brown eye is just wrong. Plus, the streets were bare ... who was she flashing? Not the poor pimply kid behind the counter, surely! As Julia says, 'they're as rough as hessian undies'.*

*S 20° 05' 32", E 146° 13' 22"   955 ft   0.0 km*
*Total: 936.1 km*

**Low point:** *A toss-up between the Red Rooster brekky and the brown eye.*
**High point:** *Cold drinks on a hot day.*

We initially headed out of Charters Towers by the road, which was really frustrating. The weather was as hot as ever. Poor old Willow was grunting as she walked along. I thought it must have been her neck troubling her but then, to my disgrace, I found some straps and buckles under her saddle blanket; she grunted less after I fixed them. Sorry Willow!

When we reached Balfes Creek we let the horses go in a small paddock next to a pet camel. Well, three horses bolted to the other side of the yard and good old Gumby cantered straight over to the camel and touched lips with him. It was then I decided who I was going to continue on with when I got to Mount Isa and swapped pack horses for pack camels. Usually horses are petrified of camels and go quite silly. But good old Gum: he loves them! I knew, however, I would have to build up strength in my legs to ride Gumby (he needed to be continuously kicked to keep him going) and not care about the zig zagging (poor fellow can't seem to walk a straight line).

The heat was starting to get to me. There was still plenty of feed, but water was decreasing in availability yet increasing in demand. Furphy was getting hot too, and because there was little water he couldn't cool down much. Dogs pant to cool down but that only works to a certain degree; they also rely on stepping into the water when they drink. I was having to stop frequently, giving Furph a drink out of the top of my hat then wetting the underside of his paws.

I was worried about the horses and the dog. My Ross River Fever (which I had contracted in 2003 and was still suffering episodes from the original infection) was making me exhausted and I was becoming stressed. With stress I get shitty, impatient and really anal about how things are done – in other words, not pleasant to be around. I think Julia was struggling with the heat as well as money worries of her own, not to mention having to put up with my anal and impatient ways. We didn't argue, just didn't talk much; we were each buried in our own worries.

### Day 83, 15 March: Jardine Valley bore

*Cooler day today because it was fairly overcast and a coolish easterly, but hot enough – I think I am getting worse at tolerating the heat. For the last few days we have had hawks of some description fly in front and behind us. I think they are waiting for us to flush out a feast for them. Today I counted over 20 hawks over head of at least two different species. It was great to get to watch them fly so close, because I could see them using their tails and wings aerodynamically to steer them around. They were so close you could just about hear their radio calls to air traffic control. Tonight has been an interesting one, to say the least. We are camped at a stock route reserve that has two yards: a bare yard with a trough and a yard with a windmill and a little feed in it. Late this arvo a woman drove up in a brand new Toyota Prado, got out and started screaming at us like a two-year-old in a tantrum. I was half expecting her to throw herself down and beat her fists on the ground.*

'What the fuck do you think you're fucking doing?' she screeched. We kept calm and told her we were camping on the reserve for the night. She was insisting that it was private property (which I thought was pretty ballsy of her since we were standing next to the sign saying 'Stock Route Reserve No.'). I explained that the DPI told us it was part of a stock route and the published stock route map must have had it wrong too. She backed down a bit and then said the trough was hers and the windmill was part of the stock route. In the end I swallowed my pride and apologised for camping on land that I knew very well we had every right to camp on. It wasn't that I was regaining some of my tolerance, but probably more that I thought she needed to save face, especially since she had said she was going to go home and tell her husband and he would probably come back with his gun! Yep, I could swallow my pride to try to avoid those pesky gunshot wounds. So we had to move the horses into the windmill yard, but she said we were allowed to leave our set-up camp by the trough. I think she was just one of those really angry people. Great welcome to Hughenden!

For the last few days Julia has been distant, quiet and not joking about. Tonight I asked her what was wrong and she replied it was nothing. Five minutes later she said she had run out of money and would have to leave when we got to Hughenden. That's tomorrow! I am not entirely sure that was the full reason. I suppose I am paranoid but I am sure I would have been shitting her with the stressed mood I've been in lately. I am so fussy and pedantic and want things done my way all the time. I know I can be hard to put up with sometimes.

So, tomorrow's ride is Julia's last one. Can I cope? My initial reaction was, 'Oh my God ... I can't do this on my own!' and then I was fleetingly annoyed with her for giving me such little notice. For God's sake Heidi, you have travelled on your own before so you know you can do it and hello, anyone who can arrive in flooded Queensland within two days of being asked to come and help is someone who leaves just as quick! I was happy to accept her rapid *arrival and I should be grateful she came at all. If she hadn't come I quite possibly would never have left Nebo. I am just going to have to stay calm and get fully self-reliant. I have already proven I can do it. But it is so hot and I am so tired ...*

*S 20° 52' 01", E 144° 22' 50"   1163 ft   24.5 km*
*Total: 1123.1 km*

**Low point:** *Julia is leaving ...*
**High point:** *Umm, that the angry husband with the gun collection hasn't returned ... yet.*

The next day I had a lot of thinking to do. I am no good when things change suddenly and I had to get my head around being on my own again. Intellectually I knew I could do it, but I was surprised to discover how much I had come to rely on Julia. But part of me was actually looking forward to the next leg, back on my own. There was never any doubt, though: Gumby and the others never really laughed at my jokes like Julia did.

# 6

# Heading west

I had decided to sell Willow. She was struggling with her neck and feet due to all the hard work and although I don't doubt she would have kept on going, it wouldn't have been fair to her. She owed me nothing, but I put $500 on her. If you sell horses for less than meat money, people take them pretending they are going to ride them and then sell them to the knackery. There is no way she deserved that.

Julia had a real soft spot for Willow, especially the way she moved her ears. Instead of putting them back on an angle like normal horses, she just turned them around still upright as though they were some sort of satellite receiving dish. Every time she did it Julia would scream, 'Look at her ears! Isn't she gorgey?' Julia called things 'gorgey' rather than gorgeous. Every time she pointed out her favouritism for Willow I would pretend I thought she was a silly horse and then spout the virtues of 'Gumby, the Best Horse in the World'.

The first day in Hughenden I walked into the post office and enquired about who I should contact to find a prospective horse buyer. Ten minutes later I walked out of the shop with two buyers coming to see Willow the next day. As it turned out, the first one to see her bought her. They fell in love with her ears and couldn't resist!

Back in town I had to do the usual jobs. The biggest part of the rest stops in town was trying to work out the next leg. I hated having to ring all the land-holders, trying to find out about future water holes and thus work out how far I could get each day. I was averaging about 25 to 30 kilometres a day. I worked out the horses needed two rest days with every five days' work. Maybe that's where the 'working week' was originally developed, back in the 'old days' when horses used to work so hard for us in everyday life. If I rode them for nine or ten days then I found they needed three or four off or they'd be knocked up by the third day into the next leg. If I only gave them a day off then they didn't recover well enough. Along this western leg the towns were conveniently spaced apart, so I would travel between them without a rest then get a good three days of rest and hard feed at the showgrounds while I did all my 'jobs'.

One thing I tried to do at every town was to write my bulk emails with my BlackBerry phone. I had no idea if anyone had appreciated them or if they were just clogging up their 'in-boxes'. But no-one complained and told me to stop, so I just kept going.

---

Hi guys,

Haven't written for a while … I am sure you are all devastated! We are on a new leg of the journey. Heading west on the Flinders Highway on our mission towards Cloncurry/Mount Isa where we meet the camels.

On the highway it's a whole new ball game … I reckon I have RSI from waving. God! Get me off this nightmare merry-go-round!! No, seriously … *everybody stop waving at me!* I am too hot and too tired and too grumpy and too thirsty to care (unless you have an ice-cold Coke).

Actually, it is quite good. I know I started this trip with the idea that I was going to avoid people, but I have been surprised. People stop and ask what we are doing and why (that's a bit of a stumper some days!) and often invite us to stay at their place or ask us to talk to the local primary school, or call in on their friend etc. Some people give us cans of Coke or stubbies or, if we are having a bad day, fruit.

Julia has now left me at Hughenden (she ran out of money – or some feeble excuse!) so I am back on my own. There are good points and bad points: it's good to be on my own, the horses carry less and I am the sole one making decisions (yes, I am a control freak) but it was good to have great company, the extra security of a second person *and* the great hardworking ethic of Julia! She made me laugh, so that was a good thing … Gumby is a great comedian but I think I would have to say Julia was better; she also held her rum better!

So now I am in Hughenden all on my own. The next leg is on a stock route *not* on the road, so different again. Looking forward to it.

Anyway, look after yourselves.

HiD

---

I got in contact with a guy called Billy from the Hughenden DPI, who was a great help. He even drove me out along the stock route and showed me where the water was. It was almost cheating! It was great because from there on, the stock route was mostly off the road, going through properties and along railway lines. As an added bonus, Billy said he would ring the station owners to inform them I was coming. So I had minimal phone calls to make. I hate the phone at the best of times and dreaded the big ring around every time I organised a new leg.

Julia caught the bus to Townsville and back out to Nebo to pick up Fizzy. She was then going to drive back to Hughenden to pick up the extra saddle and go on to Mount Isa to look for work.

### Day 89, 21 March: 15-mile bore

*Took ages to pack this morning because everything was out of kilter without Julia and her stuff. It's amazing, because I think she would have been the world's lightest female traveller but this does feel heaps lighter. Just not having to pack the extra swag makes a big difference.*

*We rode west, out of town and dropped off Willow at her new owner's place. Then Bart wouldn't walk! Zarking farkwarks Bart! I literally dragged him 15 km. I had to put a thin string around the back of his head and onto the lead rope, as well as tying him to Gumby's neck strap (sorry Gum). Poor old Gum had to tow him the whole way.*

*I am so happy we are back on a quiet track and off the highway.*

*S 20° 45' 49", E 144° 02' 15"    947 ft    23.9 km*
*Total: 1 170.1 km*

*Low point:* Dragging Bart's arse all the way.
*High point:* The tank is overflowing and wind is up so the bore is pumping. I managed to screw the poly pipe inlet 180 degrees so it's pouring beside the tank. It is beautiful; hot water pumping hard out of a 2-inch pipe ... the best combination shower and head massage I have ever had, and all under a full moon. This is what it is all about.

I was travelling along the railway one day and came across a couple of houses at what used to be a small town with a railway station. These days it only had a post office that was open between something like 2 pm and 3.30 pm on Tuesdays and Thursdays; it was a fairly quiet place. A fellow came out and started chatting.

'Where are you heading to?' Western Australia.

'Wow, that's a long way isn't it?' I don't know. Is it?

'Why are you doing this?' Just felt like a ride.

'Are you on your own?' No, I have my kids.

'Are you going to write a book?' Nope. But I'm reading a book at the moment.

'You must be so brave!' Yep, that's me. Brave all right.

This local offered me his old run-down tennis courts to stay at; a bit of feed for the horses growing up through the old bitumen cracks and, more importantly, a fence all way round. I am always keen to leave the electric fence packed up. He said I could stay there as long as Furphy didn't chase his pet rabbits. Pet rabbits? We are in Queensland – rabbits are illegal as pets and I don't think too many people around here would be too happy if you had them, but he then pointed out he meant the wild rabbits that ate his lawn and were quiet so he considered them his pets. He also said I could camp in the 'grandstand', a three-sided galvanised iron shelter that looked out onto the tennis court. I just had to be careful not to trample on a few seedlings that had self-seeded and he was nurturing. I carefully placed the shovel and rifle either side of the seedlings so I didn't accidently tread on them while setting up camp. I gave his two boys (about six and eight years old – real little devils) a ride on Gumby, then let the horses out to graze with hobbles till dark. The boys refused to go home and just chatted away to me as I was setting up camp.

It was just after sunset and getting dark, when in the shadows a snake went under Furphy and between my legs and then straight into my camp. Furphy did his usual survival technique, which involves standing stock still but looking away so he couldn't see the danger. If he can't see it then it really must not be there at all! I did my usual controlled and dignified response (which is even less helpful) when I see a snake: I rose up, hovered, running in mid-air, legs windmilling like Fred Flintstone (without the bongo music), swearing repetitively. When I finally landed and gained control of myself I told the boys to stand back, grabbed the shovel and torch and disposed of it in one swipe. Just after I did the deed I noticed the snake's markings. It looked suspiciously like what I understand a carpet python to look like, with a squiggled pattern on its back – harmless. Still, I can't camp with any snake, I wouldn't be able to sleep.

There was silence. I wondered if the boys could identify a harmless snake; then the older one piped up. 'I hope you didn't kill Dad's peanuts.' Oh my God! I thought. I've just killed their dad's pet python, called Peanuts.

'What?' I asked meekly while trying to plan a speedy pack up and escape before the boys went and told on me for killing dad's much loved reptile.

'Dad's peanuts,' he said. 'I hope they're not dead.' And he pointed at the little nurtured seedlings. Phew.

It's interesting, actually. I have grown up in country that has its fair share of snakes. I remember receiving 'disposal lessons' from Dad as a kid. At primary school the snake drill (snakes would regularly invade the craft cupboard) was that, when you saw a snake you told the teacher, who told the 'shotgun monitor' (usually a sixth grader) to get the gun and shells while the teacher watched the snake with another well-chosen student. The snake would then be shot when there was a clear line of sight. Usually the teachers were city folk, and looking back I get more nervous thinking about them with a room full of children and a loaded shotgun than a sleeping tiger snake wrapped around the blue craft paint bottle. Anyway, needless to say the old craft cupboard had plenty of holes and there were a few blue splattered snakes roaming free in the area. You can tell city folk because they all want to deal with a snake using a shotgun. Talk about overkill! One swipe of the shovel is sufficient and a lot less dangerous to people and property alike. I digress; I find it fascinating that, even though snakes don't scare me as such, every time I see one my heart ends up in the back of my throat and pounds at full speed. Apparently snakes and spiders cause an innate sympathetic ('fight or flight') nervous system response in most animals. It's silly really, because the best way to not get bitten is to stand stock still. If you're still, the snake usually doesn't even know you're there and will slither over your boots without biting you. Just have to stay still when you first see them, though. Gotta get my sympathetics under control!

### Day 93, 25 March: Cape Horn to Richmond

The stock route hasn't really been maintained so it can be a bit of a challenge to navigate. If I go off the route then I am trespassing on private property so am trying to do it right (although most land holders would be understanding and not mind). I am having to use my maps and compass to navigate, which I love; I get so bored mindlessly following tracks and railway lines.

Today was hot …. again. Surprise, surprise. The clouds came over in the arvo (unlike yesterday) so that gave a bit of initial relief, but then it got quite humid and still. Oh well, can't have everything.

The horses are a bit sore and knackered. Bart has a swelling over his wither. Not sure why; might be because he walked for two days with his head up, dragging the chain, fretting about losing Willow and the wither got too much contact with the saddle. Then again, it might be the reason why he dragged his feet and threw his head up. It's the most swollen it's been today but I put the saddle further back and he seems heaps happier.

Piglet keeps getting these heat lumps. They appear at random and seem to be in any spot under the saddle – I can't work out the reason for them. They are quite raised (up to an inch!) and hard, and some go down overnight and some don't. She is so skin sensitive – she has carried the pack for five days now and rubbed her butt raw on the britchin. The way she moves doesn't help, with quick jerky movements and short steps. I will have to ride her next time. The wound where she got kicked at Hughenden is right where the girth for the riding saddle goes but is almost healed, so will hopefully be able to ride her out of Richmond.

Gumby is going well but has lost a little weight of course; he actually looks a bit like an athlete! Hard to believe. He has been brilliant.

Piglet has decided that if she is not going to get much feed at camps she is going to eat along the way. We have an understanding that she can do this as long as she doesn't jerk on the lead rope and dislocate my shoulder. As a consequence she is no longer fussy; she eats anything as we go along, basically anything in reach.

Camping at the saleyards at Richmond tonight. A bit more exposed than the usual showgrounds so feel a bit vulnerable. I'll get used to it ... and maybe keep my rifle in my swag. Chicken Heidi! I will hobble the horses out for a feed at times during the day and buy some hay and hard feed for when they're in the yards. There is not much point putting up the electric fence because there are weaners (young cattle) in the yards that are let out twice a day for a feed and they would just knock it down. The kids will be happy enough in their hobbles. I have noticed they are not eating the Flinders grass, which is the good stuff. You can lead a horse to water ... I got chatting to one of the guys mustering these weaners on horseback. His name is Nifty and he invited me for dinner at his place. Had a great meal (an excellent rump steak), chatting to his folks who have lived here all their lives. Nifty is quite unusual. I think he is very intuitive; does a bit of healing (without telling any of the locals so they don't burn him at the stake) and seems to answer questions I am thinking but have not actually verbalised. A bit odd for the outback.

S 20° 44' 18", E 143° 08' 21"   691 ft   29.0 km
Total: 1289.4 km

**Low point:** The horses are sore and hungry.
**High point:** I loved this whole leg: great country, good food and

*water and navigating on the stock route that kept disappearing*
*on me. This is what it's all about!*

A very amusing episode occurred the day I rode into Richmond. It resulted in a 'quote for the day' from me even though no-one else was there to hear it. I was struggling to open a tight gate that had a huge pile of dried roly poly blown up against it. Roly poly is probably the Australian version of tumbleweed: a prickle bush the shape of a sphere, about 60 centimetres tall that dries up, disengages from the ground then blows in the wind to usually gather up against fences, especially in corners. It's a weed and the only animal (apart from Piglet) I know that eats it is camels. Anyway, I was trying to pull the gate towards me, not get scratched by the roly poly and push the three horses back all at the same time. Piglet was in her feeding frenzy stage and had launched forward to seize a giant, dried, round roly poly. I finally cracked it because she wasn't responding to me pushing her back and I had scratches all down my arm and face.

'*Piglet! Put the roly poly down and step away from the gate!*' I yelled in frustration. She put her head up, peering at me through the giant, dried plant in her mouth, then literally spat it out at her feet and took four neat steps straight backwards. I hadn't laughed so hard for ages. I'm not sure what was funnier – what I yelled at the horse or the look on her face as she spat out the roly poly and stepped back. It was classic Piglet style; an absolute pain in the arse but very intelligent and (sometimes) very obedient.

My horses were a constant source of amusement to me and I marvel at the relationship you have with them when you are doing something like this. I have ridden horses all my life but not until I was living, breathing and eating with them 24/7 did I experience such a great two-way relationship. It made me prone to anthropomorphising them (which I used to hate when my clients did it). It prompted me to write a few pieces for my website, which I am sure most people just interpreted as 'That crazy chick out there is now actually going really crazy!'

---

You know, I find it really interesting to see the differences in kids at something as simple as, for instance, swimming lessons. Their responses to instruction, their shyness, their reactions to others, their discomfort in their new brief bathers, their fear of water or other people or just fear of anything that isn't Mum. I was thinking about this as I was riding along. What would my 'kids' be like? And then I thought of a diving lesson. I imagine the instructor would stand beside the pool and introduce himself and say, 'Today we are going to have a diving lesson …' and before he could finish the sentence, thwack splash, Piglet would have launched herself into the pool and performed the most mind-numbing belly whacker ever witnessed and followed it up by leaping out of the pool just as fast and pushing her way back in line but somehow managing to jump the queue by three. A dive would have been summarised and demonstrated all while Piglet is trying to push further up the line, aggravating all the other kids. Gumby would be picking his nose and staring at the sun wondering if it really could make him sneeze, and Bart would be watching with a look of mild indifference. Bart would have first go and do a beautiful dive and smooth exit from the water, with all the girls swooning and the boys jealous.

Piglet would have annoyed everybody in the class and jumped the queue so much that she'd have had four dives before the rest of the class had had one. Every dive would be as equally painful to watch as the first, and after a while all the girls would start laughing at her as her baggy bathers would be choking her high up round her neck, but she wouldn't notice. Each time the instructor would try to give her a few tips, Piglet would be in the water before the sentence was finished, again with no improvement.

Bart does a couple of dives. No-one is nearly as good as he is but he does not seem to care – everything comes so easily to him. Twice while on the edge of the pool someone has brushed past behind him (probably Piglet as she is trying to jump the queue) and he has squealed in a most uncool fashion, leapt into the pool with arms and legs flailing and come up choking on water. Bart does not like to be touched on the butt!

By the end of the day Gumby has had three dives, two buckets of chips he managed to steal from a distracted mother and has been chased out of the girls' toilets because he didn't read the sign properly. Piglet has had 22 dives (eighteen ripper belly whackers, three running jumps where she forgot to assume the dive position and one where she was pushed in by a tough girl who was sick of her jumping the queue). She never really listened to the instructor, who ended up swearing under his breath every time she launched in. Bart did the required ten dives, all beautifully executed, and fell in, in an ugly panicked fashion, twice.

So these are my 'kids'. Now you know what I have to deal with every day, although it's not diving lessons but packing for about 30 km. They are a constant source of amusement, each with their own special ways, and I love them dearly.

When I emailed this to my friends I got quite a response. Everybody – except Jen Moncur, Piglet's owner – intimated they thought I should stop for a rest and that the outback and solitude was getting to me. Jen wrote to me and simply said, 'Yep, that's our little Piglet!'

By this stage word had got around about my travels and it seemed that I had a radio interview in every town I stopped at. I was not really keen and only agreed if they flogged Youth Off the Streets and gave out their phone number to get listeners to donate. I am not a big fan of the media. On the whole, they never seem to worry about the little details, like the truth. The local ABC radio stations were different, I suppose, but invariably they asked boring or even inappropriate questions. It is funny how even the media come out with the same questions as the tourists on the side of the road. But during each interview I had to concentrate to answer them correctly; I had got so bored with people asking me the same thing I decided to take on the challenge of answering the same question differently every time. I also discovered that people don't really listen to the answer you give, so I was starting to get a bit silly and give some quite ridiculous answers. But on the radio I had to bite the bullet and tell some form of the truth, I suppose.

'Where are you heading to?' Heading right around Australia.

'Wow, that's a long way isn't it?' It will be over 10 000 kilometres at least.

'Why are you doing this?' It's a dream I've had since I was a kid at boarding school. I'm also raising money for homeless kids with Youth Off the Streets.

'Are you on your own?' Mostly. I have no back-up crew or anything but occasionally friends come and ride with me for a little while.

'Are you going to write a book?' No. English was never my strong point at school and I can't see that anyone else would be really that interested.

'You must be so brave!' No, I am not. Brave is walking down a dark alley in the city of Melbourne on a Saturday night. This is safe as houses, relatively.

### Day 96, 28 March: Richmond, living at the saleyards

*Twice a day, 1000 weaners are taken out of the yards and grazed for a couple of hours then put back in. There are various guys, dogs, horses and motorbikes involved in this project. The weaners get sprayed tomorrow, then they can go over the tick line and get trucked out. They must be heading south.*

*There is a high-pressure hose on a cement block here that people use to wash all sorts of stuff. The day starts out with a procession of roo shooting Land Cruisers just before sunrise. I suppose they all then trundle off to bed. It is funny to see someone having a quiet 'end of the work day' beer at sunrise. After the roo-shooters comes a procession of council and mine workers with their utes, slashers, rubbish trucks and ride-on mowers, giving them a cursory spray. Then finally come the cattle road trains that spend up to 90 minutes washing their whole rig. And somewhere in there,*

*Heidi cools down her horses or high-pressure cleans her saddle
blankets. Interesting procession of people!*

*Nifty took me for a drive down the stock route I will be
travelling so I could get an idea of food and water. On the way
we met the owner of a station, in his digger, doing some irrigation
work. Really nice guy: great eyes, calm aura and no wedding ring.
And he had all his own teeth too! (That seems to be rare in the
single men out here.) Well, our affair consisted of a three-and-a-half
minute conversation and we are destined to never meet again. Sigh!*

*S 20° 44' 18", E 143° 08' 21"   676 ft   0.0 km
Total: 1289.4 km*

***Low point:*** *In the middle of the night, a guy on a motorbike pulled
up at my camp at the saleyards. I was fast asleep in my swag but
he just sat there chatting away. In the end I basically had to say
'Fuck off'. Not sure what was to blame, the alcohol or inbreeding.
Maybe a bit of both.*
***High point:*** *Nifty was so generous to take me for a drive down
the stock route.*

The day I left Richmond was another snake day. On the whole I didn't see
many snakes, though I'm sure I passed hundreds, but they're pretty good at
skittering away at the first noise or vibration (and three fully-loaded horses
can cause the ground to rumble just a bit). Anyway, on this day the snakes
were obviously struggling to hear us. I theorised that there was some sort of
snake convention on and they were all on their way home, drunk or hung
over, because I saw no less than six snakes cross my little track in about 4
kilometres. All of them were about a metre long and as thin as my thumb, so
I suspect they were teenagers. (Maybe they had been to a rave party.) Three
were light brown/copper colour and three were pink/red colour (the colour
of Flinders grass).

The thing about snakes is that the same species of snake can look quite
different in colour in different geographical areas. I can identify snakes at

home but I'm not so confident in other areas. These little fellas all crossed the track from north to south, further supporting my 'convention theory'. I was riding Gum and Piglet was beside us on my right, with Bart behind me and Furphy behind Piglet. Most crossed the road a few metres in front but one poor fella was a bit slow; he'd probably had too much to drink. Piglet must have stood on his tail with a front foot because the snake went spastic, turning and flipping, and just as it settled Piglet knocked it with her back foot as she continued to walk on. At this stage it had managed to move across the road a little, despite all the back flips and contortions, and had just started settling into a chosen direction when Bart cleaned it up with a front foot, setting it off again, and then with his back foot. Poor little disorientated snake! We walked on and left it behind, flicking and spinning in circles. Boy, did he have some stories to tell when he got home.

On the road I had started to develop a new disease that I named Cokeapaenia (or Coke deficiency). On hot days I drank heaps of water and electrolytes, but still could get a ripping headache. No amount of aspirin, paracetamol or codeine would touch the sides, but a cold can of Coke (the real stuff) would knock it on the head immediately. If I didn't have any Coke I would have the headache for days, from daylight to dusk. The silly thing is that I used to like Coke years ago but don't now; it's too sweet. On my ride, though, cold Coke was like crack to me! Luckily I recovered once I finished the ride.

Because of the tick line, coming into Julia Creek I had to spray the horses before I could go to the rodeo grounds to camp. So I rode through town, got the horses sprayed and managed to persuade the DPI bloke to throw all my gear on his ute and let me sit in the tray, holding the horses while he drove the 4 kilometres back to the rodeo grounds. I was knackered and didn't like the idea of putting the saddles and gear back on the wet horses to walk them back, especially since I have heard the spray can sometimes burn their skin. The rodeo grounds were being 'spiffied up' for the upcoming Dirt and Dust Festival. Even prisoners were out in force with mowers and whipper snippers.

Past Julia Creek I spent a lot of time travelling next to railway lines because that was where the stock route was. It was much better than roads. The train drivers had all started to recognise me and I am sure, back at their smoko rooms, they must have been talking about me. They started to have

*Kooltandra Siding, just north of Marlborough, Qld. Me and Furphy are nursing our sunstroke headaches after a long day on the road. The country looked like it hadn't seen rain in a decade.*

*Eungella Dam, Qld. Rest day for Bart.*

*SE of Collinsville, Qld. Me on Gum with Piglet packing, trying to decide which way to go.*

*Strathmore Station, NW of Collinsville, Qld. My plant: Furphy the obsessed, Piglet with the attitude, me, Gumby the oblivious, Willow with the ears, Julia and her hangover and Barty Butt Cheeks.*

*Jardine Valley Bore, east of Hughenden, Qld. The kids having their relaxing, end-of-a-hard-day's-work roll. The season was drying up rapidly.*

*NW Mt Isa, Qld. Getting to know my new kids. They are so BIG! Don't be deceived, I am not in control.*

NW Mt Isa, Qld. Gum and I getting to know the new kids. Gum is so little!

NW Mt Isa, Qld. Gypsy contemplating a long haul ahead of her. Her nose line is attached to her nose peg but it is not engaged, and only tied out of the way onto her headstall.

*Riversleigh Station, NW of Mt Isa, Qld. Happy birthday to me! Unbeknown to the local ringers, they were the only ones present for my 40th birthday.*

*Savannah Way, Qld/NT border. My first state border crossing.*

*Calvert Rd, NT. Bunkered down in the cold, wet mud with Gumby and my growing ombrophobia.*

*Barkly Stock route, NT. Me and the kids enduring the Barkly Breeze. The country was so open that some days we didn't even see a bush, let alone a tree.*

*Wave Hill, NT. The girls appreciating the beauty of a rising full moon.*

*Kalkaringi, NT. Having a chat with the kids at the school. Pam and Gypsy weren't so happy about stopping.*

*Well 49, the Canning Stock Route, WA. Furphy having a well-earned rest in the sand.*

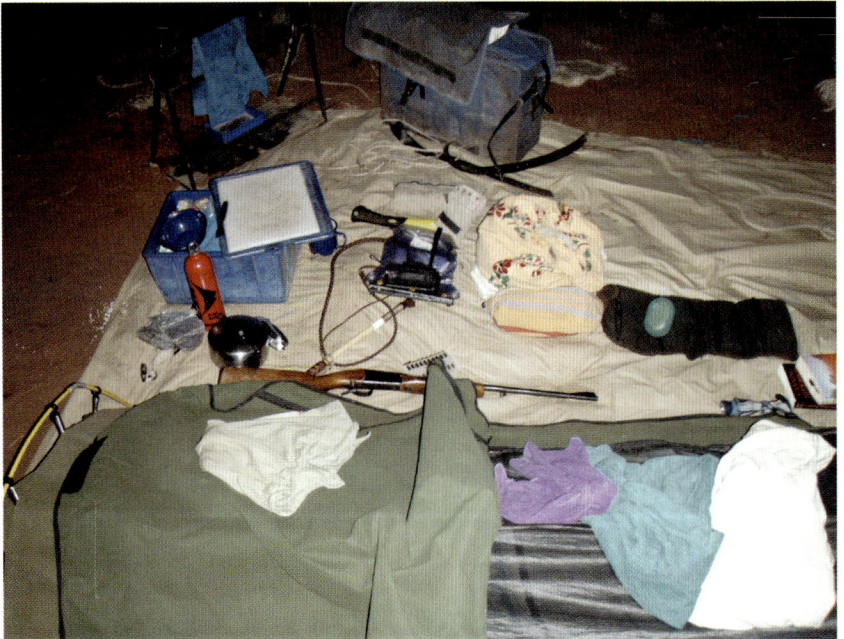

*The Canning Stock Route, WA. Every girl's dream bedside table must include a stockwhip, axe, rifle and round of ammo, at least!*

their windows already open as they passed and would wave wildly.

The last day before reaching Cloncurry, I was only about 500 metres down the road from camp and I was accosted by a stranger in a ute. He swerved to the side of the road and was out of the vehicle before it had stopped rolling. He came striding towards me, flipping open and holding out what looked like his wallet. He was showing me some sort of ID.

'*DPI – where's your paperwork?*' he yelled aggressively at me. I was caught a little off guard as he reminded me strongly of something out of a second-rate CIA movie. This guy should consider a career change to ASIO! I asked him which paperwork, as I had collected quite a bit along the way. I thought that was a fair question, but apparently not.

'*The paperwork!*' he yelled. I was staring at Piglet, hoping to God that he just wanted the certificate of tick spray and the weigh bill from Julia Creek, as everything else was buried deep in the packs, at least half an hour's unpacking away.

'*Where have you been?*' Can this guy do something other than yell? When I told him where we had been he was beside himself. I laid out the whole track from Charters for him and the more I talked, the more he got visibly distressed.

'*You've been in clean areas and you haven't been sprayed!*' Look mate, enough with the yelling, I can hear you perfectly well if you just talk like the rest of the population. I explained that I had been through my entire route with the DPI in Charters and they told me where to get sprayed etc. They had approved my plan.

'*Well, that guy in Charters is a bloody idiot!*' Still with the yelling; I thought it must have been some sort of condition he couldn't control. I watched him work himself up into quite a state, then suddenly he sighed deeply and a knowing smile came across his face.

'Oh, I see,' he said mildly, as though he had finally worked out the problem. 'Are you on any medications?' What! It took all my control to resist the very obvious response of, 'Well, you have obviously neglected to take yours!' But I stupidly said instead, 'Why? Do I look like I need some?'

Apparently I had been travelling along fat, dumb and happy, randomly crossing back and forth over the tick line, infecting the country with a plague of cattle tick that would destroy the world – and basically I achieved this single-handed! I really had to bite my tongue very hard to not say, 'Build a bridge and get over it mate!' Luckily I controlled myself. It wasn't my fault and I am quite sure the 'bloody idiot' in Charters knew the exact location of the tick line better than he did. In the end he let me go; I had to contact him when I got to Cloncurry to spray my kids, yet again. At Cloncurry, Les (who was caretaker of the local stock routes as well as the showgrounds) greeted me with already organised yards and some hay for my kids. I told him about my DPI encounter and he just laughed and said, 'Oh yeah. That would be Neil. Don't worry about him. He takes himself far too seriously and everyone just ignores him.'

I had started to find myself constantly managing Piglet's ailments. Her sore feet were understandable, because the country was starting to get a bit rocky, and were easily fixed with easy boots. She seemed to have a constant stream of rubs and lumps and rashes. A lot of my buckles were brass which, if up against her grey coat, left green stains (much more than they did on Gumby for some reason). I was hoping the marks would grow out because I wasn't keen on handing back a green horse to Jen!

Piglet always had the odd bite or kick mark from Bart, but it wasn't his fault – she drove him to it. In the yards at night she would hassle him, trying to claim 'top position', until finally Bart would put her in her place. She would then go and bully Gumby, who was quite happy to be bottom of the pack. In the end, even Gumby lost his patience and would put her in her place too. She was her own worst enemy. The leather britchin plate was starting to rub the top of Piglet's rump and she was fairly bald all round the back of the britchin area, despite the lamb's wool sleeve to protect her. I think it was a combination of thin Arab skin and the way she moved. She was always rushing and rocking and bouncing, never just strolling along. She often tripped because she didn't place her feet carefully enough due to her rushing. She could be sure-footed if she wanted, but I think she had this attitude that she had to be first across the line, even though she had no idea where the hell that line was.

Bart and Piglet were getting a bit sour. They had been on the road for nearly four months and were well overdue for a rest. Gumby wasn't sour, though. I don't think it occurred to him to be sour! He just kept strolling on in his own little world. Maybe I was getting a bit sour too.

We were getting closer to Mount Isa, where I would get the camels, and I still hadn't worked out how I was going to ride this last leg. The country between Mount Isa and Cloncurry is very stony and hilly (typical mining terrain) and apparently the road had minimal or no verges in some places. It didn't sound very safe for me or my kids. Mum and Dad were coming up to Queensland, to meet me at Cloncurry, for a bit of a holiday and drive, so they were going to bring up the float and take Piglet and Bart back. I was starting to worry about how I was going to do this last leg with the horses. There would also be virtually no water on the last leg.

I also found myself starting to get worried about how all this transition to camels was going to happen. I knew nothing about camels! What was I thinking? Andrew Harper said he would deliver two of his camels to me near Mount Isa, but he was so casual I was not sure exactly which month or even year he was planning on doing it. I hate being out of control, and relying on other people was hard for me. I knew Andrew was a very reliable person and wouldn't let me down despite his cruisey manner, but the stressed creature inside me was starting to rear its ugly head again.

At Cloncurry I had a few relaxing days waiting for Mum and Dad to arrive. I have never been a big reader, mainly because I am so slow (and as it turns out, I'm a slow writer too) but on this trip I had done lots of reading. I kept asking Sue, back at Mission Control, about ideas for books to read as she is an addict. I think she got sick of me in the end and thought she would shut me up by suggesting the biggest, slowest, ugliest series of books ever written (not counting the Bible that is). *Dune*: thirteen books, wading through tough language and enduring an author who I suspect was suffering psychotic events during most of the writing. The series has space travel, dimension travel, royalty and spans not only generations but centuries. The books are mainly set on a very hot and dry planet, making it necessary for the humans to wear suits that stop all water loss from their body (and that also recycle their waste). It was weird, the effect these book had on me, reading while I travelled through the hot weather. It was especially significant reading them later while travelling through the deserts with the camels on days of 45 degrees. However, I found the books quite relevant. I never would have finished the first book except I had nothing else to read; but by about the forth book, finishing the series became a challenge that I had to win. My favourite quote from the series was, 'We are friends of the stomach. We both like yoghurt.' I still don't know what that means! I think I may have read the entire series and completely missed the whole meaning in the subtext. Maybe it was about yoghurt, not interplanetary wars after all. I decided to ride Gumby to Mount Isa and Mum and Dad could be my support crew. By leaving the other horses at Cloncurry, it would only take a couple of days. Then I could go home with my parents, taking Piglet and Bart in the float. Mum and Dad had done so much for me I thought it was a bit much to ask them to float the horses back on their own. Besides the camels weren't due to arrive for a few weeks. Gumby and Furphy would then get a rest in Mount Isa and I would fly back before the camels turned up. It all sounded good …

### Day 113, 14 April: Cloncurry and west-ish

*Took off today on Gumby. The others were staying at Cloncurry and Mum and Dad were going to be my support crew. We only got 15 kilometres down the road and I pulled the pin. It was really rough, rocky, bushy, narrow and dangerous and it was only going to get worse (according to the locals). I was struggling to get into a trot because it was so rough. If I only walked it would take me a week or so and Mum and Dad can't be my support crew for that long. There wasn't room for pack horses, either. The last thing I want to do is injure 'The Gum Machine'. He has turned into a great horse. Nothing (except dogs and standing on cement) bothers him. He walks fast now, out in front and stands up for himself with Piglet when she really pushes him. He's my main man.*

*So my folks picked me up with the float and we drove back to Cloncurry. I think I will float Gum and Furphy to Mount Isa and leave them there with all my equipment, then go back to Cloncurry and take the other two home. The camels are due in Mount Isa at the end of April so it will probably work quite well.*

*S 20° 42' 13", E 140° 30' 36"   648 ft   O.O km*
*Total: 1625.3 km*

**Low point:** *Not riding the leg from Cloncurry to Mount Isa.*
**High point:** *Having the sense to stop before Gum got injured.*

On the way home I wrote another email to friends.

---

So now I am contemplating my trip from Mount Isa. I will continue with just Gumby (he drew the short straw, poor fellow!) and two camels. I am looking forward to the camels. I am a bit nervous, not of the camels but the whole new way of travelling. Anyway, what's the point if you don't challenge that ever-diminishing comfort zone? I have a theory. Your comfort zone is like an old favourite pair of bathers: if you don't keep challenging/wearing them and leave them neglected in the bottom of the drawer, then they will deteriorate, go all crispy and not accommodate you when you finally decide to get them back out and use them.
At least you can buy that bigger size of bathers each year. Not so much with the comfort zone; it's a bit harder work than that!

# 7

## Being trained by the camels

As it turned out, the camels arrived on 17 May. Dad knew a friend of a friend, Lloyd, who had a property near Mount Isa and it was arranged that I would camp and set off from there. Lloyd was great. He happened to be going into Mount Isa so offered to pick up Gumby and all my gear and take it back to the station even before I got there. I flew to Mount Isa and did six weeks' worth of shopping, picked up Furphy from the kennels where I'd boarded him and got my rifle from the post office. I couldn't find anywhere to leave my rifle when I left Cloncurry so did the only legal thing I could: took it back to New South Wales in the car and then posted it back to myself (apparently legal), to Mount Isa.

By the time I got to Lloyd's property, everyone there was having a great laugh at Gumby's expense. They knew his name because his head collar had an identity disc on it and I think that added to the apparent joke. I think they were expecting some big huge, tough horse with scars and an attitude. Poor little Gum. Everyone underestimates him. James, who works for Andrew Harper, arrived on a Wednesday afternoon with Pam and Gypsy, my new kids. Now, you have to appreciate I had not touched a camel for over twelve months, so I was a little apprehensive to say the least. They really are huge animals, especially if you are used to horses. The other thing I found difficult is that they hold their head up so high they tend to stand over you and you get the impression they can't even see you. Horses are not allowed to stand in your personal space like that because they will start to tread on you. Horses are prey animals. They can be explosive (except Gumby, of course); they need to be in case a lion comes around the corner. Camels, theoretically, are also prey animals but much less so. I think historically their list of predators is much smaller and they tend to be much less reactive. If a horse gets a fright it might jump on you in a flash or maybe turn and take off over the horizon, never to be seen again. If a camel gets a fright, it might move across a few steps, put its head a bit higher and look around; a lot less explosive. So, I was constantly (and mistakenly) expecting these camels to behave like horses do, and when they are that big you feel a little powerless!

James had to leave on the Friday so we had one day for him to hand over all his knowledge and help me get to know the 'girls' and set up their gear. Pam and Gypsy had not been worked since the last season and were a bit fresh. Also, camels like a system. They don't like change. This was very different for them. They were used to walking in a string of fifteen camels, being one of the many and just following the leader. Pam was an old professional and took in all these differences with an air of superiority, but Gypsy was a worrier, very concerned about all of these strange new things going on.

I knew Gumby wouldn't be scared so I introduced him to the camels by letting him into their yard. I did it wrong. What I wasn't counting on was him rushing over to eagerly meet them and them getting a fright. Poor old Gum – he was just being nice and friendly. From then on every time he went over to them they walked away rapidly (well, rapidly for a camel anyway).

On Thursday morning I got up contemplating how I could possibly wring a lifetime of knowledge and experience out of James in one day. Then Rowan, the head musterer at Lloyd's place, came over and told me I had to earn my keep and help them muster. I am quite sure it was a power thing. Lloyd had gone into town for a few days and left Rowan in charge. He didn't have a problem with me when Lloyd was around and I had even offered to help then, but now he was big boss man. So I had to drive around in a Land Cruiser for the day behind a mob of cattle that were being mustered by bikes and horses. I was there to carry the smoko (to this day, I can't work out why I couldn't just leave it at the yards first thing and get back to the camels). Anyway, Rowan proved his point: yes, he was all-powerful!

Meanwhile, James spent the day battling Gypsy and fitting the saddles. Maybe it was good I wasn't there to witness her behaviour, as apparently it was bad. When I returned James ran through a few things with me and did some last-minute adjustments. I couldn't believe James was just going to abandon me the very next day. I knew it would take all my self-control to not throw myself on the ground and cling to one of James's legs as he was trying to get in the truck to leave.

### Day 114, 18 May: Just up the road!

Spent the morning setting up with James and got away at
10 am. James walked back after 4 kilometres and left me to it.
Help! I started to get a cold yesterday and am feeling shite. Sore
throat, sore muscles and crap at the back of my throat (you know
how revolting summer colds, or should I say hot weather colds, are:
worse than winter ones). I had a terrible night's sleep because I was
so blocked up and spent all night turning over trying to unblock
my nose so I could breathe.

James was excellent. Really helpful and positive. I wasn't sure of
myself but he was really cruisey and insisted I could do it. What
a good actor! About a kilometre after he left me, Gypsy cracked
it and just sat down. It took me about half an hour to get her up
by hitting her butt with the bamboo end of the stock whip and all
the while saying very calmly 'up camel'. She repeated this every 20
minutes or so. She was lead camel and the first I knew of it she
would crash to the ground and just about pull me over backwards.
I didn't ride Gum at all today and basically left him to his own
devices. He just wandered along, smitten with his new friends
and totally unaware that I was progressing towards becoming
a homicidal maniac. What am I doing wrong? We got 9.93
kilometres (shortest distance ever) and that was it ... Gypsy was
going no more. At least I won in the 'get back up' department.
She has now taken to just planting the anchors and standing
stock still.

Pam is a brick. I reckon she would walk 24 hours straight if you
asked her. Furphy is the same but a bit excited since he has been
locked up for a month. Gumby is great! Couldn't work out why we
were walking so slow but just shrugged his shoulders and trundled
along.

At one stage Gypsy had crashed to the ground and wasn't
going anywhere. She was bellowing very loudly (something I don't
think I will ever get used to – it sounds so angry) and swinging
her head around from left to right like a crane. I was down the
back end calmly saying 'up camel' and giving the stock whip handle

a work out (I knew enough to know she was giving me a damn good test and she was seeing how far I would go). Then suddenly she stopped completely mid-bellow. I looked up to see Gumby, who had been ignoring the whole event and quietly grazing, pulling up some juicy grass that was wedged between Gypsy's knees almost under her chest! How many horses are that, well, I want to actually say stupid? I am not sure who was more stunned, me or Gypsy. I could almost hear Gypsy saying: 'Do you mind? I am throwing a tantrum here!'

I really don't know how I am going to do this.

S 19° 21' 55.8", E 138° 58' 45.5"   784 ft   9.93 km
Total: 1635.2 km

**Low point:** James... Don't leave me!
**High point:** I've started!

### Day 115, 19 May: Johnston's bore

Well, what a day. At least now I can get Gypsy up! But she just won't go anywhere. We had a head-on battle for two hours on the road and she just wouldn't move! I had James' parting pearls of wisdom ringing in my ears: 'Whatever you do, never lose your cool with a camel or it will set you back heaps.' I am very proud of myself — I didn't lose the plot. But ruddy hell! I tried everything: nose loop, nose line, stock whip and even just gor-rammed pulling. Finally what worked was I hobbled her and let her go, then I walked off with Gum and Pam, tied them up 400 m down the road and came back to meet Gypsy hobbling towards us. She would happily walk for half an hour then stop again ... and again ... and again! Very slow going. Only another 9 km today. God, it's a tough way to travel. I got on Gumby after I let them off to browse. I caught Gypsy when I was on Gum, and she quite liked me being up there. But Pam was not so happy about me being at eye level. Maybe she thinks that superior look of hers is not as effective.

*The camels spent their whole eating time trying to get back out the gate and go 'home'. They didn't eat much till I tied them up to a tasty prickle bush for the night. It seems to be a bit of a favourite for them.*

*S 19° 25' 19.7", E 138° 58' 45.4"　760 ft　9.14 km*
*(Ugh ... it's getting shorter)*
*Total: 1644.3 km*

**Low point:** *Now Gypsy is standing and refusing to move ... ugh!*
**High point:** *I have won in the 'don't sit down unless I tell you' department.*

One night I awoke in my swag to feel something tugging on it. There was a full moon so I could see well enough but I was a really tired and disorientated so not thinking clearly. Furphy was fast asleep on my left but had burrowed under the horse blankets so I suspected there might be 'danger' near. My hero! On my right I saw a really weird bird burrowing under my swag and apparently hunting insects in the ground. It had long water-bird legs (like an ibis), a squat, fluffy body (like an immature duck) and a head a bit like a hawk with a fairly stock standard 'jack of all trades' beak. Very weird. When I moved and shone the torch on it, it just wandered away in no apparent hurry. And just as I was falling asleep it would come back and start burrowing under my swag again. I decided I had discovered a whole new species and called it the Friendly Hawk-faced Long-legged Land Duck. When I woke in the morning I wasn't quite sure if I had dreamt it all or if I had discovered the missing avian link. Weeks later I was chatting to a local who told me it was a curlew and they were fairly common. I am such a hopeless birdwatcher. I am fascinated by both animals and flying but for some reason just seem to be totally inept at birds.

When someone asks me what camels are like I usually say a cross between a horse and a cat. They have the hard work ethic of a horse and the independence and humour of a cat. Just like a cat they can see a joke or even create one but don't particularly care if no-one else gets it. Camels are smart thinkers. As horses are responsive to the moment, camels will look at a situation, think about it and react to it later. I could see 'the girls' watching and judging everything I did and then they would decide later how to respond to me. These first few days (or weeks and months, actually) were my big test and they were not going to make it easy for me.

### Day 116, 20 May: Seymour Creek

*Marginally better day today. Still battling to get Gypsy moving but I seem to be winning. I put on a nose line* (where fine string connects her nose peg to her lead rope, so if she leads okay it does not engage but if she refuses to walk then it is pulled tight) *and thought 'Ah, this is the trick' but then she started to jack up again. After a while I realised the nose line had slipped and was too long, so not engaging. Anyway, we managed 14 kilometres today. I pulled in just before Gypsy was about to have another big dummy spit. Phew … I beat her (even though I fully intended to go another 100 metres to the creek).*

*I spoke to James on the sat phone (20 minutes — whoops!). He was great and reassuring. Just what I needed. James confirmed mainly what I thought: Gypsy was testing me out and it sounds as if I might be slowly winning. I need to shorten the nose line and try Pam in front, though. Thanks James. After talking to James I didn't feel quite so stupid.*

*It's nice country here but a bit stony for my liking. James assured me the camels would be okay with the stones but it is very different from horses with their hard hooves. I don't think the camels can travel in as rough/steep country as horses, or that may just be when they have the packs on. Those packs are so high on top of the camels, making them look prone to tipping over. Their centre of gravity is so high compared to a horse.*

*I am struggling with how little they are eating. I am used to horses that are happy to graze all day. The camels just seem to eat for an hour at sunrise and an hour or two at sunset and then just pick at the tree they are tied to for the night. It feels very strange to a 'horseman'. But James assured me it's all okay.*

*S 19° 20' 12.9", E 138° 58' 34.5"   719 ft   14.0 km (yee-hah!)*
*Total: 1658.3 km*

**Low point:** *Battling with Gypsy ... still.*
**High point:** *Talking to James and now not feeling quite so stupid.*

I found it really hard to get used to what the camels ate and how little they ate. They prefer to eat shrubby bushes and even trees. From what I could tell the pricklier it was the better they liked it. Very different from horses. So, with my choice of camp I had to find feed the horse could eat as well as what the camels would like. That became a bit tricky at times, but actually having the camels carry water (instead of having to find it at every camp) was enough to make up for it. I could start choosing camps that had no water, so it was all about food. I calculated I had about seven to eight days' worth of water-carrying capacity (if the camels didn't drink) but initially I wasn't going to make the camels carry a full water load and I started out watering them every two to three days. It wasn't until I got into actual low-water areas that I increased their times between drinks. You can't just take a camel that has had water every day and make it go cold turkey by depriving it of water for fifteen days; you need to work up to it so that the animal's metabolism can adapt. Anyway, that wasn't an issue. I carried a few days' water just so I had flexibility for my camps but not so much that it gave the girls unnecessary work at this early stage.

On the fourth day with the camels, I had a huge breakthrough that kept me on a high for days. The camels were out browsing with their hobbles on but I had to keep a close eye on them because Gypsy was still wandering off for 'home' when she thought I wasn't looking. So I took my stool and journal to where the camels had found a few juicy prickle bushes and settled down to write. I was having a bit of a confidence crisis. Could I really do this camel thing? Was I ever going to get it right and earn their respect? I knew enough about camels to know they would work till they died for someone they respected, but if you weren't doing it right … well, why would they bother? Was I going to be good enough for the girls? I was midway through a whingeing sentence about how I thought I was losing the 'camel battle' when Pam hobbled over. She sniffed my face, my journal, Furphy (who was sitting next to me with his eyes closed – if he couldn't see her, she mustn't be there!) then positioned herself and sat right next to me, facing in the same direction. I felt so privileged. Pam was a very aloof camel that I think would rather do the job without people around at all and here she was, voluntarily sitting right next to me. We sat there for 20 minutes staring ahead at the fiery sunset, just sharing a moment. She then rose and hobbled off to browse with Gypsy again. She never did that again, but I am quite sure it was intentional. I think she came over to have a quiet chat to the rookie: 'You're okay … you're doing fine.'

From the start I had trouble with the saddles. Horse and camel packs are really different and people pack them using very different principles. Horses have to have everything symmetrical, with very accurately weighted packs. If they sit asymmetrically at all, then there are sore backs to deal with the next day. They need their girths done far tighter than the normal saddle and they like to carry the weight more at the front rather than the back. Jockeys are very forward on their horse, to bring the centre of gravity forward. Camels may have the pack saddle sit askew, but you fix it by packing the weight asymmetrically to straighten it. I think cameleers tend to put more weight at the back than the front if they have to choose. Their jockeys sit behind the humps. The saddles also go further back.

I was having trouble with Pam's saddle as it was rubbing her pelvis on the left. One of the problems was that she was so tough she wasn't 'telling' me when she was sore. Every couple of days I would try a different strategy but I was never entirely happy. Gypsy's saddle appeared to fit and not rub (I'm sure she would have told me about it) but I kept losing the saddle blanket out the back or it kept slipping to one side. Very frustrating.

Phone reception was getting few and far between so I was taking any opportunity I could to send emails out on my BlackBerry.

Hi guys,

Well, I have officially done it. I've gone crazy. I left last week with the camels and have so far gotten about 150 km. It is pretty slow going but the girls are unfit. They haven't carried a full pack for a while and haven't worked all day like this since last year, so we are taking it steady. Yesterday I had to cross two creeks – couldn't walk in ankle deep water across the causeways as they are so slippery with slime. So I launched into waist-high water that had quite a strong current and rocks and weeds underfoot. Gumby, the courageous little man, didn't even hesitate and was walking in front of me unassisted as I was battling the camelids! Pam was a little unsure but allowed me to drag her in (which is generous, considering her packed weight totalled nearly a tonne). Then once she was in the water she wasn't waiting around for Gypsy to throw a tantrum on the banks; she just heaved her in kicking and screaming.

It worked really well except on a little island where both camels hit a tree with their packs so hard that once we got to the other side I spent 40 minutes resaddling them both. Could have been much worse as I don't know if these girls have ever crossed water like this … well they have now!

 Their saddles are very different from the horses' saddles. I am getting better at fitting them and loading them properly. The actual saddle itself weighs about 35 kg (or feels it anyway!). It is an art to get a saddle on top of the camel on your own. You have to do a bit of a 'clean and jerk'. It is big and bulky and you have to hold each end (about a metre apart) and then lift it up onto your knees, have a bit of a regroup, then lift it up onto your waist, another regroup, shuffle to the camel's side without frightening her, regroup, and then haul it up and over the hump, which is still a fair height off the ground even though she is sitting down! Ugh! And then Gypsy has the hide to groan as I am picking the saddle up! Pam is wonderful; as I am staggering towards her she leans her hump towards me, making it easier to put on. So that's where I am up to: battling the elements (or, should I say, camels!). Out here reception is few and far between so communications are limited. I think I might have to resort to getting passersby to take my Blackberry for a drive to town and drop it back off to me on their way back. That way I may might at least get a few emails sent! Will see how I go.

HiD

---

I was heading north towards the Gulf region and the Northern Territory border, following a stony dirt road that led to the tourist destinations of Adel's Grove, and Kingfisher Camp. The traffic on the road consisted mostly of 'grey nomads'. They would all stop and ask the usual questions.

'Where are you heading to?' Geelong.

'Wow, that's a long way isn't it?' Just a stroll in the park.

'Why are you doing this?' Just taking the dog for a walk

'Are you on your own?' No, I've got a friend with me – Oh my God, where has he gone?

'Are you going to write a book?' Yes, it's a murder mystery.

'You must be so brave!' Not even on a good day.

Changing the subject I asked my usual: 'What's been happening in the real world?' Apparently, Paris got sentenced to 45 days' gaol for not wearing her undies … or something like that.

The grey nomads all started calling me 'the camel lady'. I thought that was really odd. When I had four horses no-one called me 'the horse lady'. Actually, I don't think anyone has ever called me a lady! For some reason it really grated my cheese that they called me the camel lady. Why didn't anybody call me the Gumby lady? Or maybe they did behind my back.

I got an interesting insight into the whole grey nomad phenomenon. A lot of them get so obsessed about the cost of everything that the trip seemed to be all about the challenge of spending as little money as possible. I would ask what their trip to wherever was like and I would get a rundown on the cost of every caravan park and service station within 300 kilometres. I would learn about all the deals and tricks: if you book in for three nights here you get the fourth free but you do it on a Sunday because the cost of fuel goes up on the Monday and doesn't come down till Friday, but then on the weekend the caravan toilet dump point costs an extra $2.50. Oh yes, I learnt all the tricks.

Everybody would stop and take photos. I hate having my photo taken! Most were polite and would ask but some wouldn't. When you think of it, it's a bit rude taking a photo of a total stranger without even asking. I think it is, anyway. But some people were so amazingly rude, I am sure there are a few photos out there of me with my mouth wide open and a look of total disbelief on my face.

I have decided there are three types of travelling tourists: the nice ones, the rude ones and the fools. The nice ones (most of them) who'd stop for a chat would slow down respectfully, ask if they could take a photo and wait till I'd walked away before they would start up the car so they didn't frighten the camels. The fools were okay, because at least they kept me amused. But the rude ones were a different story. Several times a car would drive past and stop about a hundred metres ahead. People would pour out of the car and set up the video. They would film me walking closer and closer to them until I got to within about 10 metres and then they would leap in their car and drive off, showering me in dust. Now those were the rude ones!

The classic tourist experience I had was so amusing that I couldn't get angry about it. I was walking on the side of a very rough, stony road south of Adel's Grove. The camels didn't mind the traffic as long as it went past them and didn't hang around. Gypsy used to get quite distressed when cars drove slowly behind us or even beside us. Anyway, on this day I could hear a four-wheel drive and caravan come up behind me. We were right over to the side and the road was particularly wide. I was walking with Gumby beside me on my left and had the camels' lead rope over my right shoulder. I thought the vehicle was taking a long time to pass and I could feel Gypsy getting stirred up at the back. Even though she was tied to Pam, not me, I could still get a feel of how she was travelling through Pam's lead rope. I looked around to see what Gypsy was doing and saw the vehicle slowly driving beside us. As the front seat came level with me, the car slowed down to my pace. It was so close that, if I put my right arm out I could have knocked on the window. I could just see through the tinted, closed window a video camera held up by the passenger. I felt like a fool having this close-up video taken of me, by a total stranger, as I walked along. Poor old Gypsy was going spare because the caravan was travelling right next to her. I was just dumbstruck. After about 50 metres the camera was put down and they drove off in a shower of stones and dust. Afterwards I couldn't stop laughing; I imagined the dreaded photo night the rest of the family would have to endure when Grandma and Grandpa got back. The whole family would be sitting around watching the darkened close-up profile of some stranger leading a couple of camels for three minutes. The good grandchild, politely trying to feign interest, would ask who I was and what I was doing. All they would be able to say was, 'We don't know.' What was the point?

One thing I learnt on my trip was how much you miss when you're in a car. I have done a lot of driving through Australia and seen a lot but it was nothing compared to the relatively short distance I have travelled with my kids. There is even more to see when you are always on the lookout for water and different feed for camels and horses. You really see the weather patterns progress in just one day and you get an appreciation for the different soils and how this couples with the different terrain, flora and fauna. In other words, you learn to read the country and see changes in a matter of a few kilometres rather than hours of driving.

### Day 120, 24 May: Riversleigh Station
*Happy birthday to me, happy birthday to me, happy birthday to old bag Heidi, happy birthday to me! Wacko! 40 years! What a ridiculous age! I didn't seem to think it would happen to me. I know 50 won't come ... I will die before then but that's okay. I have done/am doing everything I have ever wanted. How many people can say that? Why am I talking about death? Had a good day today. Gypsy only dropped down once while walking and Pam wasn't so hard to drag. We did a good distance but the packs are fairly light. I filled up the water tonight so that should be interesting tomorrow. We are camped near Riversleigh homestead tonight so they picked me up and took me in for a feed. I was secretly hoping for a birthday beer but, typical luck for me — it is an Aboriginal-run property and is dry. Apparently cola cordial is as good as it gets. The place is managed by some whitefellas, Kylie and Lance, and has blackfellas working on it. They are mostly kids who have been before the courts and were given a choice of gaol time or work on Riversleigh. They were nice kids. Dessert just*

*so happened to be a chocolate cake so I pretended it was my birthday cake.*

*Gum is turning into a camel. He eats anything! He eats trees, dirt, dead leaves, saplings ... the only thing he doesn't eat is prickle bush. He gives it a go every now and then and longingly watches the camels devour it. The needles that are exactly like sewing needles without the eye are just too much for him. Poor fella. The food is not too flash for him.*

*S 19° 01 46.8, E 138° 44 22.    3460 ft    16.0 km*
*Total: 1719.1 km*

**Low point:** *It has to have something to do with the number 40, surely!*
**High point:** *I suppose ... I made it to 40? That's a good thing, isn't it?*

It's strange but I found that with the camels I preferred to walk and lead Gum and Pam. With the horses it was a lot easier to ride and lead. With the horses, the packs would give you a bit of a beating when you were on the ground all the time. At least if you were riding you only got bruised lower legs. So when I had horses I was in the saddle for much of the time.

With the camels it wasn't until the ninth day that I got on Gum, and that was only because I was starting to struggle with shin splints. Trina chased up some osteopathic advice from her brother-in-law and apparently I had been curling my toes under as I walked. Once I was told this I realised how true it was. The ground was so stony that I had developed this habit. She told me about some exercises he'd suggested and they really helped. They involved walking with my toes pointed up in hyperextension but this was very difficult to do without doing the same things to my fingers and hands – I looked quite ridiculous. My legs felt a lot better but I still had to do a bit of riding. Pam didn't like me up there with her. She couldn't hover over me and look down her nostrils at me. It's all about the position of power!

I stayed at Adel's Grove, a tourist resort in the middle of nowhere, for a few days. They were really lovely people with lots of tourists going in and out. The guys at Adel's Grove treated me so well. They never charged me for food and even ran a raffle one night to raise money for Youth Off the Streets. They made $242.05 by raffling off a T-shirt and cap. I also found out that Hells Gate Roadhouse, further north towards the Gulf of Carpentaria, had just closed down so I wouldn't be able to restock there. So the people at Adel's Grove put out a box for packet food donations. It was great! I got surprise peas, pasta and sauce, rice and even cappuccino and mocha sachets. It was great to see such generosity. I only had to throw out a couple of the things: I draw the line at anything over three years out of date!

I had enough stores to get me through to the time when I would catch up with Ken Horkings, who had joined me at the beginning of the ride, and his wife Shirley. They were heading north for holidays and were going to camp with me on the way up for a night or two, as well as drop off some essentials that I'd asked Mum to collect together. I needed some good walking shoes because as much as I love my RM boots they were not really made for walking around 20 to 30 kilometres a day. I had also given my stock whip a bit of a workout and the leather was coming off the handle. Without the leather, on a hot, sweaty day the handle would be too slippery to crack the whip properly. I suppose it had served me well, since I did get it for my thirteenth birthday! So I needed another stock whip. I was also devouring the novels. Mum had become a regular at the local second-hand bookshop, where she would buy books and then post them on to me. I would read and then burn them as I went so the girls were not carrying excess weight. I also had some horse food on order. As accommodating as Gumby was by eating anything, I had ordered some hard food for him. He deserved it. Camels could carry a lot more than horses, and carrying a 20-kilogram bag of horse food could be managed easily.

Even so, I still carried the same lightweight food for myself: cashews, trail mix, dried apricots, pasta and sauce, rice, sachets of flavoured tuna, cheese, butter and a pepper grinder. It was a habit and certainly good enough for me. With the camels I did start carrying one weighty luxury – 'tinned' plums (in a screw-top plastic container that could be reused) and tubes of condensed milk. When I was feeling particularly tired or cold or down or old, or even just lacking in self-control, I would have a bowl of plums covered in condensed milk. Yum … sweet enough to choke a pig!

At Adel's Grove I was camped in the hangar and the kids were loose on the airstrip. The girls spent their whole time right down the end of the strip, up against the fence, trying to get 'home'. Gumby seemed very disappointed with his attempts at getting them to talk to him and in the end he hung around with me in the hangar. Rod, the manager, took me for a flight in his Cessna 152 over the whole area. We followed the path I was planning on taking up to Kingfisher Camp, flew over the local mine and saw Lawn Hill National Park from the air (and it looked just like that: hills of lawn). When we came in to land the girls had, for the first time, ventured down the strip and were right where we wanted to land. The advantage of a little Cessna is that it can land on a postage stamp, so we just flew low over the girls and landed at the end of the runway. They were not too happy and so scuttled back down the end again.

The flight really blew away the cobwebs. I really enjoyed it. In fact, it was the first time I had enjoyed flying since before I was in the air force. When I was a kid I used to dream I could fly. In any dream, as long as I could launch from a box or get a running jump, I could get airborne with my arms out and escape any monsters. It was great. When I started flying for real, I suddenly stopped being able to fly in my dreams. It was a bit sad but I loved real flying so much it was a small price to pay. I graduated with a commercial pilot's licence just after the nationwide pilot's dispute in 1989 and jobs were near impossible to get, due to an excess of overqualified pilots in the market. For twelve months I dropped parachutists in Victoria, towed gliders in South Australia and chartered a wool buyer through central western Queensland to properties when they were shearing – and none of it was paid work.

In desperation I applied for the Royal Australian Air Force. That was a whole different kettle of fish. I stepped into a world that had the overblown egos of *Top Gun* and the repressive sexist attitudes of the Australian Football League meets *Bewitched*. In the RAAF I learnt all about egos. I learnt that a big ego really only means insecurity and that I, that is, a female, was a huge threat. After all, if a female could fly these military jet aircraft that meant that the guys' penises weren't as big as they thought! The way to fix that was to get rid of me, the threatening female. So I was bombarded with resistance and harassment for the eighteen months that I served. Women in the air force are fine as long as they know their place, which really means being an education officer or nurse. I even had high-ranking Squadron Leaders on active missions to catch me doing something wrong so they could kick me out. One of them used to get to base an hour early and sit in his car in the car park near the gates, waiting to catch me driving onto the base (we weren't allowed to stay off-base at night if we weren't married). This guy was actually great for my morale, because I used to hide my bright yellow ute all over the base at night instead of putting it in the officer cadets' car park, so he would think I was off-base. I'd then watch from my bedroom window as he arrived before 6 am every morning and settled in for an hour of boredom watching the gate. When our flight marched to work we passed his car, so I used to hide in the middle where he couldn't see me. It was one of the few wins I had in there so I had to take joy from it.

I loved the aircraft I flew, a Pilatus PC-9, but the continual harassment wore me down. In the end I hated flying and was doing it badly. I failed two flights in a row, which I quite rightly deserved to fail, and they finally managed to achieve their goal: they kicked me out. Mind you, it wasn't everybody who hassled me, just the pilots with their fragile little egos. Whenever I think of my time in the RAAF I am reminded of one of the cleverest jokes I have ever heard:

Q: What is the difference between God and a pilot?

A: God doesn't think he's a pilot.

I would just like to apologise to all the nice pilots out there. I am sure you three are lovely and I recognise that it is unfair to generalise.

So, that flight over Adel's Grove was the first I had enjoyed in years. It is great to see the country from above, especially since I had ridden through it. It was also a little demoralising as I saw a week's worth of riding in just a short joy flight. I left Adel's Grove feeling very slow indeed.

We continued north towards the Gulf of Carpentaria and the landscape was becoming even more tropical. I knew I was coming into ironwood country. Ironwood is a tree found in patches in the north and is one of the few plants toxic to camels. In fact, it is very toxic. There is some story about a guy who took a string of camels through ironwood country. He stopped one night and tied his kids to some innocent-looking eucalypt-type trees; he woke the next morning to find more than half of them dead. Any locals I came across would retell this story, substituting their own embellishments, but none of them could actually identify the tree. You know, once you lose all your horses in less than a day to something like salmonella it makes you a bit gun-shy. Actually, gun-shy is the wrong word – more like completely paranoid. I was therefore pretty stressed. I had only a couple of pictures of the tree and was imagining that everything from a willow to a Bathurst burr was an ironwood incognito (I do acknowledge my botany is pretty poor).

### Day 127, 31 May: Feral Bulls camp

*If one more person warns me about ironwood I think I will force feed it to them – once I have identified it, that is!*

*Gypsy has an infection in her nose peg so I've covered it in Traumeel. Seems to work nicely. Pam is urinating a lot – not in volume but frequency. I must look up about cystitis in camels. She is still working hard but very grumpy with me. When I touch her neck she threatens to bite.*

*Today I met a couple of blackfellas who live in Darwin but are travelling to Doomadgee for a few of weeks. Something to do with training some young locals to help with their employment. Anyway, these guys were really nice. It was a bit embarrassing, actually. I was riding on a 4WD track and the warm morning sun was shining on my face. I was dozing and getting very wobbly on poor old Gum. He was doing his best to keep 'catching me' as I swayed out too far to one side. Next minute I woke as Gumby pulled up, nearly sending me headfirst over the handlebars. There, only a couple of yards in front of me, was a vehicle with both its occupants leaning on the bonnet. They had been driving towards me and saw my stupor so decided to stop, since I obviously wasn't in control of my driving! Anyway, they plied me with cold Coke. That woke me up.*

*The camp seems to be surrounded by bulls. They have been bellowing continuously since sunset and are getting closer and more agitated. The camels don't like hearing bulls bellowing. Not sure why, but it makes them restless. Furphy is hiding under a saddle blanket and Gum is oblivious. My family! There are piles of* horse manure everywhere, thus stallions. They must be brumbies. Normally I would be wary of them coming in and upsetting little Gum, but they won't come anywhere near 'the girls'. I wish the bulls had the same idea.

I am starting to get a bit freaked by this mysterious ironwood. I just want to be able to identify it.

Furphy is becoming a feral little jerk. As soon as I say 'up camel' he barks brainlessly and runs around in true untrained kelpie fashion. I am a bit surprised and very pissed off. In hindsight, this started developing when Gypsy was going through her stages of poor behaviour — throwing herself on the ground bellowing, and me saying 'up camel' trying to get her to move. It was all too exciting for him and now he has developed bad habits. His only endearing features were his camp guarding (but now he even tries to get Gumby out of the camp) and his being not brainless. God, I have even busted the well-trained kelpie.

I have been thinking lots about travelling the Canning Stock Route. Can I do it on my own? Do I have the guts? The skill? The stupidity? Do I take Gum? He drinks a huge proportion of the water and will make it logistically a lot more difficult for me but I need him, mostly for his humour and light-heartedness. Gum can find a joke in anything. My sanity will be a lot safer if I take him. In the last two days Gum, Furphy and I have used a total of 20 L of water a day! I can't believe how little he drinks!

Oh well, got plenty of kilometres to worry over that one.

S 18° 14' 37.0", E 138° 29' 50.2"   208 ft   23.7 km
Total: 1836.5 km

**Low point:** Pam's cystitis? And grumpiness.
**High point:** The way they went today ... Gypsy didn't throw a tantrum.

Finally I met a station owner who could positively identify the dreaded tree. My suspicions were confirmed: it was a fairly innocent-looking plant that was tempting to tie a camel to after a long hard day, so I was pleased I was finally in the know.

I was seeing fewer and fewer people, which I was fully enjoying. Along the way, lots of people asked if I got lonely out there. When I would say I didn't, they invariably responded by saying, 'You must like your own company'. What a strange thing to say. Does that mean that *they* don't like their own company? Is that why people need to be with others? To block out that person they don't like – themselves? It's a bit sad really, if you don't like your own company, because there is one thing for sure: you're never going to get rid of yourself.

I was finding, however, that with fewer people to talk to I would engage in mind games with myself. Lots of maths calculations in my head (I suspect that, even though I do 'like my own company' I must be a pretty boring person!). I would spend all day working out current speeds, average speeds, next ETAs, final ETAs and even future dates when I would end up at certain points throughout the rest of my trip, allowing for varying speeds and setbacks. Yep, on reflection … I am pretty boring.

So, the miles rolled by and pretty soon I had arrived up at the NT border. I was surprised to realise this was my first state border crossing in my trip. I was looking forward to the Northern Territory. I had this naive, and since disproven, idea that the NT dry season weather varied from sunny, fine and 29 degrees to sunny, fine and 31 degrees. How little I knew.

# 8

# Ombrophobia

One of the things I had been most looking forward to on my ride was the Northern Territory: great country, great people and great weather. Well, I suppose two out of three should have been okay but the weather nearly killed me. Maybe that is exaggerating but it certainly was a huge mental challenge. There is a seasonal phenomenon misleadingly called the Barkly Breeze that challenged my world for over a thousand kilometres. It starts in about March and stops around November; so basically if it's not the hot and unbearably humid wet season, it is blowing a gale. It was a consistent and persistent south easterly that blew 24/7. It was quite cool so even on sunny days I wore my jumper and neck roll.

The Barkly Breeze started to drive me crazy after a while. If someone stopped for a chat and was leaning out of their Land Cruiser window talking to me, I had to use all my self-control not to reef them out, leap in myself and shut the windows. I just wanted it to stop blowing – for just a minute! I now understood how this sort of persistent wind, without relief, could contribute to mental health issues. I kept thinking that, because of its name it would stop once I left the Barkly Tablelands … not so.

However, this 'breeze' was not my only environmental challenge. The area seemed to be reminiscent of Victoria with bushfires, excessive rain and freezing temperatures.

### Day 137, 11 June: Bushfire camp

*All day I have been watching smoke over the hills in the west. The country I walked through has had recent fires and there is not much feed left for the kids. Choosing camp was a bit tricky. I don't want to camp too close to bushfires but the wind is behind me and I need to pass through them in a day so I can camp safely on the other side tomorrow. I find judging a bushfire's distance quite hard.*

*Fires here don't seem to have the same intensity as at home. Everyone takes them very casually, too. They don't burn the trees much and no-one seems to fight them. I stopped early so I was behind the fire. Now the sun has gone down I can see several spots of flames. I will get up every couple of hours and just check there is no wind change and they are not getting any closer. If my calculations are correct (and they are most likely wrong!) the fire is about 2 km away and won't be able to get here, as it would have to burn back on previously burnt ground – enough of the blasted fire, Heidi! Get over it.*

*The last few nights have been cold. Last night about 5 degrees and there was a really heavy dew – my swag was still wet when I unrolled it this arvo. I don't like the cold.*

*S 17° 11' 43.4", E 137° 44' 06.0"   544 ft   27.0 km*
*Total: 2073.7 km*

**Low point:** *Fire ... going to be a long night.*
**High point:** *Met up with the two guys from Darwin again, on their way back from Doomadgee. Still really nice guys. Gave me another couple of cold Cokes. Also gave me a Cherry Ripe they bought especially in case they caught up with me; how thoughtful is that? They must be gay.*

I managed to get through the night, as well as the fires the next day – all quite uneventful but the southerner in me finds it impossible to be casual about any bushfires. We were all getting into a pretty good rhythm. Gypsy had stopped testing me (mostly) and I was actually warming to her. She was quite affectionate (especially compared to cold-fish Pam) and always very concerned about getting my approval. We were covering about 25 to 28 kilometres on most days and I was learning more about pain-free saddle fitting for the camelid. We were heading due west pretty much all day, every day, which made the south easterly Barkly Breeze easier to tolerate. Furphy was settling down and behaving better, but that may have been because I was tying him up to a tree 50 metres away before I sat the camels down in the morning. I was nervous I was going to forget about him and leave him behind, so I would tie Gumby near him. I wasn't going to forget Gum!

For about the last 10 kilometres walking into Calvert Hills Station we had a very nice-looking escort. A large, healthy-looking male dingo followed along beside us, about 40 metres away, for a couple of hours. He was just checking us out, curious about what we were doing. I found it interesting that he was not concerned at all about Furphy, who was travelling about 40 metres ahead of us. Furphy, of course, refused to look over his right shoulder. A couple of kilometres before the homestead our travel companion disappeared into the bush. I had the distinct feeling we had been escorted off his territory.

Calvert Hills Station was owned by an old American guy who said he bought the property because he'd had a fight with his father one day about how to cook a steak. He figured if he bought a cattle station then his father couldn't tell him what to do with his own barbecue. Bit of an overreaction to a family tiff but it was well worth it – it was a brilliant steak. His skills were second only to my father's steak-cooking skills. I was greeted by a station hand with a python wrapped around his neck (he had found it in the paddock earlier that day) and several backpackers who came from all corners of the world. The manager and his wife were great and told me about a short cut I could take through the property rather than continuing on the stock route. I filled my jerry cans with water and we set off again the next morning.

Clouds were starting to roll in every afternoon, but I couldn't wait around at Calvert Hills and sit out the potential bad weather. It would waste too much time. Also, I had arranged to meet Ken and Shirley Horkings on the Nicholson River on 16 June. I just had to get over my ombrophobia. (How did we all operate in the pre-Google era? All I had to do was type in 'rain phobia' and within a second I got some word that sounded like a Mexican dance and means 'shoulder' in Portuguese.) Anyway, I just had to brush aside my fledgling ombrophobia and push on.

Catching up with Ken and Shirley was great. It was strange because their presence linked this experience of mine to home. Before then it had all been quite surreal. We camped at Nicholson River for two nights and Shirley spoilt me with great food like meat and vegies. The family from nearby Benmara Station came over one afternoon and we had a barbecue, and they brought Gum some food. He was very happy and so was I because he was losing weight and I was getting a little concerned. The Benmara guys drilled me with the usual.

'Where are you heading to?' Hobart.

'Wow, that's a long way isn't it?' Not as far as Iowa.

'Why are you doing this?' TV got boring.

'Are you on your own?' Everybody is always on their own.

'Are you going to write a book?' Yeah, an instructional on the bonsai vegetable garden.

'You must be so brave!' I am camping in your backyard and you think it's brave – what don't I know?

Changing the subject, I asked what had been happening in the world. Apparently Lindsay Lohan had been arrested for DUI and was admitted to rehab. Hang on, hadn't I heard this before?

A guy from the DPI also came out and sprayed the kids for ticks since I was heading back into a clean area. Before they were sprayed, I asked the guy if he had worked with camels before and he announced he was an expert because he used to work with them in Dubai. I was a little bit sceptical about this as he was insisting on patting Pam's flank, even though she was clearly very angry and about to let fly. I think the only reason he got away with it was because Pam was so stunned she couldn't decide whether to kill him with a bite or a kick! I tied the girls down so they couldn't get up, but they weren't very happy. Poor old Gypsy wanted to lean on me afterwards, for security, but she was wet and toxic so I wasn't too keen on the idea.

While we were camped there the weather became even more threatening, and the morning Ken and Shirley left it started raining. As I watched their ute disappear over the horizon I had this stupid abandoned feeling, which I hadn't experienced since my boarding school days. I had to contain myself from running down the road after them screaming, 'Don't leave me'. They took the horse feed (so we didn't have to carry it) to drop off in portions every 27 kilometres for the next leg of the trip. So I set off again on my own, dragging my feet, with an ominous feeling.

Pam was quite flighty for the first few days but then started to settle. She didn't like the wild weather. Maybe she had that same feeling as I did. It rained about 10 inches (according to the nearest rain gauge at Walhallow

Station) in the next week. It was a pretty tough week, actually. At the time I thought it was a real physical challenge but in hindsight (even as early as when I got to Anthony Lagoon Station the week after) I realised that I had not been mentally prepared.

As I understand it, one way of getting over a fear or phobia is overexposure to that which you're afraid of. Maybe that was what God was trying with me. If that was the case, I think God should leave the psychology to the professionals and just stick to what he is good at – miracles, propaganda and wars. My rain phobia was only validated over the next week. I still managed 180 kilometres in eight days but it was a huge challenge. The Barkley Breeze didn't slow down and it mixed in well with the huge amounts of rain and temperatures with an average range of about 4 to 13 degrees. I bunkered down for two days and tried to wait out the rain. The theory was that I could keep all my stuff dry (or not so wet) by setting up a good camp, lighting a fire and sitting there till the weather cleared. That didn't quite go to plan.

It wasn't any good travelling in the wet because of the type of soil in the area. The road was very slippery for the camels; with every step their feet would skid. If their feet skidded out to the sides instead of forward, they were at high risk of doing the splits and fracturing their pelvis or shoulder. They could walk better on the black soil on the side of the road – but when the black soil was wet it would build up on their feet, mixing in with the dry grass we were walking through, and before long all of us (including the dog) were wearing what I called 'booties'. When I was a jillaroo in Queensland we used to have to smash these dried up 'booties' off the sheep's feet after a rain. Otherwise their feet would wear down underneath and break through the booties, which would create a heavy cement-like bangle that would then rub and cause fly strike and infection. However, things weren't going to get that bad with the camels, because I wouldn't let it, but it did make travelling slow, heavy and tiring for all of us. Also, Gumby couldn't travel well on the black soil on the side of the road. After rain black soil can be treacherous, with plenty of sink holes. The camels had big feet that didn't sink down so much, but Gum's little feet would dive suddenly straight down and he could easily have broken a leg.

My feet, though, travelled the worst in this wet. It didn't matter where I walked, my feet would be tacked up by collected mud and I would literally have basketballs on my feet. I had to walk with my feet wide apart, otherwise one would catch on and glue to the other as I swung it forward and I would end up flat on my face. It would take longer for me to remove the bulk of this mud with a screwdriver than it did to collect it by walking along. In the end, I rode the whole time. If I got on Gum without cleaning off my feet properly, the weight of these mud balls would start to pull off my boots and weigh my heels down so much the back of my calves would start screaming at me in a few short minutes – let alone the extra weight Gum had to carry. Poor Gum.

So I rode Gum on the edge of the road and led the camels, trying to encourage them to walk to the side (not behind, as they were used to) on the black soil. Furphy made his own way. Every now and then I would get off and get the mud off everyone's feet with a screwdriver, doing mine last, then I'd get back on Gum and go again. Sometimes the rain was so heavy that I would marvel at how lucky I was to be riding a horse that didn't realise he was one. When rain is really heavy, horses tend to just turn their bum into it and refuse to move. Gum hadn't learnt that trick so he just continued walking, shaking his head intermittently as his ears filled up with water.

When we were camped I could huddle under my hoochie in semi-shelter but the poor kids had it bad. A lot of places they couldn't go off the road very far, especially with hobbles on, because of the mud and thick, dry grass. There were very few trees and bushes so the camels only had the dry grass to eat and they weren't keen on it. Generally, they could only venture as far as the borrow pit on the side of the road because the grass wasn't as thick and the sink holes not as treacherous. I had to really control myself not to take off their hobbles, and I kept saying over in my head Trevor's words of wisdom: 'Don't do something different because you feel sorry for them; you will later regret it.' I am quite sure if I took the girls' hobbles off they would have left me in a flash ... they were too smart to hang around in this situation. Gum might have stayed, but I didn't want to risk losing him; he was the only thing keeping me sane.

To top off this wild, wet, windy, cold climate was the type of country. People describe it as 'open downs' country, but this really just means 'flat and not a bloody tree or bush in sight'. Not good country to be in during this weather. We were so exposed. Some days I just kept walking beyond 30 kilometres because I was trying to find a camp that was a bit sheltered for the kids. There is nothing sadder than seeing a soaked and bedraggled camel sitting in the mud, shivering so hard that her whole body is shaking. I will never forget the tragic look Gypsy could conjure up on her face when I used to get up and check them in the night. Another difficulty with no trees or bushes was that I had nothing to tie the girls to! I had to become quite ingenious to work out a secure ground tie. It was times like these that I felt I had taken this trip too far. I deserved to suffer, whatever happened, because it hadn't my choice to be there but my kids had never done anything to deserve it. They just worked really hard without question.

### Day 146, 20 June: Freezing rain camp

Oh my God (or whoever) it's zarking freezing! It rained last night but most things are still pretty dry. I contemplated staying put and just battening down the hatches but it started to clear so I packed up and left. Well, it drizzled all day. And cold. I can only think of two occasions when I have been as cold: 1) riding through the Vic Alps when it snowed and 2) camping somewhere in Victoria (again) with the RAAF.

The poor camels are freezing — when I loaded them this morning they were shivering all over, especially Pam. How cold and wet can it get before the camels can't cope? I wish my sat phone was working. I would like to ring my camel advice hotline and have a chat to James about camels in this weather.

Even Furphy is looking tragic. Gumby is coping the best. Not sure if he has realised yet that it has rained. He has leftovers from the food Ken dropped off so he is pretty happy, actually. We didn't reach the next drop-off point tonight, though, so hopefully the food there hasn't become cattle fodder.

There is plenty of feed/dry grass but the ground is so slippery with big holes that the girls don't like it. When I unloaded Pam this afternoon she struggled to get up because she just kept slipping in the front feet. Not sure what I can do about it.

Most of my clothes are all wet and the bloody Drizabone leaks badly and should really be called a 'wetasashag'. I was so cold today that I just ached all over (still do). I have had about five cups of tea tonight, which means I will have to get up all night and go to the toilet. S'pose I have to get up anyway to check the kids.

I am starting to get a bit concerned. If it is raining tomorrow I won't go anywhere ... maybe. Do I stay to minimise the risk of slipping and broken bones or do I keep going so they can at least warm up a bit when walking and keep going to fresh food? Wonder what the best decision is? I always find hindsight is the way I make my best decisions, but I don't have the luxury of hindsight — if I did I wouldn't be zarking wet and cold still! This is the first time on my trip that I am a bit worried. Are our bodies going to be found in a couple of weeks, when 4WDs can get through, as little frozen popsicles on the side of the road? Don't be stupid Heidi ... it's only water and low temperatures. It just feels as if this is the whole world and we are never going to get out of it. Never see the sun again? The girls wouldn't be happy!

S 17° 51' 17.4", E 136° 29' 02.5"    818 ft    20.6 km
Total: 2259.7 km

**Low point:** Rain, rain, cold, wind, rain, cold, rain, wind and the feeling that it will be like this forever.
**High point:** We are all still alive ...

### Day 147, 21 June: Freezing rain camp, day two

I didn't go anywhere today. The weather is still pretty filthy, though not as bad as yesterday. At sunrise I put up a road block to stop any passing traffic — actually didn't think anyone would be able to get through this road, but I managed to snare the manager from Calvert Hills and his wife. They said the weather was shocking even in New Zealand! They also said more rain is forecast. Ugh! I asked them to ring Mum and Dad and let them know I am okay and to ask them to buy me a Drizabone, a tent and to rustle up a sat phone that works. This is what my life has come to: I have finally admitted I need a tent, as opposed to hoochies. Who would have thought I learnt that lesson in NT?

Last night I was thinking I needed to be rescued out of here, but not so now. It has stopped raining so I managed to get a fire going (used about 400 ml of my shellite: bummer). It wasn't too easy, as all the wood was soaked through and I am no good with fires at the best of times (I am ashamed to admit). I have only just mastered burning my toilet paper properly!

The camels somehow survived the night but are 'not happy Jan'. The ground here is slippery, with long grass and big, hidden sink holes, so not a good combination for the girls with their hobbles on. I spent all day changing the kids' tethers, eating and reading. I managed to get nearly everything dry with the fire – happy about that!

Didn't rain most of the day today but started up just as the sun went down. My camp seems to be shower-proof but I really do need a tent ... yuk. Not sure if I am glad I got a weather report or not – it wasn't good news. I haven't told the girls yet; they won't be happy.

Zarking fardwarks. I just want the bloody sun to come back out. Is that too much to ask? It's not meant to be this wet here at this time of year. It's not meant to be this cold ... ever! At least I don't think I am going to die, like I did last night (I should forgive myself for the occasional irrational moment). I am fairly isolated out here and don't enjoy not having a working sat phone.

Okay, time to shut up.

S 17° 51' 17.4", E 136° 29' 02.5"   818 ft   20.6 km
Total: 2259.7 km

**Low point:** Gumby looking very skinny.
**High point:** Got the fire going. Shiny!

Also, a little fat, dull-coloured bird keeps flying around my camp. He is very quiet and friendly and even let me pat his feet. I think he was trying to cheer me up.

There are many camping do's and don'ts. I am quite sure I've broken a number of rules myself but there are a few I think really should be adhered to. One of the most hideous things I would come across in my travels was escaped toilet paper. It would blow in the wind, wild and free, getting caught around plants, decorating them like a travesty of a Christmas tree. Or sometimes it would not blow away and stay forever on the ground for future generations to accidently stand on. People don't understand that just because you've parked on the south side of the tree, and thus completed your business on the north side, it doesn't mean everyone parks there. Some people park on the north side of the tree, hop out of the car and stand right in your toilet! And don't think a couple of inches of dirt on top are going to help. The unacknowledged truth is that dingoes love to dig up and eat our excrement, in the process setting the toilet paper free to travel wherever the wind will take it. And, may I say, dingoes are better at digging than we are, so don't think you are ever going to 'out-dig' them. Yes, dig a nice deep hole to drop your 'produce' in (to at least prevent someone stepping in it until the dingoes come along to feast on it) then *burn* your used toilet paper, drop any leftover ashes in and fill in the hole. Easy peasy! Just try not to start a bushfire.

> **Handy hint no. 8:** To be a successful 'toilet paper burner' you need to give up old ways of being a folder and become a scruncher. Folded toilet paper doesn't burn well and may lead to frustration, burnt fingers and even a regrettably messy situation. Scrunched up toilet paper allows oxygen in and you get maximum burn-off.

> **Handy hint no. 9:** Sorbent burns better than Kleenex.

I suppose people call the Barkly Tablelands remote or isolated, but it isn't really. You just have to drive further to get to the pub. The people out there are really friendly and would give a stranger their last stubby from the fridge. Even though their next-door neighbour might be a hundred miles away they still know them well; much better than in the city. I marvel at how people live in town and don't even know the person their house shares a wall with! What a sad way to exist.

I think the weather started to make me feel a bit desperate and 'trapped'. It seemed that the wind and cold and rain were never going to stop and the road we were on just went on ad infinitum. I once heard the brilliant Stephen Fry talk and he likened depression to bad weather: when you're in the middle of it there seems no way out and it will never end, but it *is* going to end, just as the sun will always shine again after a storm … one day. It's funny, because out on the Barkly Tablelands I came to an inverse conclusion: bad weather is like depression, because you just can't see how it could ever clear up again and stop raining, but you know things will have to brighten up and get 'happy' again … one day.

Out there, this sort of rain stops all form of transport. The roads become impassable and such low cloud cover makes movement by air out of the question. I knew no-one would be driving on the road but the lack of traffic still gave me an uneasy feeling. Normally this stock route would get about one local vehicle per day. I just had to keep repeating that I wasn't lost, I had plenty of feed and water, I wasn't even very far behind my original plan of travel and no-one (I think) had ever died in the Northern Territory of prolonged hypothermia. But my mental discipline faltered and I allowed myself to start to feel very isolated. I didn't even know if Paris was still in gaol …

### Day 149, 23 June: Creswell Downs camp

*Bit of a mental struggle today, especially in the morning. It seemed to drag on and on and I just wanted to be anywhere but here. I am thinking lots about giving up. Bloody pathetic — the hardest thing (and I hate to admit it) is that I am alone. I was alone when I thought I was going to die of hypothermia, I was alone when I was making decisions on whether to keep travelling or stop, I was alone, alone, alone! I can't believe I am saying this; me, who loves being alone, loves my own company, hates people! I think it is the weather too. No rain today but very cold with wild wind. It seems so unfair to have this weather up here. God, I am a whingeing child!*

*S 17°56' 54.0", E 136° 12' 57.3"   778 ft   30.9 km*
*Total: 2290.6 km*

**Low point:** I am losing the plot.
**High point:** Can see a star tonight, fighting through the cloud.


### Day 150, 24 June: No trees camp

It's official: God is killing himself laughing up there. Today has gone from good to bad to worse to zarking disaster:

Good: Packed up and left by 8.15 am.

Bad: Decided to take the road to Walhallow to get me to civilisation (and shelter) a day earlier but got a couple of k's down the road and realised it was turning into black soil country. Couldn't do that to the kids, so turned back.

Worse: Had to camp in the middle of nowhere. No trees, no shelter, not even a bush to tie the girls to! I did about 6 k's more than I wanted but was desperate to find a shrub of some sort. In the end we couldn't go on. The camels are tied to their saddles, which are staked in the ground. They are sitting on the road, in the mud and rain. I hope Gypsy doesn't chew the wood on her saddle; she often chews trees she is tied to. Gumby is tied to a rope attached to a stake in the mud. I am under a hoochie only 2 ft above the slushy mud that is in the borrow pit beside the road. I can't get it any higher because I have run out of the taller stakes. So I am lying in a ditch on the side of the road, soaking wet and it has just started pouring down again!

Zarking disaster: I had one last hazelnut/coffee/chocolate powder drink that someone gave me and decided to drink it tonight to warm me up. I have been saving this up for when I really need it — the last supper, so to speak. I was so looking forward to it. Once it was made, steam rising off the boiling, aromatic nectar, I proceeded to tip all but a teaspoon over the last of my dry clothes I had just changed into. God is laughing up there and I don't like it.

I am smelly and skanky but too cold and wet and tired and pissed off to have a tub. I will be spending all night getting up and checking the kids. What if Gypsy starts to eat her saddle — they are pretty hungry! I have to keep saying to myself, 'Only two more

*camps and we will get to Anthony Lagoon Station.' Hope they
are welcoming.*

*Gypsy has quite a sore right hind leg; I suspect it's her foot.
Gumby is sore in his front right pastern and left stifle and is
carrying his tail high. Pam's left front foot has been really worrying
her today. My new shoes that Ken and Shirley dropped off are not
waterproof, not mud-proof and not grass-seed proof. How could
they possibly be marketed as hiking boots? They are also too small
and my little toes are being compressed down to nothing. Maybe
lucky my feet are numb with the cold. It's going to hurt when
they defrost!*

*S 18° 02' 39.5", E 135° 56' 44.5"   743 ft   34.5 km
Total: 2325.1 km*

**Low point:** *I don't even know where to start.*
**High point:** *Ah ... we are still alive? Or maybe that is a low point!*

On the eighth day the rain cleared and the sun defrosted us. All of a sudden
life was easy again. About 5 kilometres before we got to Anthony Lagoon
Station I saw my first vehicle in what seemed like an eternity. Anthony
Lagoon Station is about 300 kilometres due east of Elliot; still a long way
from nowhere. The station manager told me he had heard through the bush
telegraph that we were coming his way. He commented on how sore my kids
were and announced we would be staying at the station for as long as it took
for them to feel better. He said he would put hay out for them in the yards,
where there was shelter, and I would stay in the guests' quarters. I love
outback people.

By the time we limped in to the homestead it seemed we had an entire
footy team watching our arrival. I unsaddled the camels while Scotty the bore
whore (that is what he was introduced to me as) took Gum and unloaded
him. The manager informed me the Borroloola police had just called and
asked if they had seen me, as I was registered as a 'missing person'. How
could I be missing if no-one was expecting me? I was too tired, too sore, too
cold, too windblown and too relieved to care. I just wanted to settle the kids,

give them food, water and shelter and go inside and enjoy a dry lack of wind! I would sort it later.

I was led to the yards where the manager had put some hay out for the kids. As we rounded the corner, the manager was saying he wasn't sure how much camels ate and he could put some more hay out the next morning. I found myself standing in front of 3 half-tonne piles of hay as tall as the camels! 'Is that enough?' I heard from behind me. Oh, the joys of outback generosity and hospitality …

# 9

## Visitors

The first thing I did, even before having a hot shower or a beer, was to ring my parents. They had just been notified by the police that I had been 'found'. I felt so bad. Mum was playing it down, saying she knew I was fine and hadn't really been very worried, but I knew that wouldn't be entirely true. Yet again I questioned whether I had the right to put my family through this. Luckily, they had only been informed I was missing earlier that day so they didn't have much time to brew many ulcers. I think the managers of Calvert Hills got quite concerned about me in the weather and went looking for me. However, the road was basically impassable by four-wheel drive and the cloud was too low to do any sort of aerial search, so I am not sure how effective their 'search' could have been. When they couldn't find me they reported me missing to the cops. I fluctuated between feeling grateful and guilty for their concern and effort, and annoyed for them stirring up a hornet's nest and worrying my family for no apparent reason. I was walking along fat, dumb and happy (well, maybe not so happy), not realising all the commotion going on around me.

All my family could do was sit and wait it out, and have faith that I was capable enough to survive such weather. I think Mum was quite annoyed by the police because they kept telling her I was totally unprepared. They said I had no camping gear, no wet-weather gear and no sat phone. I can see why they thought this. I'd asked the Calvert Hills manager to ring my parents to tell them to get me a new Drizabone and a tent, and the police just extrapolated from there. I think Mum took personal offence at them saying I was ill-equipped and tried to tell them I was very well prepared and experienced. I suspect it fell on deaf ears, but I suppose you can't blame them. There would be all sorts of idiots who travel through the country by various means without the right gear and knowledge, and the police would end up having to bail them out of sticky situations. I even heard of one guy who apparently pushed a shopping trolley from Darwin to the Queensland border, where he was turned back by the Queensland police. All I could picture was a pissed off guy pushing a trolley with a bung, wobbly wheel through the outback, constantly berating himself for not turning back sooner and swapping the trolley over when he first realised he'd got the dodgy one.

At Anthony Lagoon I went out each day and checked the kids. Gum started to brighten up and was no longer sore but the girls remained very reluctant to move about. I ended up staying six days to give them a rest. In the end, I left because their improvement stopped and I started to think they needed to move a bit and get circulation going in their feet to help healing. I decided to travel just a small distance each day so I wouldn't stress them too much but we could still get back into a routine. Camels love a routine, so much so that they hate days off. They were starting to get a bit angry with me and I could tell they wanted to get going again, even though they were still sore.

### Day 157, 1 July: Anthony Lagoon

Well, I've been here five days and starting to get a bit twitchy. The manager and his wife have been great. Their son works on Camfield (another station along my route further west) so will probably meet him later. The food here is great and the accommodation is brilliant. Not a single breath of wind in my room; I am loving the calm around my ears and regaining a bit of sanity that blew away in the Barkley Breeze, but I just need to get going. I have been on the Internet getting details of all the local pastoral companies and wrote a letter to them (which I was quite impressed with, even if I do say so myself) asking for donations to Youth Off the Streets. I find it really hard to raise money because I can't persistently hassle people and companies by email and phone, because I am just too busy surviving. My requests usually fall on deaf ears and I can't follow them up with harassment because I am back on the road again, out of communication range. Hopefully something will come of these letters. I suppose I can only try.

Today I went out in the paddock with Skeeter and Scotty to pull some others out of a bog. Very open country. Apparently one of the problems they have here is known as McLeod's Daughters Syndrome. That stupid show is enticing ill-informed young females

*to go out and work on these places. My God! What are they
thinking!*

*S 17° 58' 38.2", E 135° 31' 56.6"    698 ft    0.0 km
Total: 2389.3 km*

**Low point:** *Sore camels. May take a while. Ugh!*
**High point:** *Great people and hospitality.*

Mum and Dad had planned to take a holiday up north and meet up with me
for a while. They were due to leave home about the time I was reported
missing but ended up being delayed, so they left the day after I spoke to
them from Anthony Lagoon. Originally we thought we would meet closer to
Elliot, in the centre of the Northern Territory; but with the delays from the
weather and then resting the kids, I was still nearly 300 kilometres east. They
borrowed my uncle's Land Cruiser tray-back, called 'Elsie', which was fully
decked out for outback camping. They had never been camping in their lives
before so had to borrow all the gear, including swags. I was mesmerised at all
the gear they carried and was excited at the prospect of a bit of 'luxury
travelling'. They arrived at Anthony Lagoon in time to experience the great
hospitality I was enjoying and we set off the next day. Dad told me he had to
drive to Elliot, a seven-hour round trip on dirt roads recently trashed by
unseasonal rainfall, to pick up a surprise parcel for me. What the? Why
didn't they just bring it with them like they did the 'kitchen sink'? It was
decided Dad would leave at 4 am and Mum and I would set off walking.
Dad would meet back with us about midday, just when we would be looking
for a camp. What could be so important that he had to pick it up that day
and leave so early?

### Day 159, 4 July: Turkey's Nest camp
*Oh my God. The surprise was Tonia and Sam, (two of my sisters).
The day started with me packing up slowly and leaving at about
10.30 am with Mum. We were about 7 km down the road (at
about noon) when Dad met up with us after his trip to Elliot and
back. He stopped and Tonia leapt out ... I was gobsmacked ... then*

*Sam comes running out from the other side of the Cruiser! How
excellent! They are going to be here for about four days. I am so
excited. They flew to Alice Springs and then bussed to Elliot, then
waited two hours in the dark for Dad, then drove for three hours
squashed in the front seat of the Elsie. I think Mum was pleased
to stop walking so she jumped in the ute and Ton and Sam walked
with me and the kids. Pam and Gypsy were a bit 'Who the hell
are these silly women disturbing our day's work?', but I think they
warmed to them.*

*S 17° 56' 12.4", E 135° 23' 54.7"   710 ft   16.7 km
Total: 2405.0 km*

**Low point:** *Sorry Pen and Trina* (my two other sisters) *weren't
there.*
**High point:** *Ton and Sam, of course!*

The first night my family camped with me was quite hysterical. For once *I*
was the expert in something and advising *them* of my useful handy hints for
the beginner camper. Somehow the simple task of rolling out four swags (I
don't include mine in this event) became an inter-territory incident. Poles,
pegs, hoochies and ropes got mixed up and all sorts of shapes and sizes
resulted. At one stage three people were claiming they were sleeping in Dick's
borrowed swag. If that was true it must have been fairly crowded!

### Day 160, 5 July: Another busted arse windmill camp
*Last night was an 'adventure'. Tonia kept having nightmares,
screaming hysterically in a very scary manner. Once she did it just
as Gumby was having a leisurely roll right next to us, on the other
side of the barbed-wire fence. In all the chaos and confusion Gum
got tangled in the barbed wire and Tonia fought her way out of the
swag (still asleep, I think) running off into the dark yelling 'Torch,
Gumby, fence'. Poor Gum had his left hind caught in the middle
barbed wire and he just waited while I cut him out. He had cuts
over his rump and lower left hind. He was so good, didn't panic*

*(not like Tonia!). He is such a dag. He was just trying to camp as close as he could to us. He pulled up pretty good today. I was worried about cellulitis as it happens with those sorts of wounds but nothing has eventuated yet.*

*It was great walking with Sam and Tonia. Livened up the day and stopped me over-thinking and doing pointless maths equations in my head. I had to wear my RM boots today as my new hiking boots were just too painful, but for some reason I think my feet have swollen ... maybe I'm pregnant?! I think I'll call him baby Jesus!*

*The camels still have sore feet. Pam occasionally lifts and holds up her right front foot and Gypsy can't decide which back foot hurts more. Poor girls!*

*Caught up on all the family/friends gossip, with Tonia's and Sam's interpretations. It was great. Was even informed of world events. Yep, people are still bombing and killing other people all over the world. Glasgow airport is the latest one. Will humans ever learn? I am quite sure they won't.*

*I am feeling a bit spoilt ... all right, am feeling very spoilt. Mum and Dad are doing the camping thing the usual Douglas way — very organised with lots of food and equipment. We are eating (and drinking) like kings; I love car fridges! Tonight we had a beautiful camp oven roast and vegies and champagne. Can't get any better than this.*

*The wind seems to be getting even worse if that is possible. Maybe I just got soft at Anthony Lagoon Station.*

*S 17° 56' 12", E 135° 23' 55"   710 ft   13.6 km*
*Total: 2418.6 km*

**Low point:** *Girls feet sore this morning.*
**High point:** *Ton and Sam here ... I'm still gobsmacked!*

That first night we camped at the turkeys nest with 'the busted arse windmill'. When getting directions from locals they would talk about 'the busted arse windmill'. Initially I thought that was the windmill's name, like the Dougy

Walters Bore or the Dead Dog Yards. I thought it was strange that quite a few properties had windmills of the same name ... then finally thick old me realised they called it that because that's what it was ... a busted arse windmill. Since most bores are now operated by a diesel pump or solar panels, windmills are not maintained and slowly deteriorate.

A 'turkeys nest' is not necessarily a home for a big bird. It is a large circular dam that is pumped full from a nearby bore and surrounded by a fence to stop stock coming in and getting bogged in it when it gets low. Water is piped downhill into a trough with a float on it.

Most nights we camped at a turkey's nest yard and so the next leg of the journey was one long 'busted arse windmill' tour. However, it had its advantages because the camels could walk around (although still with their hobbles on because they could have easily stepped over the barb-wire fences without any problems) and eat whatever was in the yard.

The country started to get to me after a while. It seemed like thousands of miles of flat, open downs country with not a stick of shade or shelter to hide behind. I really appreciated my family being with me, breaking up the slow, grinding torture that this leg was evolving into. It seemed I'd been heading west for an eternity. I was desperate to do even just a 20-degree alteration in course but it wasn't to be. So we continued on, westerly, constantly chasing the path of the sun.

Tonia kept announcing: 'This is exactly what I imagined the Northern Territory to be like.' Really? I didn't see any sign of tropical country, waterfalls, salties, or even much in the way of barramundi fishing! I hate to think how excited she will be when she sees the 'real' NT. Although Ton was brought up in the country like the rest of us she is probably the sister who most took to city living. She was very excited about 'pulling on the old boots' and getting into the camping/outback thing. On their last night, half the gear had been dumped by Cherub Creek and Mum and Dad took Elsie back for the rest. I arrived to find Sam pointing to a snake trying to burrow into one of the swags on the ground. You know, I'm not too excited about snakes trying to share my swag. This one seemed quite determined and a little angry. So I somehow managed to wrestle the shovel from the top of a somewhat indignant Pam, who couldn't understand what my hurry was all about and why I had not asked her to 'hoosh' (sit).

After disposing of our unwelcome guest Tonia proceeded to pose for photos. The first was her standing in a very casual country style pose with the snake hanging off the end of the shovel. She announced, 'Move over Crocodile Hunter, the Cherub Creek Hunter is here to stay.' She then started to get a bit carried away and by the time she was finished we had a range of ridiculous photos. There was one of her pointing the .308 rifle in the air, with classic shooter's stance and our friend draped over the end of the barrel. We also got one with her holding my Ka-Bar knife with the snake coiled around the blade. At one stage she was standing triumphantly with the snake hanging by the tail in one hand and stock whip in the other. The final, and most perplexing, one was of her holding a fishing rod with the poor demoralised snake hanging from the line. In the cold light of day I am not too sure if those photos come out much for public viewing. The hysterical thing is I don't think the 'Cherub Creek Hunter' has ever killed anything in her life!

My Ka-Bar was my pride and joy. I had it in the RAAF and used it when I did the air crew combat survival course. It is a great knife and could probably tell more stories than me. I have used it to cut down young trees with a 5-inch diameter trunk (admittedly it took a bit of effort), dig holes, cut surgical sutures out, open cans and kill animals such as calves. It is what you call an all-rounder. A fighting and utility knife, the Ka-Bar was issued to American Marines and Navy for years. It is quite solid and has a sharp point on a double-edged blade and is about 30 centimetres long. Apparently the Ka-Bar got its name from the manufacturer when they received an illegible letter from a satisfied customer relating the story about how the knife saved his life when he was attacked by a bear. All they could decipher was 'k a bar' which they eventually worked out was meant to be 'kill a bear'.

The differences between the types of people and their attitudes from state to state fascinated me. I used to pack my .308 rifle in a leather scabbard on top of the pack horse but it would be covered by the swag. All that could be seen of it was a short leather cylinder that poked out the back. It could have been anything to the unwary passer-by. However, New South Welshman and Victorians would immediately comment on my rifle and express their surprise that I would be carrying one. I don't even know how they knew it was a rifle. They never commented on the Ka-Bar I had strapped to my right hip. When

I got to Queensland (literally when I stepped over the border) people would physically step back and eye me with suspicion. I invariably would forget I was wearing my Ka-Bar (putting it on my belt each morning came as naturally as putting on my undies) and was perplexed at their body language. The Queenslanders didn't care about my rifle at all. When I had the camels in the Northern Territory I had the rifle in its scabbard hanging off the near side of Gumby's saddle, for easy access. The only thing locals would notice is that I didn't have a cold beer on me and they would produce a couple out of their Engel car fridge and insist I take them, as though it was a matter of survival. Even though horse and rider were draped in guns and killing knives, the grey nomad, for some reason, would only comment on my stock whip, which I hung on the left side of my belt. I still haven't worked out that behaviour! Thinking back on it now, I concede we must have looked like some violent travesty of a Christmas tree.

### Day 24, 14 July: Newcastle Waters boundary

*The kids travelled well. Good day except for — yes — that bloody Barkly Breeze! It is a bloody howling gale. At least it didn't really start up until I was on the road so that was good. I hope I am getting nearer to the edge of its boundaries. I am so over being blown to shreds. Got an email from Trina on my Blackberry. I love getting letters from her; they are always full of info about everything.*

*Lots of open country today and, yes, I have another headache. I think my body can't decide if it is sunstroke or windstroke. I am camped tonight on the sheltered side of a turkey's nest but instead of the wind I now have the constant thumping of the old diesel pump. I am sure it will go all night. Those bore pumps around here have a gravity-fed fuel tank made out of a 44-gallon drum so it pumps for days!*

*Gumby is a funny creature. Camping at turkey's nests has made me realise how much he hangs around the camp. He tends to hover near the fence and rarely goes round the other side of the dam. I am sure that if I didn't tether him at night he wouldn't go anywhere. The problem is I suspect I would wake up in the morning with all my breakfast cashews missing and him lying beside me hogging the swag!*

*Ton and Sam gave me a Sudoku puzzle book which is great but is now really starting to shit me. I must have an addictive personality (possibly already proven with champagne) because I stay up all night and do Sudoku. I have decided I just have to bite the bullet, hurry up and finish them then burn the completed book. That should fix it, surely.*

*Mum and Dad left today. For some reason I didn't feel as bad as when Ken and Shirley left me, but back then I think I subconsciously knew I was in for a tough time. It was great to see Mum, Dad, Sam and Tonia and share this with them but now I am looking forward to being on my own again.*

*S 17° 55' 57.9", E 133° 57' 16.4"   704 ft   23.5 km*
*Total: 2579.4 km*

**Low point:** *Family is all gone.*
**High point:** *Trina's email.*

So my visitors left me. We were alone again. I have always been a bit hopeless with change and found it would take me a day or two to get used to being on my own. Travelling with a support crew was so luxurious and I loved it, but it really did feel like cheating and taking the easy way out. Holiday over, nose back to the grindstone, I continued heading westwards towards those sunsets.

# 10

# Hitting the wall

Not long after Mum and Dad left me I reached the boundary of Newcastle Waters Station. Ever since I was a kid I'd known that Newcastle Waters was a huge property somewhere in the centre of NT. In fact it is over 10 000 square kilometres in size and carries 45 000 head of cattle. The boundary grid was an unexpected challenge to which Gumby rose magnificently. Actually, I did something that I never thought I would even contemplate doing with a horse and I am sure all horse people would think I had lost the plot completely in doing it.

Grids are a row of spaced pipes with no soil below, which stop stock (but not vehicles) travelling through the gap in the fence. So whenever I came across a grid on the road I would have to go through the gate usually found beside them. Some of the gates were a challenge to open and I am sure many had not been opened for years. Occasionally the corresponding gate was a kilometre away from the grid and I would have to walk up and down the fence looking for it.

The boundary grid at Newcastle Waters had a brand new fence either side of it and no sign of a gate. I followed it both north and south for many kilometres looking for a gate but couldn't find one. Normally at this stage I would cut the fence, go through and then strain it back up again, good as new. I had carted around a set of wire strainers for just the occasion and although I only used them a couple of times and they were very heavy for my kids to carry, they really were essential. However, this fence was brand spanking new with five strands of high-tensile barbed wire. Usually there are scraps of wire on the ground that I can use to strain it back up again but obviously these fence contractors were very good at their job as there was not a single morsel of spare wire. I really couldn't contemplate cutting such a work of art without being able to repair it properly.

In the end I had a close look at the grid itself. I have long discovered that if you want to solve some problems you have to look at them from every angle. It was made up of large bore pipes about 150 millimetres in diameter but not very far apart. The giant-sized camel foot would, I figured, easily span across two of these so if I could persuade them, the camels could walk across it. But how was I going to get Gum across? I stared at Gumby for a while, contemplating what a wonderfully quiet and sensible horse he was. In the end I felt comfortable with giving it a go. I fronted Gum up to the grid and slung his lead rope over his neck. I then proceeded to circle him in a clockwise direction, picking up each foot and placing it further forward: left front on a pipe, right front on a pipe, right back forward, left back forward, left front on another pipe, right front on a pipe, etc. With each foot placement Gumby would just watch what I was doing. So as I slowly circled him he would follow with a perplexed gaze. He never once resisted or changed the position of his foot from where I placed it and in a matter of minutes we had walked across the grid. He had complete faith in me and trusted me that he was going to be okay, and I had complete faith that he would do as I told him and wouldn't panic. As far as I was concerned this horse was priceless.

Then I fronted the girls up at the grid one at a time and both had the same reaction. They initially stopped and gave me a look of 'No, we are camels, we don't walk over grids'. Then after a quiet word from me, saying it would be okay, they walked across. Camels are very precise with their feet and do a lot of feeling through them so they could feel the support of the pipes under their feet and therefore trusted me. That was a really satisfying feeling, especially considering the resistance and testing they gave me just one month previous when we started.

So we managed to walk across the grid. I was so proud of my wonderfuly sensible and trusting kids, and hoped I would never have to do that again.

### Day 171, 16 July: Old stock route camp

*The country is slowly changing — more trees and less wind-blown and 'godforsaken'. I have seen lots of wedge-tailed eagles lately. I saw a group of about seven at one stage, all within 50 metres of each other. I didn't think they were such social animals.*

*Followed the old stock route north, like Mathew the boreman directed me to. It was great and Gypsy was very happy with the sandy track that was soft on her feet. She travelled so much better.*

*We stopped at camp at about 3 pm and I let the girls graze in
their hobbles. They didn't march off on me like they have been
lately so I was much happier. For some reason I take offence and
worry excessively about how they are coping when they try to do
the Harold Holt. I didn't tie them up till sunset and they were both
quite happy. Tonight has been a smorgasbord for both Gum and
the girls.*

*The soil here at camp is also sandy but hard – a very nice
change. I was very worried today; there was cloud till about 1 pm. I
think I have a cloud phobia now! I'm turning into a phobic mess.*

*Have reception for my emails today because we are pretty close
to Elliot. Not good enough for making any phone calls, though. I
haven't had reception since 15 May. I need to start replying to all
these emails. There are lots of responses to my last bulk email so
maybe some people are reading them!*

*Today I saw a tiny newborn calf all on its own. It had sunken
eyes, couldn't walk and was badly dehydrated. I think Mum had
abandoned it. I suppose she may be coming back but I doubt it; he
looked too far gone. I wanted to shoot it to prevent the inevitable
prolonged death but I have no right to, so had to keep on riding.
Hopefully I will see the boreman again and tell him about it – he
could shoot it. I hate seeing young suffer like that, even if it is all
part of Mother Nature. Sometimes she can be a bit harsh, I think.*

*S 17° 39' 47.8", E 133° 40' 35.6"    718 ft    26.3 km*
*Total: 2626.7 km*

**Low point:** *My back was extra sore today, whether I rode or
walked. It started hurting after about only 2 kilometres.*
**High point:** *Relaxed camp with plenty of food.*

One beautiful, warm day, while striding along the sandy tracks, I was bored
and thought I would take advantage of being in phone range. I was riding
Gumby and just turned around and took a photo with my phone, looking
straight down Pam's lead rope to Pam and her pack. It was a great photo,

with the rope in the foreground being out of proportion and out of focus. So I texted it off to basically any mobile phone number I had in my contact list. I was so excited but I think I only got one immediate reply: Lavinia, a vet nurse I had worked with, sent me a photo back. It was of her car parked in Ballarat, with snow falling on it. God I love my life, I thought. Where else would you want to be and what else would you want to be doing? Certainly not driving around Ballarat at that moment!

That night I wrote a bulk email:

---

Hi guys,

Well, I made it to Elliot (or near enough, anyway) … finally. I think that makes me halfway through the Northern Territory. How exciting! I was looking forward to Elliot as I haven't seen a town since Mount Isa on 14 May. I was planning a shopping spree Paris Hilton would have been proud of but, alas, there are only so many tacky fridge magnets and crude stubby holders from a service station that one can justify buying. Actually, Elliot is bigger than I expected. It has three servos. I was going to stay out the back of one thanks to Stewy and Lee and have a hot shower, but the camels would have freaked in their yard. Gumby would have been happy as there was a broken down bus in there and he would have made himself at home on the back seat.

Even though the Barkly tablelands were a bit tough to cross (hundreds of km of no trees and a howling gale) it was made much easier when my parents turned up and 'support crewed' for me for ten days. I think I put on weight! It was brilliant. Also Dad got up at 4 am one morning claiming he had to get to Elliot to meet the bus to pick up some freight. I was a bit confused at what a stupid thing he was doing and he returned with two of my sisters. It was wonderful; for five days they walked with me and I caught up on all the gossip and news. It feels really good that they can now picture better what I am doing. What the hell am I doing? I sometimes wonder. With my parents came a ute and fridge, chairs, table, champagne – you know, all the basics. It made me realise how cushy it would be to have a back-up crew (there would be no hope of that weight-loss program succeeding). All those people who do those amazing things like ride horses from Broome to Cairns (or roll around Australia because one leg is shorter than the other) and use back-up crews – it would have been easy peasy. They cheated! I only cheated temporarily.

Well, I am leaving phone range tomorrow and may not get back into range till Wiluna, in WA in November, so you can all breathe a sigh of relief that you don't have to endure another of these emails for a while.

HiD

I didn't realise what a big tourist trap Newcastle Waters was. I rode in to an area just outside the main gate where there was parking, tourist information boards and historic buildings. The homestead/living area itself gave the impression of Fort Knox with unwelcoming gates but I can't really blame them, judging by the number of tourists buzzing around like flies to a maggoty sheep. Of course, when I rode in I couldn't get them off me either.

'Where are you heading to?' Insanity.

'Wow, that's a long way isn't it?' Actually, not as far as you think.

'Why are you doing this?' Sanity just seemed so, well, sane.

'Are you on your own?' No, I'm with my imaginary friend, Barry. Say hi Barry. Sorry, he's quite shy.

'Are you going to write a book?' Yes, it's going to be called *Insanity Through the Life Stages*.

'You must be so brave!' Well yes, I draw my strength from Barry.

I was invited through the gates by the manager and put up in guests' quarters, which were very luxurious. Even had a TV! I find it interesting that if you haven't seen television for a while you lose your immunity to the complete twaddle shown on it. I had no desire at all to see how Aleisha was going on *Big Brother*, how the world reacted to the last *Harry Potter* book release, or even that it had been announced that Russia was hosting the 2014 Winter Olympics.

The place was fairly quiet because nearly everybody had gone to the Katherine show, which was obviously the social event of the year. I think the only people left were the boremen (who had to keep working – you can't neglect those bores) and a couple of shady looking characters who I suspect probably had an arrest warrant on them and were keeping their heads down. The outback would be the first place I would go to if I had the law after me.

I just had one rest day. I discovered the bar had 'pink champagne' stubbies and I was very excited, though I'm not sure why because as a general rule I don't like 'pink'. Normally these station bars just have XXXX, VB and the obligatory Bundy cans, but apparently when someone new starts work at Newcastle Waters they are asked what their poison is and a few cartons are brought in. A guy had once come to work there and told them he drank 'pink'. How could any guy admit to that, let alone a straight guy (or a gay guy trying to pass as straight if he wants to survive) working on a station in outback Northern Territory? Apparently he drank far too much one night, shamed himself completely and hadn't touched them since, so they had spares and were only too happy to get rid of them.

### Day 174, 19 July: Newcastle Waters

*I met Ken Warriner, the managing director of Consolidated Pastoral Company (CPC) who lives at Newcastle Waters. Really nice man. I think he has been a drover most of his life so we had a great chat about life on the road. After a while I hit him for sponsorship: he gave me $1 per kilometre for the first 5000 kilometres. Yeah! I finally made some serious money for Youth Off the Streets. Thanks Ken.*

*Ken's wife, Sally, was doing the bar tonight and she gave me three pink champagne stubbies to pack. Shiny!*

*S 17 22 17.5, E 133 24 35.5   713 ft   0.0 km*
*Total: 2676.3 km*

*Low point:* A bit weird because hardly anyone was at the station —
they were all at the Katherine Show.
*High point:* $5000 ... yeah!

Armed with my pink stubbies and a $5000 promise I decided to move on.
I only stayed a couple of nights; there was no reason to loiter any longer.
I was looking forward to the next leg because it promised to be less open
and windswept and much more interesting country. I was half way across
the Northern Territory and that fact alone was quite motivating.

### Day 175, 20 July: New Hickety's bore

*The road was good today leaving Newcastle Waters. Still bloody
windy but doesn't quite cut through you like it did on the Barkly.
Apparently this wind won't stop until Top Springs. I am getting
to the stage where I am thinking the world will always be bloody
windy. The Newcastle Waters manager showed me a different way:
I head northwest through Newcastle Waters, across the northeast
corner of the Tanami Desert and then into Dungowan (also a
CPC property) and come onto the highway 55 kilometres east
of Top Springs. I am looking forward to saying 'I did a bit of the
Tanami'. Silly really ...*

*When I arrived at today's camp, Ken, Sally and a friend
pulled up and we chatted. The friend asked me to sign her copy
of Outback magazine as it contained and article on me (how
embarrassing) and gave Youth Off the Streets a $50 donation.
I have never really understood the whole autograph thing and I
certainly don't understand why anyone would want my signature —
they couldn't even cash much of a cheque with it! Oh well, I got a
50 buck donation. I can never refuse that!*

*Tonight I cooked my tuna and rice while drinking one of my
pink stubbies. Wow, does this stuff go straight to your head when it
is warm. Now just got to work out what I will do with the empty.
I think I will carry it in a saddle bag and get the first passer-by
to take it. That might be a few days. Sorry Gum, you'll just have to
carry it ...*

*S 17° 17' 01.6", E 133° 13' 42.0"   717 ft   23.3 km*
*Total: 2699.6 km*

**Low point:** *The embarrassment of signing the magazine.*
**High point:** *Seeing Ken and Sally again – nice people and got the opportunity to thank them for their hospitality.*

I was always really paranoid about how my kids were going. I was concerned about their eating habits, any rubbing or pain they were enduring and what their physical and mental condition was. Maybe it would have been a lot easier if I didn't worry but I would not have been very happy with myself. My kids worked so hard for me and my prime goal was to support them, making it as easy as possible for them. Basically, the trip became one huge animal health management exercise.

Up until now I had pretty well ignored my own health and personal requirements. The only reason I tried to keep myself healthy and pain free was so nothing would interfere with looking after my kids. After the first few days with the girls I had changed them around so Pam was lead camel. I don't think this was Andrew's original idea, as Pam would have made the perfect anchor camel at the back; she wasn't flighty and would be able to keep my very short string of kids anchored. It didn't work that way, though. Pam was a bit of a drag-along camel and Gypsy refused to drag her. Also, Gypsy was freaking out up the front and needed a camel ahead of her. So Pam went in front and Gypsy literally hid behind her. The trouble was, Pam was trashing my back. I found the best way to lead camels was with the rope draped over my shoulder. But when Pam slowed down it would pull on the top of my shoulder and I would have to lean forward a bit. My shirts would wear rapidly on the left shoulder (obviously the one I favoured) so I used to reinforce the material with a denim patch. Some days Pam really dragged the chain and I would get quite sore. She was losing condition and slowing down a bit – or maybe that was me.

Anyway, my back really started playing up and I was becoming a rapid fan of the Aspalgin that some passing bush nurses had given me. Sometimes I really had to push myself to unsaddle the kids before I would fling myself on the ground and rest my back over a pile of sand to try to relieve it. At times like this I really missed my good friend, Jeff Morrison, an osteopath for humans (as well as an animal chiro) and an absolute magician; my back desperately needed him. He used to threaten that he was going to come and camp with me for my 40th birthday and bring a bottle of Bollinger and a dress for me to wear. I think he was serious but sadly it never eventuated. I knew that one visit from him would fix my busted back but I had to settle for the camping chair Mum and Dad left me that had a back on it. Up till then I had been sitting on a stool that was easy to carry with the horses. My chair with a back was the one luxury I made the camels carry. Sorry girls, but I am sure it meant I was less cranky.

I used to also get quite bored sometimes. I could never work out why I found some days fascinating and stimulating, and I would even be reluctant to pull up camp, and some days I would be bored out of my brain by 10 am. To pass the time I used to do mind games or sing, or tell the kids about a great (or terrible) movie I once saw, giving a blow-by-blow description. Sometimes I would choose a theme such as names from Harry Potter or types of infectious organisms and try to think of one starting with each of the letters of the alphabet. I would tell Pam all about A for aspergillus, B for brucella and C for clostridia; or maybe U for Umbridge, V for Vernon Dursley and W for Weasley.

Pam really objected to my singing. In particular, she hated *Bohemian Rhapsody* with a passion. I don't know whether it was the words she objected to (or maybe the fact that I had trouble remembering all the words) or whether it was the tune itself. I suppose it could have possibly been that I struggled a little to keep up with Freddie. Either way, as soon as I started singing 'Is this the real life …' Pam would jerk hard on the lead rope, putting me in danger of dislocating my shoulder.

Pam also objected to me giving her instructions when I was listening to my iPod. She would tolerate me listening to the iPod as we walked along but if I told her to do something like 'hoosh' when I had the headphones in she would just give me a superior look, raise her head to full height and look away. When I finally did pull my ears out (even with music still blaring) I would ask her again and she would lower her head and place it right in front of my face and give me that well-loved look of 'So did we learn something from this?' and then sit in obedience. Gotta love Pam; she was hard but she didn't expect any more of me than she did of herself.

The continual grind of being on the road was starting to wear me down. I think it was starting to wear us all down.

### Day 178, 23 July: Tanami Desert camp

*Camels were happy because it was great sandy ground. Gypsy is tired but well behaved. The morning took forever! I was singing Bohemian Rhapsody by 9.30 am. The day got better faster, though. I am on serious water rations now, not just practice. It will be interesting to see how fast we go through it. I have been monitoring Gumby's water intake when I can and it seems he hardly drinks anything for a horse. Am I miscalculating or has he been hanging around the camels too long? Just gotta make sure the camels don't get to Gumby's bucket.*

*This country is great — lots of trees and shrubs. It certainly doesn't feel like a desert.*

*The other day I crossed over the Ghan railway line. I can't believe people pay more for a one-way train ticket from Darwin to Adelaide than for a flight from Melbourne to London. Why doesn't anyone come with me? It's a lot cheaper and you see heaps more! Gumby hasn't eaten much grass today or yesterday. I didn't hear him graze much last night either. He mustn't be well but his gut sounds are good. He still breaks into camp and tries to steal the leftover horse feed that Mum and Dad dropped off at Elliot for me, so he can't be too bad. Maybe he is a bit depressed. I have to keep chasing him out of camp and Furphy goes right off.*

*I am really enjoying this desert leg and so are the camels. It's beautiful country, soft sandy ground, great tucker for the girls and no more Barkly Breeze. The last couple of days I have really noticed the silence — I'm sure it's just because there isn't that howling wind. I love no wind!*

*S 17° 18' 20.2", E 132° 27' 40.2"   811 ft   28.5 km*
*Total: 2783.8 km*

**Low point:** *Gumby's depression – I think it is the equivalent of a normal horse going sour.*
**High point:** *No wind!*


### Day 179, 24 July: No camel food camp

*Got up this morning and – shock horror – Pam has no hump! Where did it go? It was there a minute ago! Looking at her she is a bag of bones – I think. Gypsy is still the same – I think. Oh God, I can't tell. I have spent all day freaking over how my girls are looking that I can't really see through objective eyes.*

*While packing this morning, putting the water jerries on Gypsy, a Land Cruiser came flying up the track. I camped right on this track last night because the flora was so thick we couldn't really get off it, plus it is a desert track between two properties (i.e. basically a private track) and I never expected traffic. I tried to wave to the guy to slow down while hooshing Gypsy down and holding onto her untied water. I decided Pam would have to fend for herself. He didn't see me. To this day I am not sure how you don't see two camels, a horse, a dog and a human waving wildly, that are on the same 9-m wide track as you! He finally saw me when Pam got up and crashed into the back of Gumby, gear flying off her unstable saddle. So he stopped. Apparently the stock camp from Newcastle Waters was heading to Dungowan to do some mustering for a few weeks. I had to quickly finish packing the kids as there was more traffic to follow and I couldn't be sure those vehicles would be any better driven.*

*It was another of those very slow days. The first 10 km took an eternity. At 12 km we went through a gate, which I think was the Dungowan boundary. The country hasn't changed much but I do miss the desert already. I think I must be a 'desert bunny'. It was wild and beautiful country. The sounds were amazing – even the flies. I think because I spent so much time in the wind and now it had stopped (or I have left it) I am amazed at how I can hear everything. Not only has the wind stopped but the days and nights are hotter. There is light dew in the morning but that is because it is so still.*

*I had a really sore back this morning by 9.30. It is getting worse. Normally getting on or off Gum only fleetingly helps. However, today when I got on Gum at 8 km it instantly got better and stayed better. All I can put it down to is the fact that, for the first time I had the rifle on Gumby hanging off the near side of the saddle. This caused the saddle to be skew, which fixed (temporarily anyway) my back. The trouble is I am sure it is not good for poor Gum. I am sure he will have sore ribs, wither and lumbars tomorrow. I will have to work out how to carry the rifle on him without unbalancing the saddle. How did John Wayne do it, I wonder? Maybe he didn't care about busting his horse and just got a new one every movie.*

*I put the rifle on Gum today because I realised I didn't know the wild camel status around here. I needed something to protect my family if an amorous bull camel in rut launched through the bushes at us. I needed to be prepared, just in case.*

*S 17° 09' 49.0", E 132° 21' 22.9"   851 ft   28.1 km*
*Total: 2811.9 km*

**Low point:** *Goodbye desert.*
**High point:** *The kids behaved surprising well with the wild driving of the ringers. It could have been quite ugly.*

I was fascinated at the sudden change in the country once I entered Dungowan. I had left the red sand and thick scrubby bushes that hummed of the wildlife of the Tanami and entered much more sparse country. The ground was hard and eroded from the rains it gets in the wet, the eucalypts were taller with little ground cover and herbage, and the birds and reptiles were quiet and shy.

On the way through Dungowan I met up with the manager and his wife, Ron and Sue, and their kids. They were really welcoming and generous as only outback people are. They offered me all sorts of things ranging from collecting water for my jerries to steak for me and a bone for the dog. Sue put together a list of names and phone numbers of property owners/managers for my future travels and gave me a rundown on who they all were and what they were like. Looking at it closely later, I realised the list extended all the way across into Western Australia: 700 kilometres. From this I developed another of my brilliant but unproven theories. Everybody knows twelve of their neighbours in each direction. In the NT this might mean 700 kilometres of knowledge. In southern New South Wales it may mean 60 kilometres of knowledge. The exception to the rule is town living, as towns are like intensive farm piggeries. The breeding sows have no real say over where their pen is or who their neighbours are and nothing in common with them. They can't even turn around or crane their necks high enough to see who their twelfth neighbour is. There is too much noise and stimulus so they just put their heads down and await their next meal to pour from the automatic feeders. What a dull life.

The weather started to heat up, which I certainly welcomed. I hadn't quite defrosted mentally since my stint on the Barkly Tablelands and was desperate for some good solid heat. I used to calculate how many days till the next 'civilised' break where I could do my washing, restock my food etc. I had three long-sleeved King Gee work shirts and two pairs of RM Williams jeans cut off as long shorts. I would arrange it so that I wore two shirts for the bulk of the portion of each leg, so the last shirt would have only been worn for a couple of days by the time I hit civilisation. You know things are bad when you can smell yourself, but it's even worse when you no longer can; it means your nose has given up warning you of your poor hygiene habits and has decided to shut down till the next wash.

### Day 182, 27 July: Ripping headache camp
The kids went well today, despite me.

For some reason the word 'skanky' keeps cropping up in my thoughts. Today I wore my shirt for the sixth day; that really is skanky. It is so dirty the sweat won't dry off it and it just stays all doughy. I have limited my arm waving today as it nearly knocks me unconscious every time! If I keep wearing it, it will end up like Drizabone material. Maybe that's how they make a Drizabone …

not sure. So, a clean shirt tomorrow. Maybe that will improve my morale.

Today the heat got to me a bit; I think I made a couple of mistakes.I have been thinking I am nearly at Top Springs for too long and it really feels like I should have got there today.

I have obviously been relying on Julia joining me again and coming down the Canning with me, even though I didn't realise it. Mum told me a couple of days ago I can count her out because Phil (her father) said he hadn't heard from her in months and he can't contact her. I think it kind of hit me today. The Canning is a huge hurdle looming up ahead and I am struggling to believe that I can do it alone.

I am also worried about Pam. I think she is getting skinnier by the day but still not sure if I am imagining it. I try to give them a longer feed in the morning and night but they just stop eating after a while and seem to need a rest. Gumby is not as skinny as he got but you can still see his ribs like you can a thoroughbred — I'm sure the poor old fella has never been compared to a thoroughbred before!

And to top it all off I am ready to commit 'canacide'; Furphy has taken to running off towards cattle. If I call him he comes back rapidly, all pleased with himself. If I don't call him he turns around to see if I am watching and tries to get my attention. He reminds me of a poor neglected kid called Shane I once knew. Shane would purposefully try to annoy me and when I finally asked him outright why he felt the need to annoy me he answered honestly: 'Any attention is good attention.' This is what Furphy was doing today and it is making me feel guilty. I suppose it is my fault, I should pat him more. I need to set aside five minutes a day where I do nothing but pat him. Just another job I have to do. I am getting tired.

I have a big ugly three-week leg coming up, some of which is on bitumen. I can't even be bothered cooking and eating tonight. I will have to because that only makes this sort of mood worse.

I might just read Dune while daylight then try to cook and wash in the dark. It is a silly idea but I need to distract myself and *try to snap out of this shit mood. I am reading Dune 6 but don't recommend it because is a bit slow — what else does one expect from the sixth book of a series? Although Dune 7 does look better.*

*S 16° 38' 26.1", E 131° 58' 43.7"    725 ft    26.5 km*
*Total: 2894.9 km*

**Low point:** *Depressed — of course that's the low point! It is such a pointless, directionless, useless emotion. What a waste of brain space and energy.*
**High point:** *Sitting in the shade with a chair with a back on it, with a nice breeze, trying (but not achieving) to cleanse me and my mood and my headache.*

One thing about being on the road like this is you just have to keep going. When I was on the Barkly Stock Route the only reason I kept going was that the other option was to stop and that was only going to delay us getting to shelter, feed and general sanity. Once at Anthony Lagoon I forgot the edge of despair I had endured and didn't really consider stopping. I think it was a bit like childbirth. In general, if you ask a woman who is in the process of giving birth if she will do it again she will reply something to the effect of 'Take my ovaries now and while you're at it take his testicles, too' while pointing to a poor, innocent-looking male. But, like slow learners in a banjo shop, they nearly always end up going back for seconds, and maybe even thirds. I was hitting a bit of a low again and at one stage the main driving force was to get out of this godforsaken situation. But I think this time, deep down, I knew I was still going to go back for that third and fourth child, the pain of parturition soon forgotten.

# 11

## Catch up with the sun

I followed the Buchanan Highway to Top Springs at the intersection with the Buntine Highway where there was a pub, service station and truck stop rolled into one. This seemed to be a main meeting point for all locals (i.e. people from as far away as 350 kilometres) and tourists. I had dinner with Sue and Ron and their kids (from Dungowan station) at the pub, which was great. I had met a few faces on the road already and was feeling a bit like a local.

I was surprised at the number of blokes in NT and Queensland pubs who had fractured their spine while bull riding at rodeos. Maybe it was your outback bullshit story that guys told to impress the women, but I don't think so. *All* these guys had been flown to a Brisbane hospital (they must be experts in spinal surgery by now) and *all* of them had got sick of hospital and discharged themselves early. What were they thinking? I wouldn't mind so much dying in a bull-riding accident (theoretically, that is, because I have no desire to ride a bull. I hear they are pretty hard in the mouth and don't neck rein too well) but ending up a paraplegic or quadriplegic because you got bored in hospital and left before you were properly healed? How is that fun?

At Top Springs I met a guy who had been the under-18 Australian Champion Bull Rider and won a 'scholarship' to America to continue his craft. His sponsor was Jack Daniels, which was ironic given the age of the competition. They paid for his insurance and he talked about how it was hard to afford it if you didn't have sponsorship. I am not a big fan of insurance companies but can't really understand why any would touch a bull rider. Surely there is only one direction that career is heading and you can guarantee there will be a payout in the end. But maybe I am just a coward and a cynic.

I was getting more down. I couldn't work out how I was going to travel the Canning Stock Route on my own and without any support crew. It is 1800 kilometres of desert with one remote community in the middle. All the wells are basically tourist sites so reliable information on their water status was difficult to ascertain. Dad spoke to me on the phone one day when I was feeling particularly negative. I tried not to convey my feelings but don't think I succeeded.

'Someone here will just have to go over and meet you when you are halfway down!' he announced. I was too weak to say no. My family does so much for me and at this stage I was feeling very much the spoilt black sheep of the family.

Mum and Dad had actually driven as far as Top Springs when they had come to visit and left a bag of Copra (horse feed) there for Gumby. He was very pleased about that. He loved his Copra and since I had been carrying it and feeding it to him his weight had held on a lot better. I tried Pam on it but she looked at me as though I had offered her a marrow bone to eat. Some days she was just too proud for her own good.

I had been having an ongoing battle with Pam's saddle. It seemed whatever I did it still rubbed her so I got James to send me a whole new canvas padding. I dismantled the old one and stuffed the new one as best I could. I should have done it sooner. Pam was much happier and, thus, so was I.

I left Top Springs on 31 July and a few days later I was finally feeling motivated enough to write another bulk email.

---

Hi guys,

Well I am sitting here in the dark with a selection of friends (mosquitoes, flying ant things and Gumby) waiting for the full moon to rise. I love the full moon although I have to admit it is so bright I sometimes put a hankie over my face to sleep. It is amazing sleeping outside, as every now and then you wake up and see that the stars and moon have shifted and you get to learn their patterns a bit. I am even good at guesstimating the time when I wake up. I have no idea how I do it but I just can.

It was quite a warm day (maybe 36°C?) and I have been drinking all day but still thirsty so having a great cup of tea. You know you don't appreciate the little things till they have gone. I lost my enamel mug while crossing the top corner of the Tanami and now a cup of tea involves risking third-degree burns while drinking out of an enamel saucer. For some reason I feel Asian when I am doing this! Do they drink tea out of a saucer?

I am now about 60 km west of Top Springs (a pub/servo) and have about 550 to go to get to Wolfe Creek and start the Canning Stock Route. And before you ask – no, I didn't see the movie for the very reason I knew I was going there. This leg is basically 'follow the road' most of the way so am going to try to find a better, more interesting way on old tracks through the properties. I get so sick of trudging down the roads! I met a few nice tourists the other day but one of them sent my whole self-identity into a tail spin. He said *I* was a tourist. No! Not me! He then donated $50 to Youth Off the Streets and made me talk into a video. I hate cameras and start a full 'fight or flight' sympathetic response in front of videos. Ugh! I offered to prostitute myself instead but he just laughed. How rude! I was deeply offended until I realised the shirt I was wearing was on its fifth day of travel. Oh well.

Gypsy got two large bald patches the size of dinner plates either side of her hump. The tick spray they had to endure back on the Barkly Stock Route scalded her. Anyway, I think hair is finally growing back! Thank God, as I didn't fancy handing her back to Andrew, her owner, with great big bald patches. However, I have a terrible suspicion it is going to be white hair – Good look Gypsy!

Furphy cut the pad behind his dew claw and I fear the world seems to be coming to an end. Every time he moved last night there was yelping and screaming and I kept thinking he was being attacked by an axe-wielding maniac. He is not a man of courage I am afraid to say! Especially after the other night. I woke to hear a strangled barking noise (not Furphy) and found a dingo a metre from my swag, looking at me, and Furphy *under* his blanket. I chased the dingo off with the stock whip before Furphy would surface. Great protector, that one!I have been missing my iPod terribly. I posted it home so Harry (my nephew) could burn on the new *Harry Potter* book (read by Stephen Fry) and he will post it back … to somewhere.

Gumby must have three speeds or styles of walk, because as we are going along one of three tunes to the rhythm of his walk sneaks into my head and then I can't get rid of it. It would be all right if it was *Hotel California* or *Eagle Rock*. But I get either *Pop Goes the Weasel, Yakety Sax* (the theme music to *The Benny Hill Show*) or *Skip to my Loo*. I mean to say – why would someone write a song about a kid busting to go to the toilet? And did someone feed their weasel too much cabbage and onion? Anyway, I can't get these tunes out of my head once they are there unless I can sing out loud another song over the top of them. Quite tragically, the only song I seem to remember the tune and words (mostly) to is *Bohemian Rhapsody*. And I tell you Pam does not appreciate my Freddie impersonation. She always pulls on the rope whenever I start up.

I will get to Kalkarindji community in a few days and will have range to send this. The communities are always good for sending off my mail and catching up on phone calls. I think there is some government initiative that states that remote communities should have a Telstra tower.

Anyway, thanks again for listening.

HiD

---

A day out of Kalkarindji I woke to have that eerie feeling that someone was staring at me. When I opened my eyes I found Gypsy, Pam and Gumby all looking at me with great intensity in the full light of day. I had slept in. I felt really sick and blocked up and was lying in a sea of sweat. This wasn't your ordinary cold; it was industrial strength. I finally worked out where I had got it from, too. When I caught up with Ron and Sue, one of their daughters had a cold – obviously my lack of contact with the human race had made me even more vulnerable. I felt like shit. The poor kids were starving so I let them off for a feed and had a late start to the day. Gum had to carry me most of the day because I could only walk about 500 metres and my 'batteries' would run out.

About 10 kilometres out of Kalkarindji, still in the middle of nowhere, I realised I would have reception so cranked up the old mobile. It was windy and I had my hands full with reins and Pam's rope so put my earphones in and tucked the microphone into my shirt. I was talking to a friend, another Julia, who is always up for a laugh and we chatted away happily for ages. When I reached the grid of the Kalkarindji boundary I stopped at the gate and Gum put his head down to graze. Julia was in the middle of a hysterical story about a horse she had done a chiro on and I was trying to contemplate dismounting without getting caught up in the reins, Pam's rope or my phone. I threw my leg over, got it completely tangled in Pam's rope and fell backwards, A over T, flat on my back. My left leg had twisted and jammed in the stirrup and my right leg was caught up in Pam's rope. Gumby looked at me out of the corner of his eye, not pausing at all in his grazing quest and Pam looked at me briefly, giving me that haughty glare I had grown to love and then looked away raising her head high and thus lifting my butt off the ground. I was totally at the mercy of my kids. Meanwhile my phone had gone flying and I could hear a high-pitched squeak in the distance: 'Heidi ... Heidi ...? Hello?' I don't think I had laughed so hard in a long time. I must have looked ridiculous!

I finally managed to extricate myself from Pam and Gum, rescued the phone and proceeded to go through the gate while telling Julia, through convulsive laughter, about the sight she had just missed. Once I was through I got back on Gum, carefully, and sat up only to be confronted by about half a dozen blackfellas sitting on a small knoll about 20 metres in front of me.

'I'll ring you back,' I said to Julia.

How embarrassing! When you fall over like a fool and have a friend with you it is not so bad and you both have a bit of a laugh. And when you fall over and no-one is there to laugh with, it is embarrassing but okay because no-one is there. But when you do it and there are people watching from a short distance ... that's when it is hard to hold your head up. However, I stopped for a chat and they were very respectful. They didn't mention what they had just witnessed; instead we discussed the weather and how far it was to the community. As embarrassed as I was, I would love to have seen the whole episode. I don't think I could have been so controlled and not brought it up if I was one of the witnesses. Well, that was my first fall for the trip. Not exactly heroic and spectacular.

I stayed at Kalkarindji police station and the kids were in a great paddock with high fences and lots of food. My cold developed into laryngitis and I had very little voice for two days. There went all my plans for making hundreds of phone calls.

### Day 193, 7 August: Kalkarindji

I woke up yesterday morning with no voice and a shocker of a night's sleep. This morning is only marginally better. Hopefully Furphy's meat-flavoured Vibravet (antibiotics) I started on yesterday will start to kick in. I have lots of phone calls to make about the future path and water on the Canning so this voice isn't helping at all. I managed to speak to Sheryl, the rocket scientist, and ordered some supplies from Coles in Kununurra. God knows what I am going to get! Ken and Shirley are going to pick them up on their way home from their holiday and I will meet them on the road in a couple of weeks.

The thing I hate about getting back to civilisation is that I eat too much and I eat bread, which only serves to grind my guts and my metabolism to a screeching halt, making me feel all doughy. Yep, that's why they call it 'dough' — because it makes you feel doughy! Also, when I am in civilisation I start to develop a bit of a reluctance to launch back out there (it seems all so hard from the civilised side of the fence) so then I feel guilty and then I feel stupid etc. Yep, I am an eejit!

This arvo I ventured down the street for the first time. I went to the little food store and did some limited shopping. When I was in *there, contemplating the colour of my new pannikin a wizened old blackfella with about three teeth left came up to me chuckling.*

*'You that woman who rode from Rockhampton and picked up camels in Mount Isa.' It wasn't a question, just a statement.*

*Stunned, I asked him how he knew.*

*'Oh, rumours everywhere. You crazy lady. Australia is a big place. Too big to ride. You very crazy lady,' he grinned. With that he turned and wandered back down the aisle, chortling away. It was then I realised that those polite locals I met up with earlier may not have said anything to me about the ridiculous event they witnessed but I could be sure that everyone in town knew exactly what happened!*

*I know the old blackfella was laughing at me, not with me.*

*S 17° 26' 48.2", E 130° 50' 20.0"   551 ft   0.0 km*
*Total: 3096.1 km*

**Low point:** *This bloody cold.*
**High point:** *Meeting the old black fella in the store (despite him laughing at me).*

It seemed the further I travelled the more I became aware of the history of each area. Admittedly I had very little interest in history at school. In my defence, I could not see much importance in learning that eleven southern American states had seceded because they wanted to continue abusing their black slaves or even that the great Church of England was founded by an unfaithful megalomaniac having a guilt trip about the possibility of killing one of his many wives. For some reason it never really felt relevant to me and my life. But out there, history seemed so near and had consequences that I could see.

Wave Hill Station, where Kalkarindji is, made headline news in 1966 when its indigenous people, the Gurindji, walked off the station and refused to work. They wanted wages (they were only paid in rations) and better treatment from the station they worked on, but the main issue was land rights. This set the ball rolling and eventually resulted in them being granted title to the land and recognition as the traditional owners. Such a summary does not demonstrate the significance of the string of events, but suffice to say that this community was thought to be the pioneer for inspiring other communities and indigenous rights throughout Australia. Paul Kelly and Kev Carmody captured this in their song *From Big Things Little Things Grow*, a tune I have liked for years but never actually realised what it was about.

The police station is on the eastern side of Kalkarindji, so on the day we left we had to walk right through the town. In the middle of town, a woman who said she was the principal of the school stopped me and asked if I could walk to the school and show my kids to her kids. Pam and Gypsy were behaving a bit out of sorts after having a couple of days off (which they hated and it would take a bit to get them back into the routine) and as they were in town. Gypsy was right up Pam's butt as she was extra nervous of anything that could be behind her. I was still a bit dodgy from my cold and keen to just get out of town and start walking to settle the girls. Besides, I hate the unexpected interruptions in my well-laid plans. I politely declined, citing the girls being unhappy, and walked off. My conscience, however, only let me get 50 metres down the road. I mean, what the hell was I doing if I couldn't share this with kids and a town that had generously made me welcome? I really had to keep working on my 'flexibility with plans'. Just because I was cranky and the girls a little flighty didn't mean I couldn't do others a favour. So I walked around to the school and fronted up to the outside fence. There was a road behind us that was carrying a surprising amount of traffic. Gypsy was not happy and stuck to Pam's butt like glue.

An old fella passing by stopped for a chat and a sticky beak.

'Where are you heading to?' Serendipity.

'Wow, that's a long way isn't it?' Depends which route you take.

'Why are you doing this?' Looking for a husband.

'Are you on your own?' Until I find a husband.

'Are you going to write a book?' Yep. It's called *Chance Favours the Prepared Mind*.

'You must be so brave!' To stand stationary with these wild kids screaming and running towards me? Yep, I must be. I rapidly gave him my camera and asked if he could take some photos. The kids came from all corners of the school – they were like budgies to a dish of water in the desert. The girls' eyes grew bigger and bigger as screaming kids launched onto the fence and started climbing. Thank goodness a teacher appeared out of nowhere and gained rapid control, announcing threats to any child who crossed the fence. I did a little talk and the kids asked lots of questions. To this day there is nothing that makes me smile more than these community kids' wide grins, white teeth flashing and cheeky eyes glinting. After, I reflected that somewhere in teenage-hood that wild, free glint in their eye seems to dissolve, leaving behind a world weariness.

The old fella gave me back my camera, saying sheepishly, 'I think they worked out', and I was on my way. As I walked out of town I was feeling much better and I think we all had a lighter step. That night I ate dinner and sat down to view the photos of such an uplifting experience. I had 22 close-up photos of the old local from Kalkarindji, with mouth open and a look of intense concentration on his face. He fell for the old digital camera facing the wrong way trick ... bummer!

The principal of the school gave me a $50 donation for Youth Off the Streets. I realised that every donation I had received from Northern Territorians was $50 or more. I couldn't believe their generosity. It seemed the less populated or the less affluent the area, the larger and greater in number the donations. An interesting commentary on humankind. Later, when I went through a part of New South Wales that had the worst drought-affected land I had ever seen, I experienced incredible generosity. Property owners were insisting on feeding me, handing over more food for me and my horses and donating $50 even though they had not had stock on their place for up to three years due to the fact that dirt is not very nourishing.

When I was at Kalkarindji police station the Underwood boys stopped for a chat, telling me about water and the track ahead. They were heading into Katherine for a family reunion. A couple of days out they passed me again, limping home a little worse for wear with two of them lying cast in the back of the vehicle. Patrick, the driver, insisted I stay when I got to his place, Inverway. The Underwoods are probably best known from Terry Underwood's bestselling book called *In the Middle of Nowhere*. This is about her life as a nurse who married a patient (yes, another spinal injury) from the Territory and her journey from Sydneysider to remote cattle station owner.

Terry is also known for her photography skills and being an ambassador for Year of the Outback.

You wouldn't meet nicer people. Apparently this family reunion spanned across the country (I discovered one family member was returning from my home area of Tocumwal) and lasted for what seemed weeks. I suppose when you travel that far to catch up with all the family you hang around for a while. Basically, from Kalkarindji to near the Western Australia border I kept running into various members of the family. There were hundreds of them, with an Underwood baby under every bush or so it seemed. I met all the sons, babies, cousins, aunts, etc. I was starting to feel a bit like an Underwood myself, they were such a welcoming family. I would travel along and a passing car would screech to a halt and out would leap an Underwood of some description, who would give me a rundown of the path ahead and hand over a few cold beers. They would then take my empties left from their last encounter and shoot off in a cloud of dust.

### Day 197, 11 August: Perfect camp

*Had visitors at camp today – Cody, Alex, Jeffery, Delton and Latoya. A carload of blackfella kids stopped to see the camels. I am hidden off the road so they must have good eyesight! Four boys about ten years old came in like a whirlwind and rushed up to my kids, who were in a turkey's nest yard. Poor Gypsy, she likes surprises less than me. The woman had them under control though ... they were just being boys. They climbed all over the pack saddles so I took a photo. As soon as the photo was taken they all wanted to have a look at it. We may be in the outback but they can spot a digital camera a mile off! There is something good for the heart seeing young blackfella kids laughing and smiling. It's quite infectious.*

*This camp is brilliant: a turkey's nest with great camel and horse feed, a good fence, fresh tasty water and short green grass for me to camp on. All I need is a bar fridge full of Bollinger and I will stay here a month!*

*The other day I was packing up and the kids were grazing for brekky and there was a loud 'bang' – both Gum and Pam spun* and jumped and I turned to see a puff of smoke float away. What the? Furphy had run back to the saddles and buried his head under a blanket and Gypsy continued browsing (that reminds me, I must check her hearing). I finally worked out it was one of those big green, fungal puffballs exploding. I have seen them the size of softballs pushing up through the bitumen.

My back was really sore again today. I took some codeine which helped. I think I am back to full fitness after that filthy disease I got at Kalkarindji so happy about that. I am looking forward to getting to Inverway, then I will be halfway to Bililuna from Top Springs.

This morning Gypsy spat the dummy again while saddling. I don't know what her issue was. She doesn't seem sore and her feet seem okay. All I can think is that she is throwing a tantrum when I saddle Pam and not her. When I am saddling her she is fine; it's when I am doing Pam that she is impatient and chucks a wobbly. She has such a fluid personality, always changing and evolving. I am sure I will discover what her problem is and I bet she never had a problem with it before. This morning both front legs were tied down (when sitting the front leg can be tied so the knee cannot unbend from its fully flexed position and the long end of the rope goes over the camel's neck and ties the other knee flexed; this prevents them from extending their knees and being able to stand). Several times she ended up on her side floundering. I really do think it is attention-seeking behaviour!

S 17° 40′ 36.7″, E 130° 00′ 39.4″   1296 ft   24.6 km
Total: 3200.0 km

**Low point:** Bloody back... stop whingeing Heidi.
**High point:** Smiling kids in my camp.

I had an old sheepskin that I had cut up and attached to Gumby's saddle which served many purposes: it stopped my bare legs rubbing on the saddle, it stopped the saddle getting too hot to touch in the sun after I had been off it, it stopped me getting all sweaty, and it even padded my butt to help with saddle sore. People used to ask me all the time if I got a sore bum with all that riding. I would say 'no' because I thought I didn't have a right to complain about a sore bum if Gumby wasn't going to complain about a sore back. But the truth of the matter was that I *did* get a sore butt, just as anybody would get sore sitting in the same position all day, every day. I had done my fair share of riding for entire days but that was doing things like mustering. When you are going at the one pace, just walking, you get sore feet and a sore bum. I used to move about a bit in my saddle – take my feet out of the stirrups, throw a leg over the pommel – but I knew it was harder work for Gum and after a while my bad 'position' started to hurt him. So I did a lot of walking. When I had the pack horses, walking was a pain because they would smash you about with their packs, especially when they were tired; so I used to walk only a third to a half of the day. I loved walking with the camels, they didn't crowd you at all. The girls had as big a personal space as I did, so I walked about two-thirds of the day.

Personal space is a funny thing. I remember as boarders, when our parents used to come and pick us up from school, watching through the upstairs window as the adults met and shook hands. The handshake revealed so much about the person. The farmer would lean so far forward his back foot would come off the ground; he would shake with an outstretched hand, then go back to his position of distance. A group of farmers would stand in a 3-metre diameter circle and talk quietly about how the season was going. Even the fact that they all suffered a fair level of tractor deafness would not encourage them to come in closer or talk louder. On the other hand, the parents of the 'day bugs' stood in a circle tight enough to know what they'd each had for dinner the night before. They did not have to move their feet to shake hands, elbows still tight by their sides, and they'd even get the other hand to clamp around the outside of the shake in a death grip. They weren't going to let their new acquaintance get very far away at all. They would also talk loudly as though they were competing for noise. There was the occasional 'wet fish' shake that amused us all. It would just flop around and do anything the other hand dictated. We concluded that this was more of an indication of personality rather than environment. It was always amusing to see a sheep farmer from southern New South Wales meet a doctor from Toorak; it would

CATCH UP WITH THE SUN

be totally awkward and unbalanced. Although the doctor would talk loudly and edge closer and closer, the farmer still wouldn't catch a single word. He would just nod politely, inching backwards.

Ken and Shirley caught up with me on their way home from their holiday, just east of the Western Australian border. They had picked up my order from Coles in Kununurra. Good old Sheryl! Somehow, an order for one pen turned into a packet of 20 pens, a kilogram of dried apricots became 3 kilograms, eight rolls of toilet paper turned into sixteen and 2 kilograms of mixed dried fruit and nuts arrived as 5 kilograms of lollies. Oh well, I suppose the lollies could have powered us all to Wiluna and back in a complete sugar frenzy. She added more apricots to deal with the lolly constipation I was bound to get, then she must have looked at all the dried apricots, got nervous and threw in more toilet paper. Not sure what she was thinking with the pens. I spent the whole afternoon sorting my new stores and taking off all the excess packaging to give to Ken and Shirley to throw out. As humanity evolves we just seems to wrap our goods in more and more packaging. It's depressing, really. To this day I get home from shopping and immediately remove all excess packaging off my goods. Saves heaps of room in the cupboards.

I had been a little concerned about my rifle, as I had done no maintenance and had no real interest in it. In westerns and Bruce Willis movies they always seem to be cleaning them. When I was in the military we cleaned our rifles ad nauseam, but that was the military, who also made you fold your socks into happy faces! So Ken gave my rifle a once-over, and inquired about what the camels would do if it was fired. I didn't know. Andrew Harper had told me, in his usual casual manner, that they would be fine. I knew Gum wouldn't care but thought I should get Ken to fire off a round or two while I was there, ready to calm crazy camels.

So I tied the girls to sturdy trees, Shirley whipped out the video in the hope there would be a 'show' and Ken waited for my order. *Bang!* Gumby continued grazing without flinching (surely he is deaf!) and the girls slowly looked around towards Ken with an expression of 'Huh?' on their faces. What we didn't factor in, and I think Shirley missed in her filming, was Furphy taking off at a thousand miles an hour and planting himself under the ute in a trembling mess. Still a great man of courage.

The day before we crossed into Western Australia was Dad's 70th birthday. The whole family got together in Melbourne and celebrated ... except me of course. I found times like that a bit tough, not being there when everyone else was. We all put in together and gave him the very first swag he'd ever had. Apparently he embarrassed himself thoroughly when he got it and I think was trying to set it up and crawl into it in the restaurant. He was now set for his trip with his older brother, Don, down the Canning Stock Route.

As summer approached and I was heading west the sun started setting later. I didn't notice much of a change in sunrise; maybe in my westward travel I was changing time zones at about the same rate the sunrise time was changing.

The trip from Top Springs to Sturt Creek Station was quite mind numbing. Great stations and people but the actual walk was tedious. I knew it was going to be tough from the moment I saw the first little green distance marker to Halls Creek saying 400 kilometres and I was already at Kalkarindji. Every 10 kilometres we walked past a sign with a smaller number but they just made it seem so much further: 390 kilometres, 380 kilometres, 370 kilometres ... it just went on and on. What was I doing? I was desperate to get off the road and break up this monotonous march. I really wanted to travel through station tracks but it just wasn't going to happen. Why was I doing this? Whatever had possessed me?

I seemed to constantly have *Time*, the Pink Floyd song, repeating through my mind as we walked along.

> Ticking away the moments that make up a dull day,
> You fritter and waste the hours in an off-hand way,
> Kicking around on a piece of ground in your home town,
> Waiting for someone or something to show you the way.

It is a brilliant song with a great rhythm to walk to but it wasn't until then that I actually thought about the words. Now I am not sure what Pink Floyd were singing about (I'm not sure many people have ever really known) but I had my own thoughts. I saw it as a bit of an explanation for my ride.

I have accused many people, including myself, of just trudging through life. It can be easy to kick back and settle for the position you are in because, well, that is just the position you are in. I know many veterinarians who don't like their job and are smart and resourceful enough to do anything they put their mind to but keep ticking along, doing what they know and not what they dream of. When I would tell people about the ride I was going to do around Australia some would say, 'Yeah, I was going to do that'. I got sick of it after a while and would challenge them back: 'Well, why don't you?' That would make them panic! 'Oh, I can't get time off work and my children are young and my horse wouldn't make it and I have a sore back and my husband would disapprove and I am washing my hair that day and blah, blah, blah.' The best one I got was, 'I am scared of spiders so if one got on my pillow I wouldn't be able to get into bed until it left'. People just make excuses sometimes.

Don't get me wrong. I am just as guilty. It took the shock that I was going to turn 40 to make me sit up and say, 'I gotta do this now rather than dream about it for the rest of my life!'

> Tired of lying in the sunshine staying home to watch the rain,
> You are young and life is long and there is time to kill today,
> And then one day you find ten years have got behind you,
> No-one told you when to run, you missed the starting gun.

Now I had left I sometimes wondered what I was chasing. It was bloody hard work: tedious, hot, cold, tiring, dangerous, stressful, lonely (yes, a little!), expensive and very isolating. It was me versus the big void out there and a lot of the time I questioned what the hell I was doing. It seemed to be never-ending and sometimes I felt like a scratched record that no-one would come and shift forward a bit to get back onto the good part. Every day the sun rose behind me and set in front of me and I never seemed to get any closer. Why was I there?

> And you run and you run to catch up with the sun, but it's sinking,
> And racing around to come up behind you again,
> The sun is the same in a relative way, but you're older,
> Shorter of breath, and one day closer to death.

But then I started to realise what I was doing. If I couldn't make any huge gesture to the world – change it for better or worse, take advantage of this great gift of life by not squandering it away – then anything I would do didn't really matter.

So, in the immortal words of Joss Whedon's TV character, Angel:

'... in the greater scheme, nothing we do, matters. There is no grand plan, no big win. If there is no glorious end to all this, if nothing we do matters, then all that matters is what we do ... 'cause that's all there is ... what we do now ... today.'

> Every year is getting shorter, never seem to find the time,
> Plans that either come to naught or half a page of scribbled lines,
> Hanging on in quiet desperation in the English way,
> The time is gone the song is over, thought I'd something more to say.

All of a sudden the tiniest little thing was the biggest thing I could do; and it did matter. Try and work that one out.

Maybe it was the heat, or the isolation, or just that insanity was infectious and I had been standing too close to Furphy, but I was satisfied. I was doing something, even though it was just small, but I was doing something. And it *was* a big thing. Maybe the money I made could help one kid make one right decision that would steer them in the right direction and save their life or even make it a little easier.

The country had never looked so clear and beautiful. I turned southwest (finally) towards Sturt Creek Station and headed into my last port of civilisation before embarking on over 1800 kilometres of desert. It would be the toughest leg of my trip and I think I was finally ready for it. Hell, I was looking forward to it.

# 12

# Waiting

The idea, and consequent establishment of, a stock route that could move cattle from the northeast cattle country of Western Australia to the southern regions has a long and quite political history. Originally the idea was explored to link the booming goldfields of Halls Creek and Coolgardie/Kalgoorlie, which would help meet the needs of the rapidly expanding population. However, separate expeditions by both Carnegie and Wells recommended against setting up such a stock route.

The government had banned the westward movement of all cattle in the east Kimberley to reduce the spread of tick fever. The tick *Boophilis microplus* had been inadvertently imported into Australia's north in the 1870s and the government was trying to minimise its spread and thus minimise the impact on the emerging Australian cattle industry. The tick itself was not such a problem; however, it transmits *Babesia spp.* protozoa that can cause fever, haemolysis and death in cattle. In the early 1900s it was proposed that a stock route would help the east Kimberley cattle producers that had tick-infested ('dirty') cattle to market their cattle in the southwest, assuming the ticks would have died off after a long trip through the desert environment.

Eventually, on 17 March 1908 a well-construction party headed by Alfred Canning set off to establish what was later to be called the Canning Stock Route. As I travelled south down the route I followed the plight of this party in my book, *Canning Stock Route: A Traveller's Guide* by Ronele and Eric Gard. It was a brilliant and informative book and each night I would settle in my swag and read the history of the well or leg I was camped at. I found it fascinating to read the story of these amazing men while in the same environment nearly one hundred years later. I was intrigued by the fact that these men did this without GPS, satellite phone, topographic maps or solar panels. They didn't have the luxury of sturdy and light water jerry cans, lightweight comfortable hiking boots with gel-cushioned soles or ultraviolet-protection sunglasses. Hell, they didn't even have the luxury of sweet chilli flavoured tuna or alfredo pasta and sauce! They did it tough all right, and I was in awe. I think the only group of people who may have done it tougher were the few drovers who later followed, pushing hundreds of cattle south through 1800 kilometres of desert.

Sturt Creek Station was my last port of call with a 'civilised' camp (whatever that is) before I launched down the Canning. I camped there a few days, resting the kids, sorting my gear, collecting vital information about water and weather and indulging in my last 'station hospitality experience'.

'Where are you heading to?' I don't really know.

'Wow, that's a long way isn't it?' You know … it could well be.

'Why are you doing this?' Doing what?

'Are you on your own?' Well you're here, aren't you?

'Are you going to write a book?' No … the printed page is obsolete.

'You must be so brave!' Bollocks!

I had only one rest day and set off again. When I am more stressed about what is coming up I tend to launch headlong into it to get it over and done with quickly. I was starting to get obsessed about feral camels. I had not encountered any yet but my imagination was going wild about what these animals could do. The stories I had heard did not help.

It was a bit like when I first started working as a vet and calving season approached. I had never done a calving, not even at uni, and the longer I waited for my first the more stressed I got. I was desperate to get rid of my calving 'virginity'. As it turned out, my first calving was very confusing because I knew if I didn't hurry, the cow was going to spit the normal calf out without my assistance! After that I developed a caesarean fear. I finally got well and truly over that during a long weekend. I was on call and working in Myrtleford, a Victorian dairy area. On the Thursday, at midnight, I got called out to a dairy cow having trouble calving. In the vet world, in general, if you get called to a dairy calving there is a fair chance it will be in the early hours because dairy farmers check their cattle several times a day, and it will be a caesar because the farmers are pretty practiced at pulling calves themselves. If you get called out to a beef cattle calving it is usually in the evening because the farmer has got home from his day job (which allows him to sink his hard-earned money into his farm) and checked the cattle, and it's

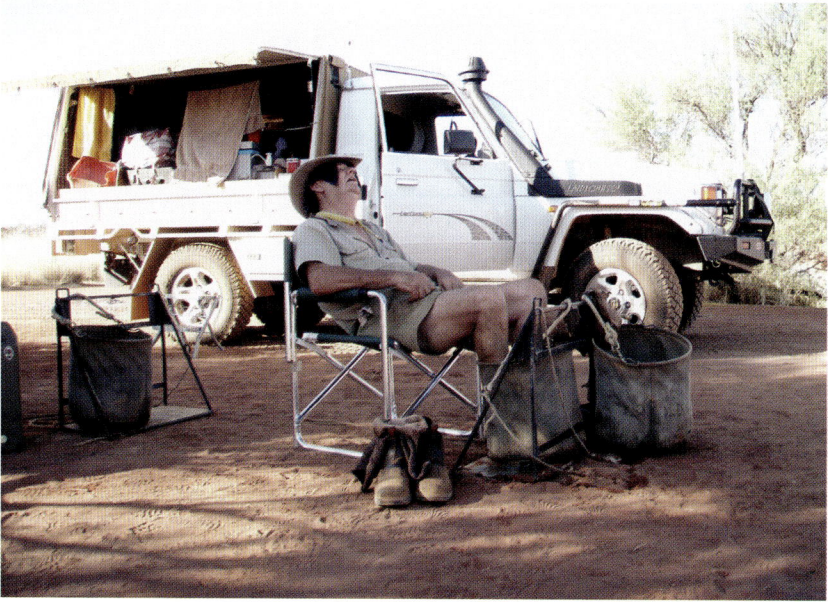

*Well 21, the Canning Stock Route, WA. Dad recovering from the heat of the day. Many days reached the mid forties, making the water in the jerry cans too hot to touch. You had to wait for the water to cool off in the canvas bucket before you could soak your swollen feet or drink it.*

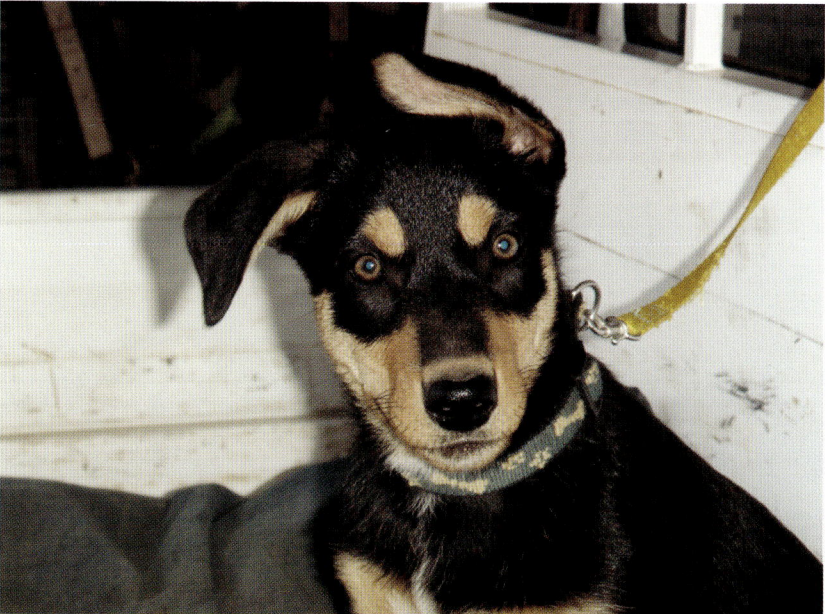

*The new recruit, Gillie Monster, having trouble controlling her ears.*

*South of Menindee, NSW. Gillie resting her sore feet, hitching a ride with Jo and Gumby. The country was suffering a long, hard drought and feed and water were a challenge for us.*

*Condobolin, NSW. Gum and Julia sharing a sandwich.*

*Deniliquin, NSW. Julia demonstrating why one should wash one's socks more than once a week.*

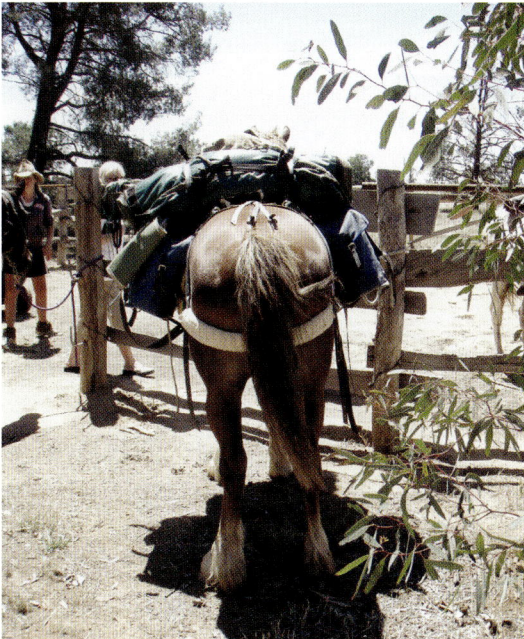

*Brigadoon, NSW. We made it. Barty Butt Cheeks to be unsaddled for the last time.*

*The Barkly Stock Route, NT. The joys of a back up crew: a quiet champagne with Dad after a hard, windswept day on the track.*

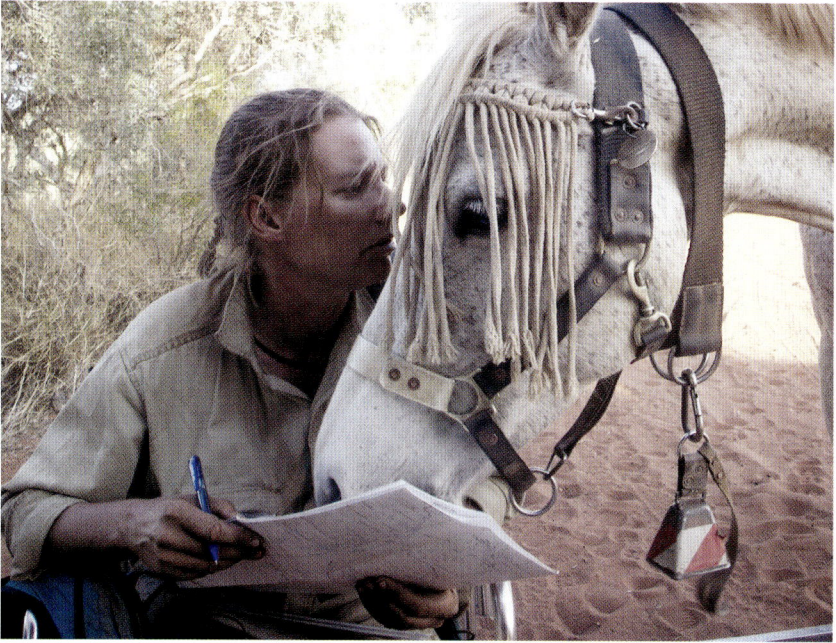

*Well 27, the Canning Stock Route, WA. Every night I sat down and worked out the next day's route. Gum sometimes gave me a hand.*

*South of Well 26, the Canning Stock Route, WA. Uncle Don cooking up a storm with his yummy loaf of bread. Every camping experience needs an 'Uncle Don'.*

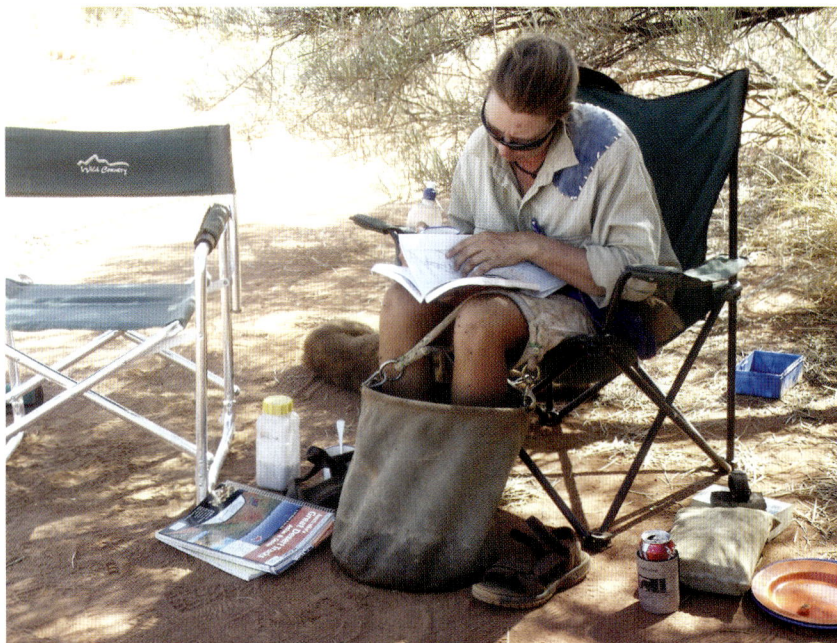

*Well 21, the Canning Stock Route, WA. Any excess water (which was rare) was used to cool and reduce the swelling in my feet while planning the next day. Luxury!*

*North of Durba Springs, the Canning Stock Route, WA. Guiding the kids off track, over the sand ridges and picking our way through the spinifex.*

*Eungella Dam, Qld. Evidence of Julia's OCD issues. At the end of every day she would scrub the kids' easy boots till they shone, line them up in some sort of arrangement, then take a photo of them. I was too scared to ask.*

*The Barkly Stock Route, NT. A quick stop to rebalance Pam's saddle. The camels hated stopping.*

*Savory Creek Crossing, the Canning Stock Route, WA. After endless days of trekking through red sand we skirted around the dry, salty Lake Disappointment and crossed Savory Creek. The salt was so intensely white that even with sunglassess on you had to squint. The salt was inches thick, undissolved in the waterholes, and had smothered any plants within metres of the edge. It looked like there had been a fresh fall of snow.*

usually a rotten calf that needs extricating because he didn't pick it up seven days ago when the cow was first trying to calve!

Anyway, back to my first caesar. The client was a great bloke called Pete and as I was performing the surgery pretending I had done thousands, I joked with him that the clinic had a policy of charging a 'snow fee'. The weather was looking threatening and we were outside at his cattle crush, my work overalls had no sleeves and I was up to my armpits in live, standing, conscious cow viscera, cutting into her uterus and reefing out the calf. This part of the procedure isn't too bad because the cow is warm as toast inside, but once you stitch up her uterus and abdominal wall you can no longer dive in up to your chin to defrost and the snow landing on your arms starts to take effect. As it was, the heifer had a hard time of it and went down and refused to get up. I was partially happy, leaving the yards with a collapsed but live cow, a bouncing baby girl and arms that weren't completely frozen yet. The next night Pete called me out again; cow having trouble calving. It was déjà vu. This time it wasn't snowing but it was wild, wet and windy. Pete proudly showed me the post holes he had dug that day and explained his plans for a shelter over the top of the crush. I did another caesar and we pushed her into his dairy where the first heifer was sitting down, still recovering from her ordeal the night before.

Needless to say, the next two nights consisted of bad weather, caesars and snap frozen fingers. Pete had worked on his new shelter in stages. Saturday night the posts were in, Sunday night rafters were there and by Monday night the purlins had arrived. On Tuesday I was pretty glad to hand over the emergency phone to the boss. The live but damaged cows were piling up in Pete's dairy and I was starting to get over the whole caesar excitement. When I arrived to work on Wednesday, the boss informed me that Pete had finished his shelter and it was very effective, as he had gone out there for another caesar. Yes, I think Pete needed to look closely at his bull selection and yes, I made the boss acknowledge his 'cushy' caesar was thanks to me and my threat of a 'snow fee'. At least all my patients had recovered and left the shelter of the dairy.

Anyway, I was getting very nervous about the wild bull camels I was bound to encounter. It was just a matter of time. Camels are different from most animals because it is the males that come into 'season' or rutt. Can you imagine an 800-kilogram sex-crazed male trying to get past you to jump your girls no matter whether they wanted him or not? Not pretty! I just wanted to get it over and done with and somehow survive the experience.

A couple of days out of Sturt Creek Station I camped at Wolfe Creek. I could have taken an extra couple of days and followed the creek in to see Wolfe Creek Crater, a well-known meteor crater that wasn't discovered by whitefellas till the 1940s. However, I was reluctant to add to the poor kids' workload. I am sure they saw no attraction in bragging to their friends about how they camped at Wolfe Creek Crater and survived! There is a horror movie called *Wolf Creek* (yes, the movie people can't spell) with a very convincing John Jarratt playing a psycho who abducts and tortures tourists near this crater. I am not a big fan of horror movies and made damn sure I didn't see the film before I left as I knew I would be travelling in the area. I look back now and regret not going to the crater to camp for a few days. I was not in a hurry and it would have been great to see, but in the end I thought I should do right by the kids. Pam and Gumby were losing weight and I was becoming increasingly concerned. A few days out of Sturt Creek Station we walked through Bililuna, the last community for about 800 kilometres, and I picked up my mail and restocked the water. With full weight on the kids, we travelled further down the track and camped at Stretch Lagoon.

### Day 216, 30 August: Stretch Lagoon

*My God, the mozzies tonight are the worst I have ever seen — even worse than on the Murray after summer floods. I am hiding in my swag while my poor kids have to deal with them all night. Thank God (or whoever) my swag has fly-wire. It is quite hot tonight and the day was in the high 30s. I saw camel tracks all day so it's only a matter of time. This afternoon Pam walked away from camp a bit and then started calling out! I am not sure who to. It was like when a horse calls out to another, but sounded more like a cow. God, I am getting more and more nervous of meeting that first bloody wild bull camel. I think I will just shoot the thing straightaway, rather than try to frighten it first, get the whole* dreaded virgin experience over and done with. I think I will call all the wild bull camels Eric. That way it will be more of a relaxed atmosphere: more comic and less threatening. I mean, how scary can an 'Eric' be?

My feet have been swelling in this heat, which is not good since the shoes are a bit small as it is. My poor little pinky toes get so squashed they come out of my shoe at the end of the day triangular. Walking is a bit hard but riding still hurts my back so I alternate lots.

Had a huge day today. I didn't plan to go so far but the poor old kids have had such little feed the last few days (shit camps) and I was determined to find them something to eat. So we walked all the way to Stretch Lagoon. We went through Billiluna and spent about two hours topping up the water, shopping (not much there) and picking up my mail. I got my iPod back ... finally. Yeah!

It is the first time I have reloaded with water halfway through the day. I have been told the camels wouldn't tolerate being half unloaded then loaded again in the middle of the day but they did well. All Pam did was intensify her haughty look but I am quite fond of that now so thought it was cute. I carried the rifle on Pam today so when I went into the community I wasn't leaving my kids alone with an obvious and 'easy reach' .308. I am a bit paranoid about the possibility of having my rifle stolen, although guns are a way of life in the outback and no-one appears to notice them.

I kept travelling on, looking for feed. There is so much spinifex out here and not a lot else. Poor old Gum really needed a good feed so I kept going till 4.45 pm (30 minutes before sunset) and ended up camping in the yards at Stretch Lagoon. There is some sort of flat, dead, prickly, unappetising weed here but all the kids are pretty happy with it. I worry when there is no food. I keep apologising saying, 'Tomorrow's camp will be better.' I'm sure Gumby doesn't understand (or maybe care) but I know the girls are saying, 'Yeah, sure, I will believe it when I see it.'

When I got here I met Kylie and Wayne and a bunch of blackfellas (mostly women) and they invited me to join them

*for tea. They were having some sort of camp and developing an
ownership map of the country between the Billiluna and Mulan
people. Then they are painting it on a big canvas map so there is
a record. As traditional owners they are concerned they are getting
quite old and their knowledge and customs will be lost when they
die. They have a great sense of humour and I just sat quietly
listening to them. I overheard them talking about alcohol and
saying it was evil and that someone (I didn't catch who) was 'sick
with it' but wouldn't help themselves. I also listened to them despair
about 'the younger generation' and how they didn't respect their
elders and involved themselves in destructive behaviour. You know, if
I closed my eyes while listening I could have been anywhere in the
country, probably even the world! Every generation seems to think
the next generation is going to destroy the world as they know it
but, somehow, it seems to go on. Just gotta have faith, I suppose.*

*I will stay here for a rest day tomorrow. We are in no hurry.*

*S 19° 40' 41.6", E 127° 35' 04.6"　975 ft　29.5 km
Total: 3626.0 km*

**Low point:** *Walking through 100% spinifex for so many miles ...
how are they going to cope? Is there going to be any feed for them
further south?*
**High point:** *Dinner with the blackfellas and Kylie and Wayne
was really interesting.*

That night Alistair, a stranger who had heard about me somewhere on the
grapevine, rang on my sat phone and said he wanted to travel with me for a
few weeks down the Canning. I was quite happy to share my experience
with anyone who was interested, but was a bit wary he might mistakenly
think it would be a 'holiday of a lifetime'. So being a bit gun-shy I read him
the riot act.

'I am more than happy for you to come,' I began, 'and I will wait at Well
49 (where there is good water) for a few days for you if you can find a way of

getting there ... however, you must only bring what I tell you, no more, no less. You will be walking 30 kilometres a day in 40-degree plus heat and you won't be riding Gumby at all because he works hard enough. It is bloody hard work,' I continued, 'harder than you could ever imagine, there is no shade, no rests, monotonous country and once you get here there is no way of getting out till you get to the next community. You can't bang out early because there is nowhere to go and no way of getting there.'

Despite this, he assured me he was fit and tough and could do it. In the end he organised a way of getting to Well 49 and said he would let me know soon when he would be there. What had I done? Could this guy cope? Or was I being arrogant to think that I could do this but someone else may not be able to? Or was I being unrealistic in thinking I could drop a Melbournite, cold turkey, into the desert to walk 30 kilometres a day in September, let alone cope with handling the camels and horse? I even wondered what the girls would think of him.

Nonetheless, I realised it would be good to have a hand when I encountered wild camels and even for lifting those heavy, awkward saddles on and off and carting the water. I was getting stronger by the day, sometimes having to carry two full jerries at a time weighing 22 to 24 kilograms each for up to 100 metres. I had worked out a strategy for carrying heavy weights a long distance. I developed a distraction technique: I would guess how many steps it would take me to get to my destination then walk that number of steps. If I didn't reach my destination then I would guess the next lot of steps and continue on. The point being, that I couldn't even contemplate putting down the jerries for a rest until I had counted the number of guessed steps. It is amazing how much more you can get out of your muscles when you don't allow yourself to think about how fatigued they are and when you have a number or goal that you are aiming for.

Even though I was not going to be in range for a long time (and thus would not be able to send any emails) I still wrote a few in anticipation of an unexpected opportunity to send them. In the end I wrote them by hand and got people to post them to Mum, and she typed them up and sent them to Sue to be put on the web.

Hi guys,

Well I've started down the Canning Stock Route. It really is amazing country and I am only 10% along it. It makes me think about when Canning and his men developed it, a hundred years ago. It also makes me think about explorers doing this sort of trip with horses and camels and having little information about the country they are heading into. People say, for instance, you don't need to follow a road but on black soil there are holes hiding in the grass that you can disappear up to your kneecaps in. Sometimes there is no sign of a hole – you just fall through the ground. In red country there seems to be a lot of stones, in the sandy country like here, the spinifex slows you down heaps (even if the horse is not complaining about the stinging spinifex needles), and if the country has trees you have to make your way through them and around them without leaving the camels' packs behind! Even here on the road the small trees are so close to the road that they are trashing my pack bags as they get caught on them all the time; that's the repairs to be done at camp each evening.

If I was an explorer I wouldn't have my GPS, satellite phone, iPod with a *Harry Potter* book reading on it, mosquito-proof swag, pasta and sauce meals and Gatorade powder. I wouldn't know there was water so many kilometres away. I wouldn't be able to get the occasional bag of Copra dropped off to supplement poor Gumby's diet. It's a hard country, that's for sure, and I'm doing it the easy way. I cannot imagine how an English explorer would like this country. I'm sure he would grow to hate it, and end up fighting it. I think the Australian-born explorers such as Gregory would have been able to cope much better with what was thrown at them.

Well, enough of the boring lecture.

So far I have had bad camps all the way down. My definition of a bad camp is one with little appropriate feed for horse or camels or both. Last night Gumby learnt to eat spinifex. Poor fellow – he eats it with all the relish of a seven-year-old boy eating brussels sprouts! He even seems to chew it with his mouth open. The camels had one lonely, edible bush within miles so that was it for them. Camels like variety but all they could do was strip this bush bare.

On the first day I passed six vehicles but since then I think I have seen two. The season is getting later and the tourists, I suppose, are scared off by the heat. It is hot but not that bad and a nice breeze whips up every now and then.

There are heaps of lizards of all shapes and sizes and I am getting to learn their marks in the sand. I'll be a fully fledged tracker by the time I've finished. I still haven't come across wild bull camels yet but it is only a matter of time as I see lots of tracks along the road.

I am looking forward to surging ahead and, if nothing else, trying to beat the heat as summer rapidly approaches.

The hotter it gets the more I dream about that elusive can of ice-cold Coke!

HiD

---

At Stretch Lagoon I developed fairly significant pain on the left side of my face. It got really painful and even lying on my right side hurt. My skin got really inflamed and swollen and would hurt more even in a light wind. By the time I got to Well 49, I was having episodes of fever, especially at night. A few mornings I woke soaked in a pool of sweat and reeling from some really vivid and wild dream that I struggled to separate from reality. It even entered my mind that the wild dreams may have been real and this ridiculous thing of camping in the desert with a horse, dog and two camels in 45-degree heat was the nightmare. Due to my lack of mirror I couldn't really see what was going on. In the end I took a digital photo of my face; it looked like cellulitis. I must admit I was a little concerned – people with cellulitis are not uncommonly hospitalised with IV antibiotics. All I had was Furphy's meat-flavoured antibiotics and his honey-flavoured non-steroidal anti-inflammatory. I took them both. They helped a bit but I was quite uneasy for a while. Then overnight my face settled down but I developed an open, ulcerating sore on my forehead. I think that was where the infection was localising. I started coating it in cattle Orbenin eye ointment (more versatile than Windex as far as I am concerned!) and Traumeel gel (my super duper, heal anything, anti-inflammatory homeopathic gel I used on all the saddle sores).

The wound reminded me strongly of a case of Barcoo Rot I once saw on a friend. It was disgusting and took a lot of drugs, time and effort to heal. My wound was skanky, ulcerative, about the size of a 10-cent piece and covered in a thick, tacky, green purulent goo; it was gross. It was right on the band of my hat so I had to walk around with my hat tipped back like some goofy Hollywood cowboy, and coat my nose in sunscreen regularly so it didn't just shrivel up and drop off.

A few days later I detected similar sores developing through my hair. I started to wash my hair and face in an iodine scrub that I used for the kids' wounds. Twice a day I would walk around my Well 49 camp for 20 minutes with my whole head/hair a yellowy tan colour, then I'd rinse it clean and dry it. I also soaked my hat as well. I remember one night thinking my treatment wasn't really working well enough, so I made the decision that if there was no improvement by the next day I would shave off my hair completely. My head sweating caused damp hair all the time and was just creating a great environment for the bacteria. A bald head would be able to dry out. I woke the next morning and, to my disappointment (surprisingly), it was improving. I think I was looking forward to shaving all my hair off! I did it once before for the Shave For a Cure charity and didn't have a single hair on my head. I loved it. It was very liberating, however a psychiatrist would have a field day with the fact that, for some scary reason, I still felt I had to wash my bare scalp with shampoo. The only thing I did not like was the glances of pity from strangers I got in public. Obviously they thought I was a cancer sufferer and that their sly glances, pained looks on their faces, and rapid retreats, pretending they were looking at something else, was their idea of being kind to those who are 'having a hard time of it'.

I won the battle, but I still had the mother of all scars on my forehead. Ironically it was directly over an old childhood chicken pox scar. I had come to enjoy the advantage of not seeing a mirror for months on end. You could go for ages without the reality of your disappointing looks interfering with your day, and you started envisioning that your looks merely reflected your being; based on that theory I thought I wasn't too hard on the eye! So after a few months of no mirror I would get quite cocky – but when I caught my first glimpse in the mirror at some showgrounds showers it was a big letdown. Curse the inventor of mirrors. I am sure if we didn't have any, our looks would not be nearly as important to people.

### Days 225–33, 7–15 September: Well 49, waiting

I have been camped here for what seems like an eternity. The days are getting hotter and hotter. I'm not sure if it just feels worse because I am not travelling. Somehow being camped during the day seems really hot, even though I have set up some shade with my hoochie. I have had lots to do but struggle to get the motivation: pulled up water from the well to fill my jerries, repaired saddles and rifle scabbard, did my laundry (and dirtied more), did a food stocktake, washed hair twice a day to disinfect my skanky head, set up a protective harness for the pack bags so they don't get trashed by the scrub on the side of the track, worked out water and camps for the next leg, trimmed Gumby's feet, blah, blah, blah and blah.

I have found it a real struggle being stationary and am going stir crazy. I have been waiting for eight days now. But I have to keep reminding myself that I agreed to wait and also I am not in a hurry as Dad and Uncle Don are meeting me in the middle of the Canning in about a month. I will have to slow down somewhere so it may as well be here. Ugh! At least I took the opportunity to order a few supplies; Gum will get some hard feed. Yeah!

Every morning and night I have to saddle Gum and take the camels (without packs) about 3 km north for their brekky and dinner. There is only a nibble here for the girls so they don't have much to eat at night when they are tethered. Gum has also run out of tether spots. I should walk it all and save Gum but I am having an episode — a Ross River episode — and struggling a bit with the whole energy and activity thing.

The other day eleven 4WDs came in at the same time (from several different parties). It was mayhem! I hadn't seen anyone for ages, then all of a sudden I was a socialite. Actually, I struggled to put two words together (must practise that talking thing). It was lunch time and they all set up their card tables and got their loaves of bread and cheese and the last of their tired looking tomatoes out and proceeded to have civilised meals. I was half expecting to see the men in their smoking jackets and women doing the embroidery. Pam and Gypsy eyed them all suspiciously from afar but Gum busied himself stealing food and escaping in his hobbles while people laughed. All of a sudden Gum threw his head up, looked around at the sea of strangers, and started calling out and shuffling around in his hobbles in a panicked fashion. Everybody looked up at him and they were all a bit nervous. I was about 50 metres away and called out, 'Gum, I'm over here'. He nickered softly and went straight back to the tasty cheese-flavoured CCs he had just stolen. He'd lost me in all the cars and people and had panicked, thought I might have left him. God I love him.

It must be hot as Furphy spends his days lying in the shade panting. Poor old Furphy's insecure personality really doesn't suit this work. He needs stability and the same thing every day. He has taken to chasing lizards. It is such a brainless activity, like chasing flying birds. It really annoys me but I hold my tongue because the camels get edgy when I yell and I can't stop him doing it anyway. It just makes me angry so I am better off ignoring it. I feel sorry for him because none of us are too keen on him.

I think when I am stationary I start to get a bit down. I am quite down at the moment. It's bloody hot, I'm bored (I've read five books since being here) and there is such shit feed for the girls and Gumby (I feel so guilty). I am starting to worry about the Nullarbor crossing. You know, this trip is just ever-increasing stress. I think one of the big advantages of having somebody with you is you can share the stress — the worries about enough food, the track you will take, the permission you need, the water source etc. Actually, being on my own (i.e. for company and security) doesn't really worry me. I just want to share around the stress! Julia wasn't much good in that department. She didn't seem to care if we camped in a flooded cemetery with crocodiles or Bourke Street Mall in Melbourne. She never once looked at a map or even asked how far we had gone. She didn't have a watch so wouldn't have known how far or fast we were going. In all, she was an entertaining, bloody hard worker. Now I feel I need more than that, although I admit I wouldn't mind a Kath and Kim impersonation or a Wheel of Fortune quip, or even a light discussion on what the magistrate should have done with Paris. Or am I being precious? Am I just looking for someone to say 'No, that's heaps of food for the night' or 'Yes, that is the better path' or 'No, they're not losing weight'. I suppose I am just looking for someone to tell me I am doing the right thing. Yes, when it comes down to it, I am hopeless. When I am moving I always say to myself 'Next camp will be better' but when stationary it tends to catch up on me. I can't seem to kid myself. Oh, shut up Heidi, I'm sick of this self-indulgent crap.

I am hot and sticky and have a heat headache ... whinge, whinge, whinge. Now I am whingeing about me whingeing!

S 20° 09' 51.3", E 126° 40' 52.3"     935 ft   0.0 km
Total: 3763.7 km

**Low point:** Ross River fever, skanky face and general blues. Ugh!
**High point:** Hopefully I will get my order today ... Gum is hungry.

Finally, Alistair arrived.

# 13

## New responsibilities

My passenger had managed to persuade a local from one of the communities to drive him four hours out to meet up with me. I had told him what to bring right down to the number of undies. I had also told him what not to bring. Obviously the sat phone transmission wasn't too good because he brought a fair bit of stuff. With my worries about Pam and Gumby struggling with this leg, I wasn't excited by the concept of them carrying excess baggage. I had to find room for a swag, a large travelling backpack, a small backpack and a 'CamelBak' (a small backpack that carries water). Of course I had suggested these things but didn't actually mean he should bring them all.

The first thing I noticed about Alistair was the huge new hat he had brought with him. It went through my mind how you could probably shelter a small family under it. Perhaps it was just as well; his skin was very fair and not suited to the burning sun of the desert. He talked keenly about all the adventurous holidays he had had while I pondered what I was going to do with all his gear.

I had to do some complicated planning to get it all onto the kids. In the end I turned Gum back into a pack horse and rigged a makeshift pack by strapping a canvas bucket either side of his saddle, filling them up with stuff and then tying a swag across the top. Good old Gum, he didn't mind. As it was, he was already carrying about 25 kilograms on his saddle in the form of saddle bags, rifle, water, etc. Poor fellow, from behind he looked like one of those overloaded donkeys led by boys wearing rags that walk on narrow, rocky mountain tracks in Peru. Well, not that I have been to Peru ... maybe I am a bit behind the times. I was very happy to see a bag of food for Gum, though. I think that made up for it. Gum was pretty happy with the deal.

From the time Alistair arrived I wondered whether I had made the right decision. One thing I knew was that I didn't need any more things to worry about.

### Day 237, 19 September, Well 46

Bad camel day today. Pam is not well and only after 2 km she sat down. We were low on water so I rearranged the jerries so she had only 100 kg and poor old Gypsy and Gum were loaded to their maximum. Pam was okay then. One thing about her is that you know she is never faking or wussing out. She hasn't been eating much lately and has been grumpy and depressed. She has taken to groaning and grumbling intermittently as we walk along — not sure if she is calling out to wild camels beyond the sand dunes, groaning in pain or so bored she is singing her own Freddy Mercury songs. I have always been worried about her. When I first got her in May she seemed to have a cystitis-type problem. Then she seemed to need three times as much water as Gypsy. She has lost weight. I worry about her kidneys. The heat seems to be really knocking her about ... I am very worried.

We seem to be going through a lot of water, I suppose because of the heat, but yesterday — 56 litres! There is a leg of 194 km between Well 46 and Well 41. How are we going to do that? We will have to stop drinking!

Furphy is getting really knocked about. He has two enemies on this trip; dingo baits and heat stress. I really don't think he is likely to take a dingo bait without my say so, but the heat stress is a real issue. He has lost a lot of weight. I am feeding him more rice than dry dog food because his dry food is a 'heating' food and rice is a 'cooling' food (according to the Chinese anyway). Also, I think his kidneys are working pretty hard so I'm trying to back off on the protein. It does not make sense with the weight loss but he is not losing it because of intake ... it's the heat. He keeps burning his tongue on hot days. Because it is out most of the time I think it is getting too exposed to the hot environment. He can't drink or eat properly because his tongue doesn't work. I think he has a damaged cranial nerve. Not sure which one — sorry, never could remember my cranial nerves for longer than the exam, even when armed with the really crude mnemonics we used to remember them.

*So when Furphy eats or drinks it takes ages and he leaves behind a
huge pool of drool.*

*At this rate of water consumption we will have to travel 32 km
a day to get to the next working well. That's asking too much of
Pam and I am not happy. To top it off, the water at this well has
a dead snake in it. It stinks and when you bring your mouth to
the water bottle you just about dry retch. I think we will have to
boil the water tomorrow to kill the bacteria. That will be a huge
job as my saucepan only holds about a litre. At least that will keep
Alistair busy for the day. We will have to have separate water:
unboiled for the kids and boiled for the humans. Some of the water
we pulled up had huge maggots and snake vertebrae in it, so I will
have to crank out the old stocking to use as a filter when filling the
jerries; works well.*

*So, Pam worries, water worries, Furphy worries. I have been
thinking that Pam will not be healthy enough to cross the
Nullarbor. Oh God! Am I just a quitter?*

*S 20° 38' 30.4", E 126° 17' 14.2"   819 ft   28.2 km
Total: 3862.9 km*

**Low point:** *I don't know how we are going to do the next leg with
the limited water we can carry.*
**High point:** *Giving the girls a drink. Pam struggles without daily
water.*

When we headed out of Well 46 we crossed paths with Canning and his first
survey expedition from 101 years ago, to the day. As we headed south
Canning and his men were heading north to what was to be Well 46. The
stock route has such a rich history that I was fascinated reading the parallel
travels of all the explorers and drovers before me. Carnegie had camped at
Well 46 a couple of weeks later in the season than us (but around a century
earlier) and he stated it was 60 degrees! That made me very nervous, especially
since global warming wasn't even an issue then. Alistair had boiled over 40
litres of the skanky snake water on the rest day and we left there with two

jerries (45 litres) of yummy Well 49 water, two jerries of boiled skanky snake water and eight jerries of 'toxic', stocking filtered, skanky snake water. But we couldn't afford to complain about the water because the next leg would be pretty tight.

My maps and other info had conflicting distances. I decided to work on the longest distance given. We had five days' worth of water so if we planned to travel for six days we would arrive at our next water supply without a drop left. I hated to travel without a safety buffer. The problem with unreliable information was that I couldn't be 100 per cent sure that the well we were aiming for had drinkable water. Anything could have happened to it since the last report I had got. It could have even more dead snakes in it or, even worse, dead birds. I was pretty stressed at this stage. Not only did I have to worry about the welfare of my kids (which was always my first priority), I now had a human to look after as well. At one stage we were crossing a clay pan and Alistair dropped back to take photos. I kept walking but he didn't appear over the dune so I stopped to wait for him. He still didn't appear so I sat the girls down and walked back up onto the sand ridge to find him. He was still taking photos and I think he thought I was crazy but we just couldn't afford to separate in that sort of country, especially with those extreme temperatures. Heat stress can cause you to make some pretty silly decisions. I think the heat was knocking him about but, to his credit, Alistair never complained. It wasn't till then that I fully realised just how responsible I was for another person. I wasn't used to it, and I wasn't comfortable with it.

The first wild camels we came across were a bit of a non-event. They hunted off very easily and, even more to my relief, the girls didn't give a 'rats' about them. Normally, horses get all skittish with strange horses, but apparently camels aren't that insecure.

As hard and tough as this country was, I loved it. I was home. The sand was a strong red ochre colour and fine and pure in texture. It was hot and dry and unforgiving but teaming with signs of life. It seemed to tell a story of the world that had passed before you; the tracks of the small lizards, the corrugations created by the wind, the burrowed holes of the bungarras, the footprints of the dingo or the tiny ridges in the sand left by the insects scooting just under the sand. If you were late the wind would erase all the stories, leaving a clean slate for us to tell our own stories on. The sand seemed to go on forever beyond the horizon with its infinite number of stories, most never to be read.

The days got hotter and the afternoons brought a stillness and occasional cumulus cloud that made me wary of the pending wet season. One of the difficulties I found while travelling was that I couldn't read the weather. I was used to reading the weather at home but every area is different and just as I would start to learn the signs I would have moved further north, or west, etc. No, I didn't have a clue and could only guess. This weather felt distinctly stifling with that feeling of 'pending doom' (maybe my ombrophobia was kicking in). I was sure it was the very beginning of the wet season to the north. A few infantile cumuli would develop in the afternoon and through the night, then burn off in the morning. The nights were mostly hot and still. The only good thing was that we were immediately cooled by the occasional cumulus scooting overhead and the girls travelled a lot better.

It surprised me how much the girls struggled in the heat. Surely camels are supposed to be good in the heat! But once it turns 40 degrees they tend to crash and burn even more than a horse. Or maybe I am comparing them to Gumby who wasn't a very good horse representative. I don't think he even realised it was hot. The water in my bottles got so hot I was tempted to throw a teabag in them.

Furphy was getting skinnier. He started making a strange clucking sound with his mouth every now and then. Poor Furph.

### Day 242, 24 September: Well 42 camp

*Pam has had a bit of a day. She was determined that any shade we went near she was going to dive into it. Today she put Gypsy to shame with the tantrums she threw. Pam was basically only carrying 83 kg of water. I walked the whole way and Gum carried a fair load. Poor Gum, he has eaten nothing but spinifex with a handful of Copra at night. The kids don't even like walking through spinifex because the pointy ends give their legs hell. According to my Canning Stock Route guide a century ago, Carnegie described Spinifex as a 'wretched, useless plant ... the most accursed vegetation to walk through for both men and camels'. He also* said 'it seems to be so arranged that it cannot be stepped over or circumvented — one must in consequence walk through it to be prickled unpleasantly'. I think 'prickled unpleasantly' was a bit of an understatement.

Today we met some tourists heading north and they gave us 40 L of water, which I gave immediately to Pam. Gypsy was so not happy with me — she threw a big tanti. Pam picked up immensely so it was worth Gypsy sulking for the rest of the day. While I was watering Pam and containing the crazed Gypsy I heard Alistair ask the people if he could get a lift with them to Halls Creek. They said they couldn't fit him in, especially since it was a three day drive. I know Alistair is struggling and so I ask very little of him around the camp or with the kids. To his credit he never complains. I don't think this is a holiday of a lifetime for him. The people said you could dig for water at Well 42 so we busted a gut to get here. It is very dirty water and there is a fair bit of digging with very slow return. I hope there will be enough clean water risen up in the morning for the kids.

It's getting bloody hot during the days. If a stray cloud wanders over we all pick up the pace and walk a bit freer. My back is the worst it has ever been because I seem to spend all gor-rammed day in 40-degree heat towing a cantankerous camel. Ugh. What happened to my beautiful Pam? I am so sore and stuffed tonight.

The dunes are killers. According to my guide, the biggest sand ridges are between Well 41 and 42 so the next leg is going to be worse. They are over 12 m high and can be less than 50 m apart. The problem with travelling with mixed kids is that horses go fast uphill and steady downhill, while camels go slow uphill and want to run downhill. So going over the sand dune I am likely to be pulled off the horse if I don't rein him in and on the other side we are likely to be run over by two tired, loaded camels 'freewheeling' down the slope.

The track seems to do a lot of zigzagging parallel to the sand ridges, so when they do cross there is less to climb. In some areas it adds a significant distance. I take direct short cuts where possible *but sometimes the track is unpredictable and hard to see. I am getting more confident to just launch off the edge. I actually love navigating off-track and it is not as if I am going to get lost, but the kids are not excited by doing the spinifex tiptoe so I want to be sure the gain exceeds the pain for them.*

*S 21° 18' 55.0", E 125° 52' 55.0"    988 ft    31.7 km*
*Total: 3982.6 km*
*Water total: 165.5 litres*

**Low point:** *My back is the worst it has ever been.*
**High point:** *Pam getting water ... that is always a high point.*

The German tourists amazed me. They come from a relatively coldish country and are happy to travel in 45-degree heat through the desert. They get out of their cars with shorts, singlets, thongs and no hat and are happy to talk to you in the blaring sun for an hour. Do they have no ability to detect environmental temperature at all? In that sort of weather, your uncovered feet get really hot and sunburnt, you take on a lot of heat through the bare skin on your shoulders and arms, not to mention the obvious self-inflicted wounds of sunstroke and sunburn when you don't wear a hat! You could almost guarantee that any tourists seen from October on were German and they didn't mind stopping for a chat in the sun.

'Vare are you goink?' Shade.

'It iss a lonk vay, ya?' Bloody oath it is.

'Vye you doink ziss?' I dunno. The heat got to me.

'You vill travel alone, ya?' Do you think anybody else would be crazy enough to walk this far in these deserts so close to summer? Apart from an unsuspecting Melbournite and a German tourist, that is.

'You vill write a book?' I would except my pen has melted

'You are brave for ziss!' Brave? To stand out in the sun? I am cheating with an Akubra hat, long sleeves and boots. You're the brave one standing there with your German accent, skimpy singlet, bare head and thongs. You're the one that is going to die, not me!

Things were getting to me a bit. I was getting shitty about everything. It was hard work for all of us, even Furphy.

### Day 244, 26 September: Wild camel camp, Well 41

*Well, today was interesting, to say the least. We didn't have to go far to get to Well 41, which was good because we only had 68 L spare. The camels went well, back to their old selves, which is probably due to their light loads, a beautiful cool south easterly and the fact that they had good feed and a drink last night.*

*There were fewer dunes to cross today than yesterday. Thank God (or whoever) ... the sand ridges between Well 41 and Well 42 are the biggest along the whole stock route, according to my guide. The topographic map says '10–12 m sand ridges' but they are starting feel like 30 m tall. Or maybe I am just over them. I am from flat country, am not keen on hills of any sort. They are a real challenge at times, especially if the kids are tired and not too responsive to me.*

*This camp is quite good. Lots of yummy feed for the kids — but with yummy feed comes wild camels. There was a wild bull camel on top of a sand dune about 200 m away but since then he has come in closer. So I have camped about 150 m away from the well to give the wild camels room to move in if they must.*

*I am now passenger free. Alistair took the opportunity to 'escape' with Klaus, a passing German tourist, even though it will take three days just to get to the next community. Why did he come? Very strange. He showed no interest in doing anything with the animals and very little interest in the Canning and its history. When we would pull up in the afternoon I would settle the girls, then Gum, feed Furphy and set up camp. Then I would make a cup of tea (I have discovered tea is the best drink ever when your hot) and offer Alistair a cup. He would accept. It fascinates me that he was happy to watch me work for an hour in the heat and wait for me to make him a cup of tea! God, I am glad I never got married. He stated he was leaving for work reasons. God, I think I must smell (oh, suppose that is quite possible). I must admit I found his parting words baffling. He said, shrugging his shoulders: 'Well, animals aren't really my thing anyway.'*

*I am up for a big night, I suspect. At sunset I could see (and so could the girls) quite a few bull camels silhouetted on top of the nearest dune, watching us. I saw them making their way down, closer, in the last light, so I can guarantee the night will get ugly. Oh well, sleep is highly overrated anyway.*

*S 21° 33' 12", E 125° 51' 00"   899 ft   19.8 km*
*Total: 4028.6 km*
*Water total: 68.0 litres... I am glad to be filling up again!*

**Low point:** *This pending big sleepless night.*
**High point:** *Making it to Well 41 ... it was a bloody tough leg.*

So I was on my own again, with one less thing to be responsible for. God (or whoever) knows I didn't need any extra worries.

# 14

## Water

About 70 per cent of the Earth's surface is covered by water. Water is everywhere and abundant … apparently. Water is absolutely essential for life, and I couldn't have it demonstrated any better than out there on the Canning. You know, you don't really appreciate something until it is gone, or at least severely threatened.

I started documenting my water stocks in my diary. I needed to keep a really close eye on usage. I also needed to keep the girls' packs balanced so had to know what weights on either side travelled well. Every morning before I loaded the girls I weighed each jerry and could thus work out how much water they contained. Water management also involved not mixing the types of water. At one stage I had good Well 49 water, skanky snake boiled water, skanky snake filtered water, salty water and Perth town water mixed with salt water. I used to label the jerries with a white ink pen.

Water management was vital. I stuffed it up once and paid dearly for it. I seemed to be drinking the skanky snake water for about three weeks as a few wells in a row were too salty for me to drink. The big kids would drink it but Furphy and I couldn't stomach it, literally. I even tried mixing in a bit of powdered Gatorade to improve the taste but the powder just sank to the bottom and didn't move. It tasted like sea water and thus my skanky snake water was my only drink until I got to Well 33, roughly the midway mark along the Canning.

One day I was plodding along doing my usual calculations. I had been having trouble with my calculations because by the time I came up with an answer I would not be able to remember what it was I had been calculating. I would then walk for another ten minutes and think, 'I wonder how far to the such and such well' and would find myself recalculating it. This happened with disturbing frequency and if I had clear thought processes I would have been concerned about it. Anyway, I came across a carload of people from Perth who generously offered 20 litres of pure, fresh Perth water. It was gold. I filled my travelling water bottles and then tipped 10 litres aside into some empty jerries on Pam. I was so excited and guzzled the fresh water, starting new calculations on whether this water would last till I got to Well 33. I never wanted to drink skanky snake again. As I travelled on, the fresh water started to take effect and a cloud seemed to lift, leaving me thinking clearer than I had for days. It was then I realised I had put the coveted Perth water in the salt water jerries and was left with salt water again … not happy, Jan! It was after this incident I became acutely aware that one of my biggest dangers out there was a decline in my ability to think clearly and make sensible decisions. It would have been too easy to miscalculate distances and end up 100 kilometres short of the nearest drinking water without a drop in my jerries.

The day I reached Well 36, on 2 October 2007, was the worst of my entire ride. It just so happened to be one year and one day since I had set off from Healesville but it felt so much further away. At this stage Healesville was just a foggy memory. This day I feared for not only my kids' lives but also my own.

I was deeply worried about the girls, who had got quite sick and I was fully expecting Gumby to follow suit.

I had done my 'homework' ad nauseam about the water on the stock route. I got local information, I asked all the tourists I passed along the way and I scoured my bible, *Canning Stock Route: A Traveller's Guide*, and any other literature I could get my hands on for any information. The trouble was that none of it was foolproof. At Well 37 I had watered the camels but should have known better. Pam had gone for four days without water and she was really struggling. But apart from her mystery kidney issues, her lack of condition alone would have reduced her ability to operate without water. The tourists who gave me the Perth water said they had cleaned out the well of all the dead birds and emptied it, hoping the fresh water coming up would be clean and uncontaminated. When we arrived, there were about 20 dead, rotting birds in it so I cleaned it out too. Pam had really struggled to get to camp and I weakened and gave both girls some of the fresh water coming up through the soil. After my horses died of salmonella in the first three weeks of my trip I had become a bit gun-shy about contaminated food and water but I just felt so sorry for Pam. That is one of the few things I really regretted.

The next day, the leg to Well 36 was quite good. Pam had water on board and had no trouble with the 23-kilometre walk. Well 36 was basically guaranteed to be one of the best waters along the 1800-kilometre track, but when we got there it too contained a few dead birds. I cleaned it out and tried to get all the water out in the hope that what was coming through would be fresh. I only had 38 litres that I could drink and a couple of days' water for Gumby. I had really relied on restocking at this well. The next morning I woke to some very grumpy camels. I had noticed Pam was a bit loose the night before but in the morning both had diarrhoea and Gypsy was putting on a huge tantrum whenever I went near her. There was no way she would let me saddle her. I had no choice but to stay put and hope they improved enough to set off the next day; but I did not have enough water to set up camp and wait for them to be fully recovered and I didn't want to chance giving Gum any of the dead-bird water.

### Day 250, 2 October: Well 36, sick camels, rest day

'If a camel gets sick I'm stuffed, if a camel gets sick I'm stuffed, if a camel gets sick I'm stuffed.' This is my little mantra that has been going through my mind constantly since starting the Canning Stock Route. And yes, you guessed it … they both got sick. Pam had a bit of diarrhoea and colic yesterday. I was worried all night and when I got up to saddle them both were sweating and Gypsy was shitting like a dairy cow. I have enough drinking water for me for four days (only just). I have decided to stay here a day to let them recover. Pam is improving tonight but Gypsy is still a worry. I know she is a drama queen but she is definitely worse than Pam. Gypsy has not passed anything since this morning so I am not sure whether that means she has started to improve or not.

I have decided I will not drink the dead bird water. I have a really bad feeling about it. I am petrified because I already gave Gumby some of the water from Well 36 before the girls got sick. The water is less smelly and clearer than Well 37 but that may mean nothing. He never got Well 37, which is what the camels got sick on, but am freaking that Gum is going to get sick as well. If Gum dies my chances of physical survival are decreased, but the chances of my mental survival are virtually zero. I can't do without him. I have spent all day imagining the trip cost me four horses and two camels because of salmonella, and maybe throw in a dog for good measure. Well 33 is about 68 km away. I think it will be asking too much of sick camels to do it in two days and then I may need to go straight through to the community (another 5 to 8 km).

I've had enough. I've been so stressed and so hot I can't stand it anymore. A side of me (not really) is hoping Gypsy won't make it through the night so I will have to go home from Well 33. That is not true ... it isn't. I'm just so tired. I am so mentally and emotionally and physically fucked that I am drinking tea with dried peas floating in it — how did they get in there? And on top of all this I have been trying to work out how to tell Mum and Dad without worrying them. I fear I am just going to burst into tears the moment they answer the phone. That's not fair on them; this is my shit Heidi, just pull yourself together. I think I will just text them my lat and long and not tell them anything. They can't help from there, anyway.

I am holding off the tears because I suspect if I start crying I won't be able to stop and they will be accompanied with a moderate case of panic, then I won't be able to make any decisions at all. As it is my decision-making skills are pretty poor at the moment; I am drinking skanky snake water and I am quite stressed. Gypsy is really quite distressed and is looking for me to 'fix it'. I have to simplify everything right down to the basics.

- I will not give Gumby any more Well 36, which means he only has two days' water.
- If push comes to shove I could make it to Well 33 in two days.
- Well 33 is about 5 km (as the crow flies) from the Kunawarritji community where I could get help to pick up any supplies I leave behind here.
- I could walk for two days without the camels, Gumby could just carry water and a few essentials rigged up in a makeshift pack saddle.

*Conclusion: I can make it but I have to leave tomorrow.*

*I have to leave tomorrow.*

*Okay. So if the camels are not well enough to carry a pack tomorrow I could leave most of my stuff behind and lead them without any weight to carry. If they are too sick to follow me even without a pack:*

- *I could let them go and hope they join up with the wild camels who could take them to water, or*
- *I could leave them tied up, making the assumption I would be able to come back for them once I get help from the community, or*
- *I could shoot them ...*

*Not good choices ... but I have choices. I still have some control of the situation, even if it is damage control.*

*I don't like it but I have some sort of plans in place. Will see what tomorrow brings.*

*S 22° 08' 20", E 125° 16' 58"   1017 ft   0.0 km*
*Total: 4164.2 km*
*Water total: 77.1 litres*

**Low point:** *Camels, of course. This is the worst day of my ride — so far. I am losing the plot.*
**High point:** *Gumby not sick yet ... But I am sure that will develop into a low point for another day, another page on my journal. I'm tired, I'm confused, I haven't had much sleep, I'm fucking hot and I just want to click my fingers and be out of here. I hate the fucking Canning Stock Route.*

After half an hour of sleep and seven-and-a-half hours of mind numbing, stomach wrenching tossing and turning I rose to find Gypsy in a more amiable mood having passed a solid manure. Neither of the girls was sweating and they complained minimally about being saddled. I had rearranged all the gear the night before, which allowed for all contingencies: essentials for

Gumby's makeshift pack, not-quite-so-essentials for a single camel (in case one was well and one was sick), and everything except the luxurious stuff like soap and spare socks in case they both could come but I wanted to lighten the load a bit. As it was I thought they were both looking pretty good. I happily spent an hour sorting it all back to my normal packing regime and easily resisted watering them before we left (even though they could have done with a drink after their diarrhoea). There was no way they were going to get water that had been within 50 paces of a bird, dead or alive!

### Day 251, 3 October: Beyond Well 35 camp

*My God! I survived today! We survived today! This is a funny game. Yesterday I couldn't see me going past Well 33. I thought I would have to be rescued. I was so down. I was sure I had killed the camels (especially Gypsy) and I just wanted to get them back to Andrew and stop this crazy shit. Yesterday I was mentally fucked. For the past few days, actually, ever since I mixed the salty water with good Perth water (which is my only drinkable water I have left now — no more skanky snake water). I think I have been mentally exhausted — lack of sleep, heat stress, worry over health of dog and camels etc. and it has been playing merry hell with my practical thought processes and logic. I am now so paranoid I put a purification tablet in the bird water to wash the dishes and have a tub. I hope to get to Well 33 tomorrow but it will be a big day. Not sure. I may take it cruisey and walk in to Well 33 with basically dry jerries (not a comforting thought). When you get down you have to be extra disciplined, I think. You must have a proper tub, cook decent meals and have a couple of mugs of tea. Otherwise exhaustion and depression just take hold and multiply, getting uglier and uglier and ever harder to shake. Heidi's psych advice for the day.*

*Hopefully I will get a good night's sleep tonight, I haven't had one for quite a while.*

*S 22° 13' 11", E 125° 03' 43"   989 ft   32.9 km*
*Total: 4197.1 km*

*Low point:* Camels don't like my choice of camp I thought it was good tucker — apparently not.

*High point:* We are all alive! All of us! We are going to make it to Well 33 and beyond. I think I've lifted out of my blues. Good on you Pam and Gyps — my heroes.

It sounds really corny but when you are out there on your own, fighting the elements, staring straight into the eyes of death, you start asking the big questions. What does it all mean? Am I going to find true happiness? Is my life worth nothing if I don't have children? What is the answer to life, the universe and everything? Why did Douglas Adams choose the number 42 anyway? When you battle with these big mind benders it leads you to further question the world, probing every unanswered corner. What would ever possess anyone to suck toxic smoke into their lungs? If God exists, how can paedophiles? How many times do you have to see *Matrix III* to understand it? Why do people hang their socks in pairs on the clothesline? I found myself just getting deeper and deeper because one question answered led to a score more unanswered. Why would anyone ever want to own a Volvo? Who the hell cares what Paris Hilton does? Why are all the shagable men married? And the biggest one of all: when is it exactly that Gumby is going to start talking?

The last day into Well 33 was a long one, 36.1 kilometres, but there was only one sand ridge so we were all pretty happy. The well had a windmill and a tank with a tap! What luxury. No winching, no pumping, no cleaning out dead birds, no decanting — not even filtering. The water was clear and clean and fresh and, as far as I was concerned, tasted better than Bollinger. There was an overflow pool which was surrounded by green grass so Gum and Furphy were beside themselves swimming and rolling and eating. We were all in heaven.

There was a set of cattle yards that were camel-proof so I could leave the girls in there without worrying about wild camels harassing them while Gum and I walked into the community. There were a couple of camels that hung around the well but took no notice of my girls. How rude! My girls were beautiful, even if they may have been a little on the slim side ... didn't that just make them supermodels? I think those bull camels must have been gay.

We had three whole days off at Well 33. Each day Gum, Furphy and I would walk into Kunawarritji to make phone calls, charge batteries, get a few supplies and generally socialise. I was very disappointed as the store didn't have Coke. Apparently Coke is bad for the kids, but Pepsi Max is not! So I drank Pepsi Max instead. It didn't get rid of my Coke deficiency headache so I wasn't happy.

The first day we rode in I found myself being followed by an ever increasing crowd of giggling blackfella kids. Finally one of them had obviously drawn the short straw and came up to me and asked if they could have a ride on Gumby. How thick was I? I had been thinking I may bring in the camels for the kids to look at but, of course, they were blasé about camels because they raided the town all the time. Camels were almost a pest to these people. Gumby was probably the first horse at the community in at least 50 years. Most of these kids had never seen a horse. Poor things. They will get a big shock when they see a real horse and discover what a doughy little shortcake Gum was. So I took all the kids for a couple of rides each. They were so polite. They oldest boy chose the order, nominating the youngest first and himself last. They all waited patiently for their go and even would say 'My go is finished now, time for the next one' when they had done a few laps of the car park. Even so, they all keenly lined up for a second ride, first checking Gum wasn't too tired. Yet again my day had been brightened immensely by these happy, grinning kids.

After three rest days of luxury I felt it was time to leave. Dad and Uncle Don had left already to meet me in a few days. They were going through Alice Springs then heading west on Gary Junction Road to come out at Well 33, but I was getting my usual stationary jitters so headed off. I also wanted to travel with them into Durba Springs. They were limited with time so I thought if I set off and got a couple of days ahead we might make it.

Before I got to Well 33 I had been looking at their arrival as my salvation. Once we were there, and all alive, I looked at their arrival as more just a shot in the arm of sanity. Boy was I mistaken! I had underestimated what four days of camping through the outback, with your brother and away from family and wives, can turn you into!

# 15

## The Two Abs

Dad and Uncle Don grew up on Kyneton Park, our home property. Their mother taught them through primary school and then they were sent away to boarding school at about the age of ten. After school they came home to the land and worked together until the farm was divided into two in 2000. They always got on well and I suspect, since the farm split, they missed each other; even though they are still next-door neighbours they hardly get to see each other. They look quite similar except Dad is a few inches taller and seven years younger. On the two-way radio even their family has trouble distinguishing between the two.

I can barely remember a fellow called Alec Betson, who worked on the place and taught me and my sisters to ride when I was a very young. Dad and Uncle Don called him Ab (because of his initials) so he promptly turned around and started calling them Ab as well. As a consequence there were three Abs on the place, which, as a child, seemed perfectly normally. After Alec left, Dad and Uncle Don continued the tradition which confused many a stranger, and even family listening to the two-way radio. Ever since I can remember, they've both suffered tractor deafness (and I suspect a level of selective domestic deafness, too). Uncle Don had succumbed to hearing aids but Dad was still hanging in there. Their deafness has always been a source of amusement to their families, because they would hear bits of whatever you said and fill in the rest, resulting in a sentence that most likely had nothing to do with what you said, made no sense at all in the context of things, but at least rhymed.

'Dad, that post isn't straight.'

'Yeah, thanks, bring over the gate.'

'No Dad, the hole is wrong.'

'No, once we get it hung you'll see it's not too long.'

'Dad, look at the level … it's not even!'

'Hi, I don't think you need the shovel … and definitely not seven!'

*'Dad, the post is on an angle.'*

'Well how did you get the wire in a tangle?

'Ahhhh!'

'Oh look Hi, the post is crooked. You need to keep an eye out for that!'

Needless to say, a conversation between the two could be highly amusing. It was also a constant source of wonder because at the end of their conversations each would somehow intuitively know what the other was trying to say anyway.

On 10 October they pulled into camp at Well 30 in Uncle Don's Land Cruiser, Elsie. Gumby saw them coming first and recognised his very own 'Mr Whippy van', calling out to it and shuffling over to them even before they had pulled up. Gum was in heaven. Uncle Don took an immediate shine to Gumby when I introduced them.

'Uncle Don, this is Gumby. Gumby this is Uncle Don.'

'Hello Gumpy.'

'Gumby,' Dad and I chorused.

'Look at you, Gumpy.'

'*Gumby!*' we repeated as Gum wedged his head in the half-open window, looking for feed.

'Gumpy, do you want something to eat? Here, I'll open the back and see what we can find.' Oh well, why bother? What's in a name?

By the time they had arrived up at Well 30, after four days of travelling and camping together, they had degenerated into a pair of snickering thirteen-year-old boys stirring each other, swearing and telling dirty jokes. What had happened to Dad and lovely old Uncle Don? Who were these children who had commandeered Elsie?

It was great (and not the least bit amusing) to be travelling with them. My mind could rest, the girls could get frequent water, Gumby had an all-you-can-eat buffet on wheels and Furphy got to sit in the front seat with the air conditioner. We were all in luxury.

### Day 260, 12 October: No-tree camp

*Not a bad day today (how many times do I start with that?). Got away at 7.15 am which isn't bad considering camp is so different and I now start the day with bacon and eggs. Looxury! Thanks Dad. The sun has been rising at about 4.30 am and I normally* get away at about 6. 30 am so three-quarters of an hour late isn't too bad.

The Two Abs brought a hand-held radio so we are able to communicate, which will be great. I feel a bit guilty that we are travelling so slowly but I think Uncle Don is enjoying having a purpose to his camping.

The girls walked well today. I got Elsie to carry some jerries — Pam really appreciated it. Saw about four lots of one to two wild camels. I couldn't even be bothered chasing them off; I just kept going. They either just stood there or walked alongside until they lost interest. Pam decided she liked the look of one and kept calling out to him. He was a coward, running in front and spinning around and then running in front again. More likely, knowing Pam, she was just telling him to get out of the way and let the real workers through. Some camels just appear mysteriously at the top of a sand dune, silhouetted against the sky, and stand regally, pretending not to look. It's all very 'movie like' (not that I have seen one of those for a fair stretch). I have tried to get photos of them but suspect it just looks like dots on the horizon. These camels don't appear as fat as the ones up north so don't feel quite so guilty looking at the girls.

Pam has completely trashed my back. I can't do it any longer so now I am making poor old Gum suffer. I have committed another unspeakable 'horsemanship crime' and tied Pam's lead rope around Gumby's neck. Good old Gum. He doesn't seem to mind. I used a wide seatbelt strap around his neck and when she drags he just lowers his head, engages his neck and pulls. I think he would make a good cart horse. I will just do lots of chiro on his neck. My back was a lot happier tonight.

Tonight the Two Abs seemed to go right off ... maybe it is the heat. For some reason Dad started doing the John Cleese walk through the sand yelling 'Don't mention the war' and Uncle Don, after he took his 'ears' out, was talking to himself. Actually, I think he was talking to an imaginary friend he calls Donny! He was saying things like, 'Well, Donny, do you think we should give Gumpy one more apple before we go to bed – he is looking hungry.' Yes, it is still Gumpy. Can't seem to get that one across. Must write it down and show him.

Gumpy, oops, Gumby doesn't seem to mind. He's become quite attached to Uncle Don (and Donny) because he has discovered what a big softy he is. Uncle Don was asleep on his swag this afternoon and Gum shuffled over and nudged him with his nose to wake him up. Uncle Don leapt up and ran to Elsie and got him a piece of pumpkin. He has Uncle Don well trained!

Today we went 4 km past Well 28 looking for feed. No shade, just low bushes. I am used to it now but with the Two Abs here I am more aware of what a good camp for humans should be. I have got into the habit of only caring about a good camp for my kids. Uncle Don has done a lot of this sort of travelling and I think he is finding it hard to change his idea of what is a good camp.

Dad has started to inadvertently call me Ab – now I am scared! I think I would rather go back to being 'SamPenTrinTon, ah ah Hi' which is what he normally calls me.

I listened to my iPod all day today (now I can charge it up easily I can afford the battery wastage) so basically danced across 27 km of sand ridges. Maybe proof I am really going crazy. I cut corners today and saved us 13 km. With more cutting corners I think we might make it to Durba Springs before the Two Abs leave.

S 22° 40' 15.5", E 123° 44' 32.8"   974 ft   27.4 km
Total: 4404.7 km

**Low point:** Not even much spinifex for Gumby – he is getting a hard feed, though. Hope he doesn't get colic.
**High point:** Uncle Don cooks a great meal every night. Tonight is chops and vegies. Just brilliant!

Even though they are off the land, the two Abs had no idea what a camel ate (which is understandable, I suppose). However, they set out to solve this problem in a very ingenious way. If you can't drag the skinny, thirsty camel to the prospective edible bush, bring the edible bush to the camel. They would drive ahead for a couple of hours then return with an assortment of broken off branches. They would hold each morsel up to Pam, assessing her response. She would turn her head away and keep it there until a tasty branch was waved in front of her, then she would casually turn back, sniff the plant with disdain and have a half-hearted nibble. The two Abs would then race back to where they found that plant and start setting up camp.

Rummaging through the gear they brought, I found a bottle of Restdown Jessie's Rosé. Don and Jo Hearn, friends from home, have a winery and produce the only wine (other than sparkling) that I like. There was a card with it that read: 'Dear Gumby and Furphy, we thought you had planned to ditch the mad woman by now ...' How rude! It's a bit harsh calling Gypsy a 'mad woman'. She has her faults but ... We drank the chilled wine, which was magical and perfectly suited the desert atmosphere. I filled up the empty bottle with the red desert sand, re-corked it and Dad returned it to them when he got back. I think they were pretty happy with the exchange.

I loved travelling through the desert country and found the sand fascinating. It was a brilliant deep, red ochre colour, especially in the morning, and would get lighter through the day. A gentle breeze would cover any tracks in a matter of hours and create corrugations that were the curse of the driving tourist. A plant that bent back down and touched the sand would move around in the wind drawing a perfect arc, and sometimes even a full circle, depending on the wind. The sand was so clean and pure. I loved it; I felt at home.

It was so hot in the daytime you couldn't stand on it with bare feet. Sometimes during an especially hot afternoon, if we stood stationary for a few minutes, Gumby would lift one leg up in the air, then alternate with the others, just like the 'dance' the shovel-snouted lizard does to cool its feet in the hot desert sand – maybe not as graceful, though. The sand radiated a huge amount of heat and I found it was much cooler being on Gumby because I was further away from it. This explained why camels legs were so long: a cooling mechanism! Poor Furphy had no hope.

I learnt all the tracks, from the bungarra (goanna) to a little bug that scooted around just under the sand surface leaving a wake, literally, of sand behind it. The only mammals there was any sign of were dingoes and camels. As I got further south, and into less desert country, the first new tracks I saw were feral cat. Then further south of that I started seeing kangaroo and emu prints.

Even though we were still walking all the way, travelling was much easier. For one, I was mentally in a much better place. But for the girls, the Two Abs carted all the heavy stuff in Elsie and all they had were nearly empty saddles. Also, we had access to more water because Elsie was doing runs forward to wells and bringing it back. This meant more reliable, much fresher water (not skanky or salty or bird infested). It also meant I could soak my feet at night again and try to get my large swollen feet down to a better size, as well as have a hot shower! Elsie had a set-up where the shower water was pumped past the motor and became hot. This was luxury beyond my imagination. I didn't feel I deserved it at all.

Up until then I had been guessing the temperature. It can be a bit hard because if you are having a bad day, and feeling the heat, you always think it is hotter than it is. The Two Abs arrived just after a particularly hot spell that I was guessing was in the low forties. Penni, my sister, had sent along a thermometer with Dad and on a 'cooler' day it was 42 degrees. So, yes, it was pretty hot out there. I then felt I deserved the privilege of whingeing and feeling sorry for myself.

### Day 263, 15 October: 44°C without a tree in sight camp

*Bloody hot day today, about 44°C. Pam struggled, Gypsy struggled, I struggled, Furphy struggled in the air-conditioned comfort of Elsie and even Gumby struggled. Lucky Dad took Furphy, otherwise I think he would have died. It was only a short day, on paper: we did 7 km across country which cut out over 13 km. The short cut was worthwhile even though it was hard work. When spinifex is old it is huge, tough, prickly and hard to pass. You just end up having to walk through it. Gum wasn't happy.*

*We pulled in at camp at about 1.20 pm but the last few km I had to ride because I wasn't sure if I was going to faint or throw up! It is actually a lot cooler on Gum because I am just a little bit further away from that hot sand. Poor Furphy would really suffer from being so low to the ground. I really find it hard to believe he is still alive.*

*Lucky good camel feed came along and we stopped. Not a tree in sight. I am a bit concerned about Gumby. The last couple of days have been slow and hard for him which is very unusual. He is also urinating heaps ... cystitis or colic? So this morning I started him on Engemycin (an injectable antibiotic) just in case. We shall see how it goes. Gave the girls an out-of-schedule drink this morning, which I think did them the world of good. We saw heaps of wild camels today (about 25) most of which, I suspect, are young males just kicked out of home and off to see the world. Was great to see them, especially since Gypsy and Pam don't care.*

*S 23° 02' 11.5", E 123° 22' 18.9"    1031 ft    22.8 km*
*Total 4480.3 km*

**Low point:** *Zarking hot. Poor Gum.*
**High point:** *Don and Jo's beautiful, refreshing Jessie's Rosé wine.*

I found desert travel so different to any other. It was bloody hot and bloody hard work. It was a long way and felt as if it would never end. There was little shade, the sand ridges were relentless, the spinifex prickled us until we bled, the sand burnt us, the feed was minimal and the water was rationed and unreliable. I loved it.

I think Gum loved it too and the girls were at home for the first time since we left Mount Isa. Only poor old Furphy couldn't quite appreciate the joys of the desert. Despite the fact that his close relatives lived in the desert quite successfully, Furph struggled.

My joy of desert travel was initially overcast by the whole pesky survival issues thing so was quite stressful. However, with the Two Abs able to travel up and down and supply us with fresh, reliable and frequent water, I could relax and revel in all it had to offer. I think I must have been a desert baby in a previous life ... I felt more at home than I had for the whole ride.

I really appreciated my support crew. Not only was I relieved of my survival stresses, but I was plain spoilt. Every morning Dad cooked me up a storm in the form of bacon (crispy – the only way to have it) and eggs (hard and turned – definitely the only way to have them). After a few days on the road the eggs seemed to scramble themselves in their unbroken shells (the road was so rough) so Dad called them Eggs Canning and served them up with flare. It certainly beat 100 grams of salted cashews for brekky. He would then help me pack up the girls (finally, someone to help lift those bloody saddles) and Gum and I would set off. The Two Abs would then have brekky at their leisure, pack up, pass us and look for a camp and collect water. At night Dad would help unpack the kids, ply me with cans of cold Coke first then champagne stubbies, and force me to sit down with a bucket of water to soak my swollen feet and a cold face washer to cool me off. Uncle Don would sneak 'Gumpy' food from the back of Elsie (although he wasn't fooling anyone) and then cook up a storm for dinner, including dessert. Most nights I had a shower, heated from Elsie's motor, which made the whole episode even easier. People often take being clean for granted and don't appreciate how good it is for your mental health.

Dad helped me out with the kids quite a lot. He would shift them from tether points, bring them in for saddling and keep an eye on them when they were browsing too far away. One day we were at a camp with very little feed. There was one largish, tasty tree and not much else so I made the girls browse away from the tree so they would have feed overnight when they were tethered to it. Pam snuck back around and was eating the prized tree so I asked Dad to take her away to where Gypsy was feeding. He lead her right past me and as her hind end came level with me she lashed out with her back leg and sent me flying, literally! No warning at all. A camel's kick has a lot of power and I thank God (or whoever) they don't have hard hooves or I may have broken a femur. Camels are incredibly smart. She could have kicked Dad instead but I am quite sure she knew who was responsible for her being taken away from the feed and she saw no reason to punish the innocent, especially when she was in easy reach of the guilty!

The Two Abs had been listening to an audio book about Lasseter's exploring adventures. Apparently he used to call his working camels 'the Brutes'. Dad loved the camels, especially Gypsy, and took to referring to them as the Brutes (only in jest). I finally persuaded Dad that the girls were not that silly and didn't like their new name so he shouldn't use it in front of them. The moment he stopped, Gypsy fell in love with him and would calm down and behave whenever he was near. I wished I'd had him at the start! Camels are scarily smart and never ceased to amaze me with their level of intelligence and ability to calculate and control their reactions to being handled. I hate to admit it, but they are smarter than horses and so keep you on your toes when you are handling them.

The Two Abs travelled with us for thirteen days – thirteen days that saved my sanity, and maybe my life. When they were with us I was able to sleep, Pam was getting daily water, I was eating meat and vegies at night and bacon and eggs in the morning, I had cold Coke and champagne on tap, Furphy put on weight and 'Gumpy' had his all-you-can-eat buffet on wheels. I was sad to see them go. Our last night was at the amazing oasis of Durba Springs, where tall white gums and green grass were surrounded by towering red rock cliffs and a deep natural spring. It was eerie to camp in this sanctuary, protected from the harshness of the desert and its heat and exposure. The next morning, as I walked out through the gap of the deep red cliffs, I felt all alone again. I had to keep clinging to the knowledge that I was only 20 days from the end of the Canning, and the desert. I was filled with a mix of sadness that Dad and Uncle Don had left and the desert was nearly over, and stress about survival, heat, water availability and the health of the kids (the usual) and joy at being on my own again. I had a lot of thinking to do about what I would do once we got off the Canning. Pam couldn't go much further and I really needed camels to cross the Nullarbor.

### Day 274, 26 October: Creek bed camp
*Fairly rocky ground and no good camel feed all day (I promised a 'Macca's drive thru' to the girls so they are not happy). Then, all of a sudden, we came across a smorgasbord for both camelid and equid and a sandy creek bed with trees for me – perfect. I would have liked to do more distance but a bird in the hand gathers no moss. Since leaving Durba Springs the other day I have had a feeling that I have left something behind. It has been with me all this time till today when I realised what it was: Furphy! The Two Abs took him, thank God (or whoever). No more frequent stopping to let him drink out of my hat, no more saliva streaks everywhere*

and no more annoying lizard chasing. He has drooled continuously since his first heat stress episode and it was only just before the Abs left that Uncle Don pointed out it had stopped. Actually, the real reason I am happy he has gone is because he wasn't going to survive much longer in this heat. As it is, he might take a bit to recover ... hope I haven't fried his organs! Poor Furph. I do actually miss him.

I get heaps of texts from Dad since he left. Initially he was informing me of where I could find feed and water down the track, now it is on the progress of their trip home. I am glad they are back in civilisation, safe from this incredible heat. I think it knocked Uncle Don around, not that he said anything. Their day at Georgia bore — where they pumped up enough water for showers, laundry and to fill all the jerries, using the hand pump that was apparently very stiff — would be a challenge for any 30-year-old, let alone a 77-year-old.

At the moment I have taken the chair about 50 m away from camp so I can sit and keep an eye on the girls browsing. Gum is back at camp eating the good grass there. Knowing Gum he will graze closer and closer to camp until 'Oops, look what I found!' Yes, the Copra. Dad left me with a 20-kg bag that poor old Gypsy is carrying — half in each canvas bucket thrown over the cross sticks.

I gave the Two Abs some of my gear to make things lighter for the girls. Now, with packing I have to consider that: Pam is chronically ill and should always carry as little as possible; Gypsy is lame on her right fore and has been getting worse with work; Gypsy is probably not going to get a drink for three days but Pam will get one daily.

So now, Pam is carrying a total of 108 kg, which includes the kitchen pack bag, ropes, my chair, the camp oven bag and six jerry cans with some water. While Gypsy carries, among other things, six jerries full of water (totalling 148 kg alone), the horse feed and my swag, which totals 203 kg. Poor Gyps.

*Had a better night sleep last night but still really tired today. It may have something to do with all the codeine I am shovelling into me to stop my diarrhoea. I have been feeling waves of nausea today. Not sure why. Maybe: It's from the same cause as the diarrhoea disease; from all the codeine I am popping; I have the DTs from Uncle Dons great cooking; I am just so tired.*

*Today I was so tired I was falling asleep on the horse. I had to walk most of the way to stay awake. Even then I was hallucinating, seeing non-existent kangaroos. At one stage I thought I was going to black-out and my vision sort of went a bit. Must be a virus I suppose ... or a stroke. Maybe I had a series of mini strokes. There is nothing like taking a minor ailment and running with it! Once I cooled off my feet tonight I felt a lot better. I think I will just stick to the diagnosis of a virus — don't want to worry those people who find this abandoned journal in the middle of the desert next to an empty bag of Copra and some Gumby bones.*

*I really need to think about what I am going to do. Pam is getting poorer and poorer and I have had to admit to myself she won't make it beyond the Canning let alone across the Nullarbor. I don't have enough money or resources to get hold of another trained camel, though, let alone get it here, and then continue on with it and Gypsy. There is also the question of what I would do with Pam. She is not mine. She is Andrew's, and she is a working camel and earns him money for his business. I have to at least try to rest her and get her health back to give Andrew a chance of receiving his business asset back. Camel transport can be a bit hard to find. Not any old stock truck can accommodate them and hardly any truckies would want to take them.*

*Money is becoming a big issue. My horses dying last year were a big cost and my savings are limited. Besides, I have only gone halfway. How depressing.*

*First things first: I need to get Pam home to rest and recuperate. How, then, can I cross the Nullarbor? Maybe I might have to skip it! No, I don't want to. I never planned to. Is this the sensible thinking traveller/adventurer in me talking or the spoilt*

*child beating her fists on the ground? I think the spoilt child! I can't*
*see any way to avoid it. Part of the skill of achieving something like*
*my goal is to be flexible in my plans and not to be bloody minded*
*about what I want. I learnt that early on with one non-weight-*
*bearing lame horse and then again with three dead horses. I must*
*be flexible, I must be flexible, I must be flexible. I will have to sleep*
*on it ... God knows what I am going to do. I do know that I am*
*not going to be happy with any solution. Ugh!*

*S 24° 08' 27.3", E 122° 12' 07.7"   1586 ft   23.2 km*
*Total: 4736.3 km*

**Low point:** *Feeling so tired ... I feel as if I am going to throw up!*
**High point:** *Great camp.*

Having Dad and Uncle Don travel with us for a couple of weeks was a huge
shot in the arm. The kids and I worked less and had more reliable food and
water and life was so much easier. But the best thing was the psychological
support. I am sure Dad would have nearly died when he first got to Well 30:
his daughter in the middle of nowhere, literally a thousand of kilometres
from any real civilisation, 10 kilograms lighter than when he last saw her, in
consistent 40-degree plus heat with nothing but a couple of skinny camels, a
dog that was trying to die and a horse that thought everything was a joke.
Never once did he express his concerns or show any doubt in my abilities
and decisions. I am sure he was suppressing the urge to grab his youngest
daughter, strap her to the back of the truck and drive her to 'safety' as fast as
he could. Seeing Dad's unquestioning faith in me and my skills was a really
proud moment for me and helped me find the strength to go on.

Pam went downhill quite quickly after Dad and Uncle Don left. I watered
her every day and she carried the bare minimum, but she lost more weight
and when she rested she would put her whole head and neck flat along the
ground. She never used to do that and I saw it as a real sign that she was
struggling mentally as well as physically. She also started to drool, having a
small stream flowing behind her nearly all the time. She ate well, though, so

I didn't think there was anything wrong with her mouth. I concluded she was nauseous, which was consistent with her whole demeanour.

The people on one of the last stations I had to travel through on the Canning to get to Wiluna had a strong reputation for being unreasonable and unwelcoming, and I had even heard first-hand about how they had threatened to shoot some working camels, even if they were tied up, wearing pack saddles and on the stock route, which is not legally part of the property. I didn't want to risk Pam going down and refusing to move while travelling through their place so I decided to exit the track further north, on a property called Granite Peak Station. It took only fifteen days to get there from Durba Springs but it felt a lot longer due to Pam's rapid deterioration. At Granite Peak, the owner Jim was very welcoming and generous, as outback people are, and offered to have my kids in his holding paddock with some hay until I sorted out what I was doing. I caught up on all the important world news, as I always did when I hit civilisation. Apparently Ben Cousins was arrested for possession after a drug search. Who the hell is Ben Cousins and why did this even get even a cursory mention, in the scheme of things?

Anyway, I had made it, and we were all in one piece. I was elated to have achieved such a feat, but also very sad. I knew I was never going to experience the desert in such a way ever again. It was over. I knew from now on my ride was not going to be anywhere near that amazing and my motivation waned. I had travelled 5013.2 kilometres. How was I going to get the energy to go any further and continue with the rest of my ride?

# 16

## In a holding pattern

Granite Peak Station is about 200 kilometres northeast of Wiluna. I stayed there for ten days while I sorted out what I was going to do. Jim was a great host, even specially ordering in a box of champagne through the mail, as a surprise. Here I was, using his paddock and hay, eating his food, sleeping in his quarters, on his phone all the time with no guarantee of when I was going to leave and he organises a surprise for me!

I went out to check the water a few times with him. Every day was about 45 degrees and the bores couldn't keep up with the stock's water consumption. Jim was carting water to a few bores, which basically kept him busy for about fourteen hours a day, seven days a week. The trouble was a fair percentage of the bore water was also watering the feral horses, camels, donkeys, kangaroos and dingoes. He had a dog trapper and a roo shooter that were kept pretty busy, but I suppose putting in bores and troughs where there would not normally be much reliable water allows all sorts of feral and native animals to live and breed.

When I rode in to the station I was amazed at what little food (or so I thought) there was. I didn't see any stock at all and thought they must be looking pretty droughty and poor. Some graziers do it tough. While I waited at the house for Jim to get in from the paddock, a beast wandered aimlessly up to me. He was about the size of a small weaner, had a mature head, a huge set of horns and a pot belly, his coat was dry and hanging over his skeleton so you could see every joint and he had long, skinny testicles that almost dragged on the ground. This was one of his bulls? I hadn't seen any of his cattle by then and if this one was anything to go by I didn't want to. The only thing he had going for him was he was very quiet – he stopped to sniff me on his way past.

I didn't dare mention the encounter because once I met Jim it was obvious he was very proud of his cattle. It wasn't till a few days later, when I went around checking the water with Jim that I saw any more cattle. They were unbelievable: huge, shiny-coated, fat, quiet cows with chunky, fat calves at foot. I couldn't stop laughing and I think poor Jim thought I was laughing at his cattle, his pride and joy. Finally, when I collected myself, I asked about the skeletal specimen at the house that could barely stand.

'Oh, no!' Jim cringed. 'You saw Brian! How embarrassing!'

Apparently, Brian was a poddy calf from a few years ago that never really did well. Drenching had nearly killed him so Jim didn't have the courage to castrate him. Brian was on a bit of a good wicket; although Jim was appalled at the idea that someone might see him as too big a softy to shoot him, even though he knew Brian was a possible source of disease for his other cattle.

I put the kids in the holding paddock (which was bigger than a lot of properties I have been on) and they ate their way through a large, round bale of oaten hay. Within a few days they started putting on weight. Initially the girls were lost, wandering the fences, looking for camp. I was tempted to take a saddle out to the middle of the paddock as they would have been happy then (they loved their routine) but I thought Jim would have thought I was crazy. Poor Gum was also a bit lost. I think he missed me (well, I missed him) and the girls wouldn't sit still. In the end he camped at the hay bale on his own and ate and drank and waited for me to visit.

I couldn't put it off any longer. I had to work out what I was going to do. After a few days at Granite Peak I jotted down a few notes to try to sort out my thoughts and come to a decision.

*I am going crazy. The guys here are great, and generous and kind and welcoming and easy-going and blah, blah, blah but I am stumped as to what is the best thing to do. I have all these thoughts but can't seem to string them together. Pam is too skinny to travel any further. I should do everything I can to return Andrew's working camels in the best possible condition. I can't travel the Nullarbor without camels or a back-up crew. I have very little money. Does this mean I can't do the Nullarbor at all?*

*I am struggling to concentrate. I want to do the right thing but my head is spinning. Maybe I should take the bull by the horns, swallow my pride and make an assertive decision. I mean, I am in it for the long haul and don't want to fall by the wayside. When the going gets tough, the tough get going so I should just take the bit between my teeth, fight the good fight and take the high road onward and upward because a stitch in time catches the worm. I know what I have to do, because if I didn't that would be like the pot calling the chickens before they hatch. So, we're agreed: I can't put all my eggs in the one basket when the shoe fits. Phew, I have sorted that so feel better. It's as clear as mud and now I just have to organise it!*

That was settled. I wasn't doing the Nullarbor, not then anyway. Maybe later … in another era.

I flew home after ten days and picked up Andrew's camel truck and Tim, my brother-in-law, and we drove 3500 kilometres back to Granite Peak Station. We stayed a day and then loaded the kids and headed east again. Camels tend to sit down when they travel so you put carpet down on the floor of the truck. I separated Gum from the girls so he could stand on the truck floor and not soak the carpet in his manure. Gum was quite happy with that as he kept looking at his reflection in the stainless steel divider and neighing. It had been a while since he had seen another horse and he was obviously keen for a conversation.

It took four days to get home. We avoided New South Wales until after we dropped Gum off at a friend's place in Victoria, because at the time the equine influenza outbreak was in full swing and there were restrictions on all horse movement in the state. With 70 kilometres to go, at Echuca, I climbed up the side of the truck to check the girls once again. They were sitting there very happily. Just 45 minutes later, when we unloaded them at home, Gypsy had a bloody nose and her lower jaw was out to one side. Her teeth were out of alignment by an inch. She must have stood up and smacked her head on the crate, fracturing her jaw. We drove all that way to return a skeleton and a broken camel to Andrew. Sometimes it just seems that the world is against you.

It quickly became clear I wasn't going anywhere fast. I had two horses in New South Wales that were illegal to move, one horse in Victoria I didn't want to bring into New South Wales, one very skinny camel I needed to feed up and one broken camel I needed to treat daily to let her bones heal before

I could return her. I stayed at home, did bits of work here and there and tried to stay motivated and organise my next move. I was stuck in a holding pattern.

I had been home for a month or so and I was slowly feeling worse and worse. The best way to describe it is to say it was as if I had blocked sinuses, my heart had relocated to my throat and I was sitting on an overworking freezer. I was getting quite vague, my head was thick and slow, I could feel my heartbeat in my jugular veins and my body was tired and hummed the whole time. I often explain to my horse chiro clients that the body is like one of those ornamental boats people build in collapsed form then push through the neck of a bottle: pull one string and the boat erects itself and stays self-supported. Everything is connected, so if you pull or break one string anything can go wrong. Anyway, one weekend, at a conference, I caught up with Jeff Morrison, a great friend and brilliant osteopath. 'You look like shit' was his greeting and before I knew it he had me on the dissection table giving me an 'osteopathic rogering', as he calls it. Because I had been stuck in pretty serious survival mode for so long, then had suddenly returned to civilisation, my sympathetics were stuck in 'on' mode and my body was still tuned for a 'fight or flight' response. Of course it isn't that simple, but Jeff adjusted me so my nervous system went back to 'normal operations' mode and within minutes my head cleared, my heart felt as if it had settled back on my diaphragm, and the humming had stopped. I don't know how he does it but he is a magician. I think in my next life I want to study osteopathy.

One day, at home, I walked out onto the veranda when it was raining and slipped, landing on the stairs with my right lower leg pointing in a very unnatural direction. A visit to the specialist revealed I needed surgery. There was no way I was going to let any butcher cut into my joints – right or wrong, I have a bad attitude towards surgeons. They really are just glorified carpenters that operate (literally) on mostly ego. Maybe that's a bit harsh, but I think they are a bit too 'scalpel happy' for my liking. I have seen it in the veterinary field, too. Anyway, I hobbled out of the specialist's office saying 'Don't call me, I'll call you'. If I let him cut into me it would be months before I would be able to leave. But if I didn't let him cut into me, how was I going to heal?

I limped home, depressed and feeling sorry for myself. I had an ominous feeling that a higher being was trying to stop me going again. It was hard enough keeping focused as I was battling the guilt of the sick camels and the dead horses and numerous favours I had received from total strangers and the worried family. A couple of days later, I went to Don and Jo Hearn's (the friends next door with the winery) for dinner. They were always good for a pep up and an ego boost. For some reason they always thought I could do this trip; they showed such faith in me I didn't like to point out the truth and disappoint them! I was still hobbling around on two walking sticks and my knee hadn't improved at all. Don asked if I wanted him to try some reiki on it. 'What have you got to lose?' he asked.

Being a veterinary chiropractor I knew what it was like to have my skills and knowledge scoffed at by people who really didn't know what they were scoffing. It made me actively decide not to rule out any ideas of other people, especially in relation to other modes of therapy, unless I had seen proof that it was a load of codswallop (not that I know what codswallop is, let alone what you would do with a whole load of it). I had heard a bit about reiki and successfully used a few techniques that I think are similar to it – but fixing a damaged ligament in a joint? Probably more out of politeness than belief that it could work I accepted Don's offer. I lay on their kitchen table for an hour or so, dropping in and out of sleep, while Don did his thing, and then went home. I did think my knee may have felt a bit better but I was probably imagining it, or maybe it was because I had been resting it for an hour. Don's parting words were: 'You will probably wake up with a really bad headache, or maybe get diarrhoea, as your body adjusts to what I have done.' What a weird skill – giving someone a ripping headache just by lying them on your kitchen table! It was the diarrhoea at 2 am that launched me out of bed. As I was rushing to the toilet I did note that I hardly even felt my injured knee.

One more treatment and five days later I barely even knew which knee it was that I had damaged. I only felt it twinge when I was trimming the third horse's feet for the morning. Maybe God had given up plaguing me and moved on to some other poor sucker.

So now I had a whole new set of problems before me. I had to get my head around travelling with horses again. When I first got the girls I was desperate to go back to horses. Camels were slow and cantankerous and big and scary, and basically far too smart for me. It didn't take long for me to appreciate their versatility and ability to carry such large loads as well as growing very fond of them (though it took a little longer with Gypsy!). I had to work out where I could start with the horses; that is, where, while heading east, does water become available and reliable enough to travel with horses with no back-up crew? After much frustrating research and 42.5 million phone calls I concluded South Australia was no good. There were basically no functional stock routes that travelled east–west and the only reliable water was in the highly populated areas which would be very difficult, unpleasant and dangerous for the kids to travel through. I finally swallowed my pride and decided I would start up again in New South Wales, where there were at least some stock routes. I then had to consider all the restrictions for travelling horses since equine influenza had hit. I was on the phone all the time to the DPI, getting information about quarantine zones and what all the restrictions were in each zone.

Since being back home, Furphy had developed a new obsession: Dad. So I found myself a kelpie pup and named her Gillie, after the best ever cricketer (sorry Don) who had just announced his retirement. Gillie was from working stock. Her mother was a kelpie and her father was a dark stranger in the night. He was unidentified but had to be one of the local working dogs, or so they told me. I have had kelpies before but she put them all to shame with her energy and nutter behaviour. I was in for a challenge.

By the time Pam put on weight and Gypsy's jaw set, and equine influenza quarantine rules loosened and my nephew had his 21st and I got my hair cut and blah, blah, blah, it was the start of April. I felt I had wasted the past four months, even though I couldn't have done it much differently, and was keen to get going.

Dad, Trina, Jo Hearn (who would ride with me for a few days), Furphy, Gillie, Gumby, Piglet, Bart, Ambrose (my polocrosse thoroughbred) and I set off in two utes and two floats to start my ride just southeast of Broken Hill. The idea was to ride southeast back home and then truck all the kids up to

Queensland where I started up the second time and head south again. That way I would be up in Queensland for the winter and arrive home in summer. Also, I really wanted to finish my ride at home. It was silly really, but after over two years riding I wanted Gum and I to finish by riding triumphantly through the property gates.

# 17

## Back to horses again

Jo and I started the new leg on 6 April 2008. We left from our camp just southeast of Broken Hill, leaving Dad and Trina to pack up the utes and floats and take them back home, with Furphy who was very confused but, I think, quite glad he was staying with Dad.

It was strange initially; we weren't carrying water, we had no camels, it wasn't above 40 degrees in the water bag and I had company that could actually speak English. All went quite well, but my biggest concern was Gillie. It took her a few days (or maybe months) to get into the swing of things: following along with all the horses, not chasing cars, not wandering too far, not getting too close to the horses' legs. She soon started to get a bit cocky and I just knew she was in for a hard lesson. At one stage she tried to jump up and snap Bart's nose. On the second day we went through a gate and had walked along another 100 metres or so. Gillie was starting to settle into quietly following along behind the last horse. Unfortunately the last horse was Barty and he didn't like anything right behind him on a good day. She must have got too close and he served her up a corker of a kick straight to her head. Poor little Gill didn't know what had hit her. She spun and raced back to the gate, all the while yelping as if she'd had her tail cut off, and planted herself on the other side of the gate, refusing to get back through. I had to leave Jo with all the horses and walk back for her – she was petrified of the horses now. I spent ten minutes coaxing her to come to me. She was so confused. It served its purpose, though; afterwards she had a healthy respect for the horses' back legs and didn't get kicked again. These are just the lessons we have to learn in life, I suppose.

I rode Ambrose. She was my hard working, 20-year-old thoroughbred mare that I knew could easily take the work, just not in the long term because she would get too light. In her earlier years she had played polo (even at an international level) and when I got her we did mostly polocrosse and some tent pegging competitions. She has a huge work ethic, so although she is very quiet she sees no point in walking when it can all be done at a trot or faster.

All her previous work had been with some sort of purpose, at some sort of decent speed and as a consequence I had to continually ride with the brakes on. She couldn't understand why we were going so slowly and was on a constant lookout for polocrosse goals and tent pegs. It didn't help that her normal, easy walking speed was 7.2 kilometres per hour, where Piglet was closer to 5.5, Bart was 5.4 and Gum was anywhere between 2.2 and 5.0, depending on his mood and the distractions around him. In the paddock she is a classic alpha mare: she had elected poor old Bart as 'stallion' and was constantly on his case to keep the rabble in line. While I rode her, however, she conceded I was 'alpha mare' and let the lower beings walk beside her, as long as they didn't get a nose ahead or smash into her with the pack. It was good, actually; my legs had never been so clear of bruises than they were packing with her. So Ambrose would usually jog for the first 20 kilometres then settle a little to a faster walk for the rest of the day.

I found getting on and off her frequently (to control Gillie if there was traffic or rabbits) started to really irritate her, but once I started doing it on her off-side too she was a lot happier. I always tell my clients they should mount from both sides but old habits die hard and I had that advice plainly demonstrated to me before I took it up myself. I could have ridden her all the way around Australia (it would have only taken about six months!) and she would have made it on sheer determination. But she is a classic-bodied thoroughbred, being impossible to fatten, and would have looked like a starved dairy cow after a few months. So just short sections of the trip for her.

Bart started getting ideas above his station (probably spurred on by the treacherous urgings of Ambrose) and was harassing Piglet mercilessly. In the end I had to hobble him imaginatively: both front legs together as well as one front to one back. That 'learned him'. Well, sort of – it didn't take him too long to work out how to get around, but at least Piglet had a fighting chance. Being with the camels for so long I'd forgotten how easy they were compared to horses. I didn't have to umpire the camels' personality clashes, they just generally worked, even with Gum and they didn't like him at all! Now that I was back to horses I had to be on the constant lookout for new issues that would pop up. The last thing I needed was injuries from silly arguments over non-existent food or who went through the gate first.

We travelled southeast through Menindee and towards Pooncarie, meeting the Darling River a few times. The drought was the worst I had encountered during the whole trip. There were some properties that hadn't been stocked for several years, not a blade of grass game to pop up in the dry. We pulled into Menindee one day, hot, dirty, dry and exhausted and received the usual third-degree from the locals. Actually, I noticed the questions were starting to evolve slowly, which I think was due to the fact that I was further along in my ride and maybe people started to think I may actually finish it.

'Where are you heading to?' Queensland.

'Are you going to write a book?' Nope.

'So did you have fun?' What? Fun? I wouldn't exactly call it 'fun'. What a weird question.

'Have you discovered the answer to life, the universe and everything?' Ah ... no. An even weirder question.

'Would you do it again?' Ah ... why? The weird ones just keep a-comin'!

'What are you going to do when you get back?' Oh ... ah ... haven't thought about that. Still got thousands of k's left.

'Will you be able to go back to work?' I'd better be. My savings are rapidly turning into debts.

When we got to Menindee we discovered there was no feed anywhere. We had done 35.3 kilometres for the day. I felt bad because poor Jo had been thrown in the deep end but she never complained or lagged behind once. We somehow found somewhere to rest the horses for a couple of days on the edge of town and a woman called Diannie (I think her name was Dianne but everyone added an 'ie' as Australians have a habit of doing), who owned horses herself, offered us her own hay as there was none for sale in town. Now I knew, in a town like that, hay would be at beyond-premium prices and said I would pay her for it. By the end of our stay we had used three of her bales (which would have probably cost her over $100) but she seemed to be avoiding me like the plague. I finally pinned her down and asked her how much I owed her. She refused to tell me so I had to get insistent. Finally she said, 'Have you seen the movie *Pay It Forward*?'

Initially I thought it a terrible idea – I was going to be lumped with all these guilt feelings about not reimbursing her. Then I thought it was a great idea. Obviously she wasn't going to accept any money, and that movie's concept quite appealed to me: some stranger does you an unsolicited favour and in return you do one for another stranger. Months down the track I was so pleased with myself as I offered a total stranger assistance by driving her – an elderly lady who couldn't drive, and her newly-diagnosed terminally ill husband – to a specialist appointment hours away. It would have taken all day and I thought I was on a winner. But alas, she had just had an offer from a friend only minutes before my phone call. Back to square one! In the end it took over twelve months for me to 'pay it forward' and I was starting to curse Diannie and her generosity. I know the whole 'pay it forward' suggestion was just to stop me harassing her and she had no intention of ever accepting any money. Country people, yet again.

Along the Darling there were some huge river red gum trees, hundreds of years old, that were struggling from lack of water. I found it quite shocking to think trees that had lived through so much change and history, unaffected, were now dying from such a simple thing as lack of water. Don, Jo's husband, caught up with us in his ute and travelled with us for a few days. That really saved us as he brought hay and could cart water if we couldn't find it at camp.

### Day 292, 10 April: Yampoola waterhole

*Tough day today. The horses were still very sore from a few days ago and were really pushing my buttons. Even Gum was out of sorts. Anyway, finally made it here. I am behind on asking the owners' permission to trespass their land and as Murphy's Law says, the more urgently you need to contact them and the closer you are to their property, the less likely they are to answer the phone. I hate all the organisation and ringing of perfect strangers that is involved in this. I am stressed again (surprise, surprise). Jo is going really well, working her butt off, but I am being my usual irrational, unreasonable, shitty thing. Ugh. Sometimes I hate me.*

*Gumby is still the best. Ambrose is still obsessed with 'doing the job'. I can't wait for her to realise that this is 'the job' – walking!*

*Don turned up today, timed perfectly as we both turned into the waterhole track. It's a dry waterhole but the best camp so far. Don and Jo did a couple of water runs in the ute using my three canvas buckets. Was a bit of a balancing act for poor old Don in the back of the ute. Some of the water didn't spill!*

*Quote for the day: 'You've always got to steer clear of the guy with the bum issue.' Jo Hearn 2008*
*S 32° 41' 38.9", E 142° 26' 3.8"    170 ft    19.7 km*
*Total: 5111.1 km*

**Low point:** *I felt bad because Don and Jo had to go and find/ferry water.*
**High point:** *Champagne (thanks Don) and nice camp.*

The horses were hungry so while Don and Jo were getting them water I gave them hay in a dry billabong and hobbled them out. I hadn't put the fence out yet but they were hungry and they weren't leaving that hay ... I turned my back for a moment and Bart, Piglet and Ambrose were at full speed, hobbling the length of the dry bed and into the trees, out of sight. It always surprises me just how fast they can canter with their hobbles on. Good old Gum was concentrating too hard on his hay to notice. I pulled his hobbles off, leapt on him bareback with a lead rope attached to one side of the headstall and kicked him hard in the flanks with my thongs. He threw his head up majestically, neighed to the disappearing horses and we trotted off slowly, wandering in every direction. Would you believe we caught up with them! I think Gum was more surprised than me. The horses seemed a bit bushed; I think they forgot what they were looking for. I am quite sure it was water but since there wasn't any for miles I think they lost their momentum. I had no lead ropes except for my makeshift rein, so I attached a set of hobbles each side to Gum's headstall, the lead rope to Piglet (the biggest pain to lead by far), two connected cow bell straps to Bart and a set of hobbles to Ambrose. I rode Gum back, juggling three hobble straps, one lead rope, a cow bell strap and four horses with no issues at all.

Don and Jo left me a day out of Pooncarie, where I had a house to camp in and rest the kids. Cindy Barber, a daughter of a friend of Mum's (who I met once when we were about two years old), was travelling up with her partner to join me for a couple of weeks. It's funny how literally hundreds of people (friends and strangers) said they were going to ride with me, and they had all sorts of plans but hardly any people followed through. Initially I was a bit nervous with all these people inviting themselves along but could soon distinguish the committed ones from the 'wannabe dreamers'. I knew the first time I talked to Cindy over the phone, never really having met her (without wearing nappies), that she was coming no matter what. I rang to ask them to bring hay and waited at Pooncarie for them. Randy, Cindy's partner, was conscripted to leave a trail of hay bales for the first few hundred kilometres of his return trip home, at prearranged camps. It never occurred to me this would be a difficult task and, me being me, I just organised it all and told him what he was going to do, without actually consulting him about whether he could or would do it. I didn't quite realise what a sheltered city boy he was. Cindy grew up on a diary farm (even though she had been infected with city living for quite some time) and it didn't occur to me she would be going out with someone who had never driven more than 40 kilometres from a post office. I suspect he thought he was in the middle of the outback and he would be found as a chalky pile of sun-bleached bones at the bottom of a dry dam somewhere. On our first day we had a bale of hay waiting for us but we found out later that Randy had got completely bushed and was found by the property owner and shown where to put it. The second day he put the bale 1.3 kilometres from the dam, so after we set up camp I walked out to it, rigged up a harness and dragged it back. That was a huge day as it was. By the end of it my back was trashed and I was completely exhausted, but taking the hay to the water was a much better option than carting water to the hay. Good old Cindy did all the work around camp that day. On the third day the hay was only 100 metres away (even though it was on a different property) but took a bit to find. Getting closer though! On the fourth day the hay was right on target.

The first day with Cindy, as we walked out of Pooncarie, Gillie had an encounter with Piglet. After developing a healthy respect for the horses' back ends, Gillie would travel in front. Walking out of Pooncarie was a little too distracting, however, and Gillie was rubbernecking at all the town dogs. A particularly exciting looking bull mastiff cross was casting very loud threats as we passed and Gillie lingered a little too long. Piglet – refusing to give way to a dog – just stood on her paw, trapping it and, ignoring the high-pitched yelps of pain, ground it into the bitumen as she walked on. Poor Gillie, she was lucky she didn't break a bone. One of her pads had been screwed half off and she thought she was going to die. First day up, Cindy launched into action, assembled a makeshift platform out of rolled up jumpers and Drizabones and attached it to the front of her saddle, then perched the patient up there, where she travelled for the next few days. I felt sorry for Cindy but she never complained. Ambrose and I took Gillie sometimes but Ambrose would only tolerate so much before she objected strongly. I (and Gillie) was lucky that Cindy is an inventor (yes, that's what is written on her tax form) and had fashioned such a great rig for the saddle.

### Day 303, 21 April: Chibnalwood tank

*Cindy went really well today. She had Gillie on her lap most of the day. She works hard, is logical and starts doing stuff before I do. I only tell her once how something is done and she does it right every time after.*

*I am still bandaging Gillie's foot. She is such a girl's blouse about it. She puts on such a huge production. I don't think I could do it without Cindy pinning her down.*

*Tonight Stephen, Natalie and Jacqui (their daughter), who live on a property we went through today, came around to our camp, dropped off our hay, cooked us up a BBQ on the back of their farm ute, plied us with beer, donated money to Youth Off the Streets and then left. Really great and generous people, especially considering the way the drought seems to be battering them around. I admire people like these guys. They just keep trying and continue to be generous of spirit. I couldn't be a primary producer: too much hard work and gambling to end up stressed and in huge debt. I couldn't hack it, especially if I had a family relying on me.*

*S 33° 55' 30.6", E 143° 01' 05.3"   172 ft   27.0 km*
*Total: 5329.3 km*

**Low point:** *This morning the sheep and lambs were surrounding the water trough. I didn't want to risk mismothering any of them as some were only a day old, so we didn't get a morning drink till we got to Arumpo.*
**High point:** *Barbecue with Stephen and his family.*

Cindy rode Gumby most of the time. I think she fell in love with him and didn't want him to 'suffer' the pack saddle. She was continually frustrated, like anybody else who has ridden him, by his lackadaisical method of travelling until one day she discovered his secret. We would ride along and Gum would drop further and further back no matter how hard she kicked. When they were a fair way behind Cindy would yell out, 'Tell me another story'. What? She was 20 metres behind me. Was my storytelling that good? Apparently for Gum it was. Cindy had discovered that the best thing to get Gum moving and keep up with the rest was me, chatting away about, well, anything. As soon as I started talking Gum would pick up his stride and actually catch up to Ambrose, who was probably travelling sideways in protest at this point, and then walk beside us until the story was finished. Surely he had heard them all before.

I soon discovered Cindy was paranoid about slowing me down. On day six I thought something was up as she was getting around a bit stiffly but insisted she was fine. When she got off the horse that afternoon she landed on one leg and proceeded to walk in a ridiculous manner, desperately trying to look normal. My keen observation skills detected that one foot never went near the ground and after much enquiring, then insisting and finally threatening, she informed me she had a bit of sunburn. Her lower leg got sunburnt in the first couple of days because her pants rode up when she was on the horse. Apparently it had got worse, rather than better, and was a very bright red with quite significant pitting oedema. I couldn't believe she had got through the day without mentioning it. It looked so painful. I know I am only a vet but it looked like cellulitis to me (or is that just about my only human diagnosis?). So, after further threatening, I made her lie down with her leg in the air, force fed her Gillies' anti-inflammitory medication and antibiotics, and covered her leg in Traumeel gel (the horses' homeopathic ointment I used for their saddle sores). She was petrified I was going to insist on stopping the ride and getting her to a doctor. Finally, the only thing that would make her behave was when I told her that if she didn't rest and take the medications I was going to pull the pin then and there and go no further! She obeyed.

It took a few days for Cindy's leg to settle down and I am still sure she didn't let on half of how ill she was feeling. I am yet to be convinced that men can take anywhere near the pain that women can (that excludes me of course; I am hopeless with pain). I suppose they need to be pretty stoic to have babies and then to go back for more!

On Anzac Day we happened to camp at the Homebush pub. Phil, the publican was great. He had a serious history of fundraising for homeless youth so was really helpful. We got there in the afternoon, when the pub was pretty quiet. He suggested we wait till late in the night, when all the locals and loggers were blind drunk (as you are on Anzac Day) and then we should walk around and 'fleece them for all they're worth'. He was right. We made a bit of money for Youth Off the Streets that night. Later I found out Phil had told everybody they should come because a naked girl on a horse was going to ride through the pub. Lucky none of the drunkards ever demanded what he promised. I think they would have insisted on getting their money back!

Phil gave us some digs for the night, which was very generous, but I ended up sleeping outside because I wanted to keep an eye on the horses. I will take a drunken fool's money for homeless kids but I don't trust them with my horses.

We made it to Balranald the next day, just as it started raining. We stayed at the pony club grounds for two days, waiting for the rain to settle. It was strange because I was starting to get into home country. I had treated horses and done chiropractic talks at the Balranald Pony Club and I ran into a few clients as well as distant relations. I thought I knew the country pretty well. I had driven the roads between Balranald and home quite a bit with work, but it surprised me how different it appeared from the back of a horse. You are more aware of the subtle changes in soil and flora, always on the lookout for good feed, water and a good place to camp for the horses.

We camped at the Moulamein polocrosse grounds a few days' ride from home. In the morning we found Piglet very lame in the back end so I treated her with everything I had, but to little effect. It seemed silly camped so close to home, unable to go anywhere. After a few days I bit the bullet and decided to just float the kids home. It wasn't going to do Piglet any good walking the rest of the way and waiting for her to improve didn't make sense. I felt as if I was cheating. Maybe it is fitting that I didn't ride into home when my ride wasn't finished. Maybe it was only right to do that just once, at the very end.

I had one leg to go – Marlborough to home – but I wasn't looking forward to it. It was going to be the dullest and most populated leg and I was starting to lose motivation.

# 18

## On the downhill run

I was wary of getting 'bogged' at home again and spent May frantically organising the last leg. I decided to truck the horses north and then ride south, but doing this was going to be expensive. My savings were disappearing rapidly, which complicated things. In the end I came up with a pretty cunning plan, if I do say so myself.

---

Hi guys,

To answer some of your recent emails: 'Yes I am still alive, just been a bit slack.'

After I got home from riding in from Broken Hill way I then had a choice:

1. I could ride up the east coast starting in Victoria and freeze my butt off trying to get to the promised land (i.e. Qld where I had started) or

2. I could truck the horses north and ride south to Vic, hoping that, as I ventured south the warmer seasons would precede me.

The choice wasn't tough! I'm *so* not a fan of swagging it in the snow so I decided to truck north. The cost of trucking three horses, me, the dog and *all* my gear was mind boggling. So I did the only thing I could think of – I bought a truck for $3500, got my truck licence and drove us all up, 1800 kilometres at 70 kilometres per hour. Wacko! Once I got over the 21st-century syndrome of being stressed because I wasn't going fast enough, then it was quite relaxing just trundling along. I named the truck Tumbleweed because it really only wanted to roll along in the same direction as the wind. On day one I got a flat and on day two I got the radiator checked (I was going through a lot of coolant). On day three I was pulled over by the cops. Was I speeding? No! Apparently when you're driving an old truck that slowly, you must be drunk. The copper was startled to read 0.0. Her parting words were 'Good luck'. That evening I spent three unsuccessful hours trying to rig a pulley system to get the tailgate up because the ratchet was getting more and more unreliable with every use. On day four I managed to wind up the tailgate and at the next town I bought a set of wire strainers (not cheap, but cheaper than any block and tackle I could find) in case the tailgate wasn't going to work. Of course, on day five the tailgate worked because I had a back-up plan. Anyway, we made it to our destination and poor old Tumbleweed has been basically abandoned at a friend's place near Gladstone. So if anyone wants to buy a horse truck in Qld … going cheap. We had a few rest days to recover from the Tumbleweed experience and set off. So far we are going well (we being Gumby, Bart, Piglet, Gillie and me). What a well-oiled machine we make!

Hope everyone is well. Some good news that may cheer you up is that I should finish this craziness by the end of the year so no more annoying emails blocking up your inbox.

HiD

---

A long-lost friend from my Perth days was living with her husband near Rockhampton and offered to keep Tumbleweed till I finished the ride. We stayed at Anissa and Ed's place for a few days' rest and then they generously drove us to a camp spot on the Bicentennial National Trail where we could start up again. There was a gap from where Trina and I had set off back at the start of 2007 but by this stage I didn't care so much. I was starting to get bit over all this hard work and stress, and was not really looking forward to the last leg.

At the end of the first day we wearily pulled into the camp that the BNT guide recommended. It was a lovely setting near the clear flowing Kolan River, with plenty of feed right on the banks and shelter for me. However, there was something strange going on and I had a severe case of déjà vu. I finally worked it out: I had been there eighteen months before. That was the very camp I had planned to leave from originally, in January 2007 with Trina, but the river was dry as a chip at that time and there wasn't any feed. After that we drove north to set off in more hospitable country. It was strange seeing it so lush and alive after seeing it dry and bare and hot. It made me think about all my camps I had had in the past couple of years. I had camped at some great places, and some shockers. If I went back again, I realised, things would be very different. The great camps may now be dry as a chip and some spots I'd never even considered might now offer relative luxury. The country is always changing, not just with travel but with seasons and time. I realised that I could continue going around in endless circles, along the same path, and still see and experience so many different things.

As I travelled south through Queensland the country became more and more populated. I found myself following bitumen roads and getting more frustrated by traffic and towns. Often we were forced into thick, long grass on the side of busy roads, which meant slow going and picking grass seeds out of the gear that night for at least an hour or so. I wasn't having any fun and I wasn't seeing any interesting country. The more populated it got the less friendly the people and the crazier the drivers.

I was starting to struggle a bit. If it wasn't overpopulated bitumen roads, the country was rough and steep. The kids were getting tired and sore and I was battling a lack of motivation. If it wasn't raining, then the dew would wet everything anyway and the weather was getting colder. My gear was constantly wet, the horses were sore, the country was uninspiring and although we were on our last leg, there was a long way to go and it seemed never-ending. Despite being in Queensland I was well aware that the southwest corner could get pretty cold, and that was where I was heading.

### Day 337, 11 July: Bunya Hole, Mimi Creek

Big day today. Piglet was being good (for her), considering the heels of her back feet are bruised. I finally have to admit to myself her feet are an issue. Just because she keeps on walking doesn't mean there isn't a problem. From now on I will keep the easy boots on her the whole time and alternate Bart and Gum with the other set.

Bart didn't like the uphill work today. He kept stopping and refusing to move on. In the end I got off Gum in the middle of a very steep hill and had a 'quiet discussion' that involved one slap on the rump with the rope. Poor fellow, I could just about hear him saying, 'No, not the bum!' He knew it meant he had to pull up his socks and he was good for the rest of the day. But I am not silly; Bart is a bloody hard worker so he must be quite sore. I will give him a chiro later. I think his back feet are a bit tender, too. Maybe I will boot his back feet and Gum's front. That should get me through tomorrow, anyway. I wasn't expecting such rough country and really need another set, but they are such a pain to carry when they are not being worn.

Last night I heard a crash and the horses got a fright. I lay in the swag like a fat, lazy cow saying, 'Steady, steady' and they settled. I woke this morning to find a tree across the electric fence and it was flattened! Lucky the horses didn't have the courage to step over the electric tape. I had brand new 'first use' batteries draining through my electric fence all night. Ugh. I can still hear the electric whine but don't have the courage to test how flat they are. Nothing much I can do about it till I get to Nanango in a couple of days, anyway.

This morning was about 3°C and this arvo probably got to about 12°C. There was a foul wind (but still a thousand times better than the Barkly Breeze). It was too bloody cold for my liking. Hopefully tomorrow will be better.

S 26° 21' 53.1", E 152° 22' 03.0"   1292 ft   29.3 km
Total: 5969.9 km

*Low point:* Bart let his socks drop.

*High point:* Bart pulled his socks up once we had a little 'chat'.
P.S. Am constantly thinking, 'What the hell am I doing? I don't
want to do this; I hate the cold and the rain and that is where I
am heading. I need a motivation injection. I need Julia again!' God,
I am pathetic. Clear skies tonight so no rain but that means heavy
dew is a cert! Might as well rain!

I found it quite fascinating that, although I was in some highly populated areas, fewer people stopped for a chat. Everyone was busy on their own mission and either didn't have time or were not interested in talking to me. I was very happy about that; I found the people far less interesting and I was on my own mission to get home as soon as I could. However, when someone did stop for a chat, I found the evolution of the usual questions fascinating.

'Where are you heading to?' Beetlejuice.

'So, did you have fun?' Yep, laughs a-plenty here!

'Are you going to write a book?' Of course! Gotta pay those debts off somehow. I thought I would call it the *Hitchrider's Guide to Australia*.

'Have you discovered the answer to life, the universe and everything?' Sure have, but the last person who did died (at the hands of a Vogon constructor fleet that were getting ready to build a hyperspace express route) just before she could get to a phone to tell someone. I'm not tellin' no-one. I'm not takin' the chance!

'Would you do it again?' God forbid! Why the zarking fardwarks would I do that?

'What are you going to do when you get back?' I thought I might try to advance my professional synchronised swimming career.

'Will you be able to go back to work?' If my togs still fit me.

### Day 339, 13 July: Nanango
*Was supposed to be two days to Nanango but came across a sign
saying 'Nanango: 30 km' so took that route. Even if I didn't make
it in that one day I would have been happy as I missed all those
bloody hills; all that steep rocky shit knocks the horses about. And,
anyway, I made it all the way. Yeah!*

The caretaker at the showgrounds is a grumpy old bugger. I felt like shaking him and saying, 'Bloody hell! Enjoy life while you can — it's not going to get any better unless you do!' (Maybe I should take my own advice.) Two minutes into our conversation he was complaining about some person who has something to do with the grounds. Three minutes into the conversation he was telling me how many millions of dollars of equipment is his (even though it belongs to the show societies, not him) and four minutes into the conversation he was telling me I could use his disabled toilet to shower/toilet. He locks the place up at 6 pm — it was a huge favour and ordeal to leave the gate dummy locked for me so I could go and buy a feed!

Anyway, the day was a pretty big one. The last 7 km was beside the highway but not too bad because there were remnants of the old road on the eastern side. The kids were pretty good, actually. Halfway through the day I took off Piglet's front boots and stuck them on Gum's back feet.

At about 4 pm we launched through some tall bushes and I got showered in some star-type prickles. I don't know what they are but they are a bastard — they explode on contact and get a really good grip on you. They are relatively easy to remove straightaway but the longer they have been there the more they break up and make themselves at home in your clothes and gear. I got covered, and then it started to rain ... I didn't want to put on my Drizabone and get the prickles in the lining. It rained heavier and heavier and I finally gave up, resigned to having to spend hours getting them out later.

Ugh! Rain, prickles, sunset approaching, busy highway, huge day... throw in a little foot binding and you've got the lot!

S 26° 40' 18.1", E 151° 59' 27.9"   1218 ft   40.5 km
Total: 6032.1 km

**Low point:** The whole rain/prickle episode.
**High point:** Made it to Nanango. Yeah!

I stayed at Nanango for three days, mainly to give Piglet a good rest. Not that it did much good in the end. The showgrounds were a couple of kilometres from town so I spent a fair bit of time walking in and out, restocking my gear, doing my laundry etc. I collected the maps Mum sent me and tried to plot out my next leg. I found myself pretty keen to head inland. I was sick of trashing the horses and, basically, I'm a flat country girl. I love being able to see an endless horizon and I was starting to feel a bit trapped by mountains and population.

I spoke to Trina on the phone and before I said anything she said I should think about getting off the BNT and heading inland. She said she thought I would get home earlier, it would be easier on the horses and that the mountains were making me claustrophobic. When did she get so insightful? Thanks Trina. The question now was, where would I get off the BNT and go back to working out my own path? If I headed west in Queensland I would have to go all the way around Toowoomba and that seemed to pose many more problems. I worked out I would start to head west once I got into New South Wales. Then the going would be much better and it should only be about three months home from there.

I was getting sick of rest days. I just wanted to get going. I thought the weather might get better and more predictable once I headed west. Rest days were often associated with a sore back/neck, bad headaches, gut doughyness and anxiety over weather, temperature and the future route. At least while in town I got to catch up on my bulk letters and web entries.

---

Hi guys,

You know, people ask me all the time if I get bored and lonely being on my own. When I tell them I am not alone but with Gumby the Machine, Barty Butt Cheeks, Piglet and the Gillie Monster they seem to look at me strangely and edge away, mumbling to themselves. I don't really understand what their problem is – that is a reasonable and logical answer, surely.

I have talked a lot about my horses but not really about Gillie, my kelpie. She is a constant source of amusement, joy, frustration, anger, bewilderment and 'what the'. She is a maniac, a dachshund, a freak, a meerkat, a nutter, a comedian, a mad scientist, an ADHD child and the smartest and hardest dog I have ever trained. Don't get me wrong: she is certainly not trained yet. She is tough work and a continual challenge, to put it politely, but if I survive her training (and that is a big 'if'), she will be the smartest dog ever. Gillie has an amazing habit of standing on her back legs. If she wants to see over long grass, or a fence or table, she simply rises up on her back legs, front paws folded neatly over themselves, and stands there perfectly balanced. I have timed her at 25 seconds before she has gone back to all fours and was reminded of those meerkat documentaries. She can see all sorts of things most dogs can't: she watches aircraft fly overhead like any other aviation nerd, she sees small strips of paper caught in the very tops of thick trees, she sees her own reflection very easily and rather than trying to play with it or talk to it she seems to innately recognise it as herself. When Gillie first started travelling with me it was open country south of Broken Hill and when a car was coming (could see them from 5 km away) I would get off the horse and call her and hold her till they passed. She had a propensity to chase cars. Now, in hilly windy country often I don't know a car is there until it is as close as 50 m away. But Gillie has learnt when cars come she has to come and stand with the horses. So often Gillie will come racing back to me and stand in front of me long before I can see or hear the car – she is my car alarm. I think she would also make a great bird dog. She trots along past long grass and for no apparent reason will stop and stare at some bush, with one front foot lifted, and then suddenly launch vertically, somehow change her direction to horizontal then land straight down on the patch with birds flying out in all directions. I'm sure I can hear her laughing as she trots away.

She really is one high-maintenance chick. She already has several names: Gillie, Gillie Weed, Gillie Water, Pinocchio, Dashy, Point Dog and Gillie Monster. Without a doubt, if I am there at the end, she will be a ripper of a dog – I just have to survive. Until then, the amusement she supplies by far outweighs the anguish.

HiD

---

16 July 2008

Hi guys,

Well I woke up this morning thinking I had been teleported to hell. Before I even opened my eyes I heard this insistent, repetitive call that nagged in the back of my mind and made me all too afraid to open my eyes in case it was true. 'Mum … Mum … Mum … Muuuuum!' Oh my God it's all a dream and I did the expected: married, kids, ball and chain, ball and chain, ball and chain! Aargh!

Then my eyes sprung open and it was all a nightmare. I was safely tucked in my swag with no-one but three horses and a dog relying on me.

But what was that horrific noise?

I didn't find out till this evening when they started nagging again. It is some sort of duck thing (sorry, not good with birds, just ask all the vet nurses I have ever worked with – especially at Kangaroo Flat vets and they, I am sure, are discreet enough not to mention 'the episode'). It's a light grey duck with a brown head and a couple of black stripes down the back. Now I am sure that many of you are thinking 'Oh for God's sake, can't she even recognise a such and such duck?' Well, no, I can't. And now I have renamed it 'the nagging, spoilt child duck'. (I apologise to a brother-in-law who will be shaking his head at my ignorance of the avian variety at this point). Anyway, the point of the matter is that life could be worse. I have been struggling a bit lately and I think those ducks put it all into perspective and I'm pretty glad where I am.

So where am I? I am out west of Brisbane at the moment. When you travel with mud maps and 1:100 000 topographic maps you know exactly where you are, but really, you could be anywhere. For instance, the other day I camped on the western banks of Mimi Creek at a water hole just before it turns southeast but I could have been in France (except no-one had a French accent). The other day I thought I could hear an awful lot of air traffic and it wasn't till I looked on a bigger scale map and realised I was not much more than an hour out of Brisbane. I knew I seemed to come across an awful lot of hobby farmers, 'blockies' (the local name for people who buy their dream 5 acres) and hippies, but I just didn't realise how close I was to the major populations. Maybe it's denial.

The kids are going well. The horses have to work so much harder in the mountains. I am not so much here to stargaze and rubberneck but am here to travel and get somewhere. So the mountains are starting to frustrate me. They knock my horses about and make them work so much harder and walk further than if we were in the parallel flat country. I loved the further out country; the outback and real rural people are always so generous and interesting. I am considering heading inland once I cross the New South Wales border, then turning south parallel to my original track. I know my horses will be only too happy if we do.

I was aware we just passed the shortest day of the year (ever hopeful of improving weather) and noticed the rapid change in sunrise. In a matter of one week the sun was rising half an hour earlier (which I was very excited about) but I also noticed the sun seemed to be setting a bit earlier as well. How depressing! Funny how I haven't noticed this before, in other years. After another week, I finally realised my gor-rammed watch was slow. How stupid did I feel, lying in my swag in the dark at '5 pm' feeling so proud for being so organised. Oh well. I will just have to be a bit more patient like I was all those other years!

HiD

---

The further south we got the worse Piglet's feet got. It was starting to give her a sore back as well. I could do a chiro but the cause (the poor gait due to the sore feet) was still there so that wouldn't do much good. I padded and booted all four feet but she was still not entirely happy. I couldn't really work out what I was doing wrong. Bart's and Gum's feet were fine. Piglet's feet wanted to grow in a strange manner and I was constantly 'managing' them.

I considered sending Piglet home and just travelling home with one pack horse. That would work for just short trips but I still had months to go that involved the possibility of snow, fences without gates, insect plagues, days of 45 degrees and rough country. I still needed all my gear for any circumstance or environment.

Despite only two easy, short days into Blackbutt, after resting in Nanango, Piglet was sore again. I had to be serious about getting her better. I gave the kids six days' rest at Blackbutt and threw everything I could at Piglet. I did her feet, chiro, anti-inflammatories, acupuncture, massage, homeopathy, adjusted the saddle fit and I even gave prayer a whirl. Obviously I was desperate. But the biggest thing I was relying on was basic rest. I really think that was what her feet needed, but deep down I knew it wasn't long enough. We took two days to get to Crows Nest but by the first morning I knew I had to do something as Piglet couldn't go on like that. We walked into Crows Nest, freshly sprayed for ticks, just as big black clouds rolled in, signalling the start of some bitterly cold weather; it was even sleeting just to the south, in Toowoomba. I had to decide what to do and, as always seems to happen, opportunity came unexpectedly knocking on my door.

# 19

## The new crew

The first morning in Crows Nest I had an interview with Toowoomba ABC Radio. It was the stock standard interview with the usual questions.

'Where are you heading to?' Straight for home.

'So, did you have fun?' As much as you can with your pants on.

'Are you going to write a book?' Not in this lifetime.

'Have you discovered the answer to life, the universe and everything?' Not in this lifetime.

'Would you do it again?' Not in this lifetime.

'What are you going to do when you get back?' Go back to life.

'Will you be able to go back to work?' That's part of life, isn't it?

### Day 353, 28 July: Crows Nest

*Zarking freezing! It poured with rain last night. Thank God (or whoever) I was under shelter in a shed here at the showgrounds.*

*I had an interview at 6.40 am (there went my sleep-in!) with the local ABC radio. I had to stand outside (the reception was poor in my shed) and the weather was freezing, with wild wind and rain. To top it off two ugly dogs came visiting and threatened to piss on my gear and pick a fight with Gillie, inside my accommodation. There I was, being interviewed live on radio in the rain and wind, with poor reception and two local grubs trying to mug my puppy and claim my gear! Anyway, the nightmare finished and I somehow managed to keep my dog in one piece, my gear dry and the interview uninterrupted and without me swearing wildly down the phone shouting something totally inappropriate like 'Git outta it, ya mongrels'.*

*Immediately after the interview I got a message on my phone to ring some old bloke who wanted to give me his horse for free. Nice strangers. However, it turned out it was a ten-year-old thoroughbred that had not been ridden for eight years and was retired from racing because he was a 'good bucker'. Yeah ... no thanks.*

*I had more visitors today, apart from the two early morning invaders. Firstly, Derek from the DPI came to sort paperwork, then Shane from the showgrounds committee came and started up the hot water for a shower, and then Sheryl from the show society came to drop me off down the street. I was then interviewed over the phone by Jim from the* Toowoomba Chronicle *and over some steaming bacon and eggs by Craig from the* Crows Nest Advertiser.

*Later this afternoon I had Robyn come and visit me. She said she heard my radio interview and popped in to offer her horse — for free. Robyn has done a lot of packing with donkeys and horses and thinks she has just about hung up her pack bags. Argee is a quarter horse gelding and is an old pro at this sort of work. Wow! Talk about unexpected opportunities come a-knocking. I am going with Robyn to Helen's place, her friend, for dinner tomorrow night. Busy day meeting strangers and in interviews etc. I feel a bit like Paris Hilton — all this attention for no apparent reason.*

*S 27° 15' 27.6", E 152° 22' 45.7"   1802 ft   28.6 km*
*Total: 6026.4 km*

**Low point:** *Having to stand out in the early morning freezing rain for a radio interview. I hate radio interviews.*
**High point:** *Robyn and her generous offer.*

I decided to take Robyn up on her offer. Argee was a big, doughy tub of lard (but only about 14.2 hands high, so not too tall for the pack) and I knew he was going to be easy to just slot in; he would get on well with the boys and, well, Piglet doesn't get on well with anyone!

I rang Darrall Clifford for advice, a brilliant farrier who lived somewhere south of Brisbane and whom I'd met at animal chiropractic workshops.

Before I knew it he said he would drive out to see my kids at the end of August. I couldn't have hoped for better guidance with Piglet and her issues. I found a paddock to leave my kids in for a few weeks and on 3 August Gillie and I hitched a ride with a truckie to Brisbane and we flew home. I wanted to give Piglet every opportunity to recover and the rest would do them all wonders. We were going well time wise, and we would still be on track to get home before Christmas.

After a few weeks at home, Gillie and I flew back to Rockhampton and stayed with Anissa and Ed. We were there for a couple of days till I got Tumbleweed back up and running. The whole time, Anissa kept telling me about a great friend of hers called Fred and how she wanted to introduce us because we would make a 'great couple'. People always find the need to pair me up. I think it worries them to see a single woman, especially one who is apparently coping without a man, and they think they have to do something about it. It went through my mind later that this poor Fred guy was probably getting the same harassment from Anissa that I was getting. Well, he was safe: he was further north so I told her he would have to wait for another opportunity because I was heading south.

Gillie and I drove Tumbleweed back down to Crows Nest and I left it on a property just out of town. Darrall came and did all four horses' feet. He told me where I was going right (Bart and Gumby) and where I was going wrong (Piglet). It was as I suspected: I had been trimming Piglet's feet but rather than helping her problems, I was probably creating them. However, I got a great demonstration of what I needed to do with her. Because I was sick of managing the horses' feet in such rough country, and because Argee's feet were soft, I decided to shoe them with Easywalker shoes. These are a synthetic shoe that would not 'weaken' the strong bare feet I had nurtured as much as metal shoes would. I decided that by the time these shoes needed to be replaced we would be in better country and they could go barefoot again. Darrall spent all day doing my horses. By afternoon we had a quiet drink in the pub and I was trying to get out of him how much I owed him. The Easywalkers were not cheap, he had driven a total of about four hours plus he had given up a whole day just for me and the kids. He refused any money, which left me feeling guilty, bad, tongue tied and incredibly grateful.

When I arrived at Crows Nest I discovered Jan, Helen's sister, had organised a fundraiser for Youth Off the Streets in the form of a school kids disco. It was great to see basic strangers working so hard to raise money for my charity. I did a talk at the school, trying to drum up interest, and the night ended up a huge success with kids asking when the next one would be.

Argee was looking like he was going to be a winner so I decided to leave Piglet with Tumbleweed, under Robyn's care, and come back after my ride finished to take them both home. On 7 September we set off from Crows Nest, heading south. Robyn came with us for a couple of days. I think she wanted one last walk with Argee as she was quite sad he was going. It was great travelling with another 'professional' packer. We had such different ideas and methods. It made me realise how I had become so driven to get to my destination and how I should maybe stop and smell the roses every now and then.

### Day 363, 10 September: Steele Rudd reserve
*I'm just loving the shod horses (don't tell anyone). Sooo much easier now. All I do is pick out their feet twice a day; no struggling to put on twelve boots on a frosty morning, no struggling to take them off when I'm knackered, no time-consuming management of rubs, chaffs, etc. and no washing of boots in the dark when I'd rather be in bed. Yeehah! I love shoes. Today was great again — but getting a bit boring really because it is so relaxing without Piglet. I really enjoy not yelling 'Piglet' all the time. We all just trundle along and the only yelling I do is at Gillie. Argee has slotted in well with Gumby and Bart — they all just cruise along. My boys!*

*S 27° 47' 09.2", E 151° 57' 43.8"   1843 ft   25.0 km*
*Total: 6107.8 km*

**Low point:** *Dad texted me a weather report. Looks like rain on Saturday and big rain on Sunday.*
**High point:** *Still revelling in the cruisey joys of my three boys.*

Penni (my sister) and Tim (her husband) were in Brisbane and I was looking forward to them coming out to visit me somewhere on the road. Meanwhile, we walked pretty well straight to Killarney, straying off the BNT, which seemed determined to keep us travelling on busy bitumen roads. As much as I loved Piglet, travelling without her was so much easier. I decided that she alone was the equivalent of three horses in relation to hard work and constant management. We made it in good time to Killarney, strolling into the showgrounds on Saturday afternoon, straight into the annual rodeo.

---

Hi guys,

Well, I think it is safe to say I don't make much of a 'cowgirl'. I had two big days to make it to Killarney, Qld, because thunderstorms were forecast. So I made a beeline for the Killarney showgrounds and the promise of shelter. When I got there I discovered I was to join hundreds of other people in the middle of a rodeo. I've never been to a rodeo before and I must say it is a once in a lifetime experience … and I kinda hope *once* in a lifetime. I think it was the continual loud American country music that really did it for me. I mean, please – I so want to hear *The Devil Went Down to Georgia* just one more time as I think that would make it an even 50! And what on Earth are you doing when you 'put cakes on the griddle' anyway? Only a country music singer could bang on and on about how the love of his life shouldn't drink tonight 'cause the liquor makes her lose her clothes … *Well just dump her and move on! Don't blame the grog – she's a harlot!*

I know it's hard to believe but when I walked in – two pack horses, riding horse and kelpie in tow – everyone was staring. I don't think it had anything to do with the fact that I hadn't had a shower for two weeks. Maybe they were really impressed by my short, fat, non-athletic looking ponies – or maybe not, since most of them seemed to have one of their own (i.e. quarter horses). Maybe they were fascinated by my hat that curled down at the front and back, compared to theirs that curled up at the sides like a leaf in a bushfire. I can't believe they haven't discovered that shape for themselves. How do they put up with getting sunburnt ears and neck? Or maybe they were fascinated with my belt with it's unobtrusive buckle rather than a spangly aluminium pie plate the size of a hub cap that they seem to all wear. And how do they bend down without slicing themselves in two anyway? No, I think they were just stunned by the sight of me because I was yet more proof of how people would do anything to get to a rodeo!

All night I had to listen to (over the top of Kenny advising me when was best to hold 'em and when was best to fold 'em) a fake American accent commentate the proceedings, calling everyone cowboys and cowgirls. Why does this sport attract such American wannabes? But, by 2 am the good old Aussie spirit had won over and those that could stand were blind, thanks to XXXX and Bundy Rum cans. The good thing about the rodeo was, I think, my horses looked at what life could be for them and they decided their lot wasn't so bad after all.

So, we are at Killarney. It is a really nice little town and we will spend a couple of rest days here before heading for the New South Wales border. It's very exciting – my last border crossing. It's great to be back on the road and I'm looking forward to the rest of my ride (especially now the weather is improving).

So this camp has been an educational experience, for I now know how to pronounce ro-*deee*-o correctly, as well as knowing when to hold 'em, when to fold ' em, when to walk away and especially when to run. I can't believe I had to walk nearly 7000 km to learn those vital lessons.

HiD

Pen and Tim caught up with me at the Killarney showgrounds. Yet again I had visitors when I wasn't actually travelling. Penni is my champagne buddy and brought some Bollinger with her; needless to say, we had a great night. The next day I left Killarney and crossed the New South Wales border at Cullendore. Pen and Tim caught up with me again and helped out with my camp. We had to 'steal' rainwater from an empty house and cart it across the road to the kids so I was pretty glad for the extra pairs of hands. Tim cooked up a barbecue treat and Pen and I reintroduced ourselves to the French champagne. Life couldn't get much better. They left me at camp that night armed with a couple of Moët stubbies to take with me for the next few days. I am quite sure the French oenologist did not have in mind that his petite champagne would be drunk warm let alone described as a 'stubby'. Oh well. I have insulted the French before and no doubt will again.

We headed south through New South Wales fairly uneventfully, and rested at Tenterfield for a few days, where I had that stupid song in my head the whole time. I only knew three words (… the Tenterfield saddler …) and didn't even know the tune so it was really driving me crazy. Coming into town I stopped a guy in a ute called Duncan and asked directions to the showgrounds. He seemed very pleasant and the next day caught up with me and said his girlfriend wanted to invite me to dinner. He picked me up later (they lived just on the edge of town) and when we got to his place he told me the girlfriend had had to leave town unexpectedly. What! So he cooked me dinner then proceeded to chase me around the house. When I said 'no' he replied with, 'Oh, I know what that means' and continued to pursue me. I must admit that sent a shiver up my spine. What a narcissistic git! I finally managed to persuade him to drop me back at the showgrounds where he then proceeded to chase me around the horse yards. What is it about a woman running away from you, screaming obscenities and abuse and threatening to call the police, that gives you the idea that she 'wants you bad'. Give me dying of thirst in the desert with scouring camels any day! Later I found out that Duncan's behaviour was not out of character. He kept ringing me from various phone numbers and I would hang up as soon as I heard it was him, but he was pretty slow on the uptake and he continued for a couple of months. Talk about make my skin crawl.

We managed to escape Tenterfield and travelled southwest through Inverell, Bundarra, Gunnedah, Mendooran, Narromine, Tullamore and Condobolin. The kilometres rolled into one and the ride was becoming quite uneventful and my journal entries were getting quite uninspiring. One day I decided I could just about write one entry that would summarise all my days.

### A day on the road

*05.10: Wake fifteen minutes before sunrise. Every morning when camping outside, my bowels start yelling at me urgently in the predawn moments. The Chinese know their stuff: the large intestine meridian is at its peak between 5 am and 7 am according to their horary clock.*

*05.14: Take the shovel for a walk.*

*05.20: Dismantle and pack up camp.*

*05.55: Organise horses; get them brushed and rubbed down, feet picked out, bells turned off and hobbles around their neck.*

*06.15: Roll up electric fence (I hate the electric fence) and pack away in bags. Pull up posts and pack away in carrying tube.*

*06.35: Saddle Gum – including saddle bags etc.*

*06.42: Saddle Bart and Argee and tighten their girths. Put tail tie in Argee's tail.*

*06.55: Load up Argee with two pack bags, shovel, fence posts, canvas buckets.*

*07.10: Load up Bart with two pack bags, swag and solar panel on top.*

*07.20: Tie a lead rope around each horse's neck with a hangman's noose and attach Bart to Argee's tail tie.*

*07.25: Put GPS on wrist and turn on, put on hat and let's go!*

*While walking I eat brekky (100 g cashews), take some vitamins and check for phone reception. I clean my teeth while* riding (toothbrush and toothpaste live in my saddlebags), spitting while leaning off Gumby. If I come across good food I will stop and let the horses pick for ten minutes or so. I do lots of staring at maps and unnecessary navigation and sometimes listen to my iPod (depending on my mood and battery power availability). I eat my lunch (100 g mixed fruit and nuts plus five dried apricots).

14.30 (approx.): Stop at camp. I find it hard to be decisive on the location of the camp as well as the position of the electric fence. I need to actually be sitting on the horse to make any sort of positive evaluation of the potential camp — bloody stupid, really. Sometimes I get to camp while walking and I get on Gum so I can make a decision. I am looking for water, lots of grass but easy to get around with the hobbles, places/trees to tie my hoochie to and hopefully somewhere flat to roll out my swag. I don't like camping near a road but sometimes have no choice.

14.40: Tie horses and Gillie up. I pull Gum's saddle and bridle off first otherwise he rubs against the tree and wrecks all my gear. Unload Bart and Argee and then take their saddles off.

14.50: Hobble all the kids and let them graze while I organise their water.

15.00: Put up electric fence and put Bart and Argee in.

15.20: Put up hoochie — this is a work of art! I have to take into account trees, position, height, ground cover, weather etc. Every camp is different and a new creation.

15.35: Lay down ground sheet underneath hoochie and then put all the gear on it to protect from rain or dew. Set up the swag and Gillie's bed.

15.45: Restock the next day's essentials into Gums saddlebags — water bottles, Gatorade, lunch, brekky and the relevant maps.

15.55: Collect water for the horses and set up their buckets.

16.10: Put thongs on. My feet are usually hot and swollen and sometimes I soak them later in the day if I have enough spare water. Feed Gillie.

*16.15: Cut grass away from the electric fence to stop it earthing and turn it on.*

*16.25: Pull off any easy boots and pick out horses' feet. Brush/rub them down and wash any sweat off with a bucket and wet towel. Treat any rubs or sores. Give the kids their electrolytes.*

*16.35: Wash the easy boots.*

*16.45: Have a few minutes resting and staring at nothing.*

*16.47: Set up kitchen and cook and eat dinner and have a cup of tea ... yeah! (Don't forget the dishes.)*

*17.15: Pack away the kitchen.*

*17.25: Write in journal and work out next day's route.*

*17.35: Put Gum in the yard and check their waters.*

*17.45: Do any repairs.*

*17.55: Have a tub in about 800 ml of water (feel much better now!).*

*18.10: Clean teeth and one last check of camp.*

*18.15: Bed. Read till sunset then sleep like a dead person.*

*What a thrilling life I lead!*

For the first time I was starting to see the end of the road. Not literally, of course – my eyesight is not that good. I was actually starting to believe I could, and would, finish. I had less than a thousand kilometres to go and I was now counting the time left in weeks. However, things started to really drag. It was so close yet so far. Julia, who rarely rang, made a timely random call and said she would come and ride with me the rest of the way. This time we only had one riding horse. I was walking half the time anyway, but it just meant poor old Gum had to carry a weight all day. I suppose that was only fair as Bart and Argee were already doing that. I made a beeline for Condobolin where we had agreed to meet and for the first time in a long while I was looking forward to my travel, not just my destination.

# I'll have an 'H' for homeward bound, thanks Glen

I immediately felt the effects of Julia's presence. We met just out of Condobolin and the very next morning I was feeling a bit dodgy. I blame her completely. We stayed there for a couple of days organising the next leg, finding somewhere for Fizzy (Julia's car) to live and waiting for the weather to pass. Julia would launch on any local she passed.

'Do you know Shannon Noll?' she would ask.

I had forgotten her obsession with famous people. I caught up on all the gossip. Brad and Angelina had just had twins; I think that made it a neat 32 kids, so far. Jen had broken up with John but there were suspicions that they would get back together. Apparently Paris had just released another song and video clip. How much can one woman embarrass herself worldwide? Surely she has paid advisors!

While in 'Condo' we noted there were two local papers. According to the locals, an elderly lady ran the original one for a hundred years or so and it was always just a four-page spread. In recent times demand had increased but she refused to get bigger, stating 'the netball results can wait till next week'. Finally some locals had had enough and started up another paper. Julia thought it fascinating that a 90-year-old lady with Alzheimer's might have been running the local paper and couldn't decide whether to call it *The Senile Times* or *The Dementia Daily*. We would be walking along the trail and out of the blue she would burst out laughing and announce something like: 'The other day I was looking through *The Senile Times* and all four pages were blank.'

**Day 437, 23 November: Ungarie showgrounds, rest day**
*Great showgrounds, nice little town, good people; thank God*
*(or whoever) because we have been stuck here for four days.*
*The weather here is shocking. There is a wild, cold wind and it is*
*apparently snowing at Orange.*

We met Pete the publican who takes the world very seriously, Georgia the gossip who cooks up a mean hamburger with the lot for $5.50, Michael the man-whore who is gor-rammed cute, Brooke in the bar with the tits she is happy to show anyone, Sydney the Salvo who is holier than thou, Derek the drunk who thinks cricket is a form of football, Cassie the cook who smokes Longbeaches like she's eating them and Barry in the bar who just has to be a woman. All great people.

The op shop supporting the local youth here is huge. Not sure how many customers it would get but Julia and I went on a spending spree. We bought Pride and Prejudice at the bargain basement price of 50 cents. We were pretty proud of ourselves until we saw the original RRP printed on it was 45 cents. It was printed in 1962 so I figure it must be American currency. Still, we now feel a bit ripped off as it was second-hand. Apparently it is my job to read it out loud at night. Julia still hasn't invested in any glasses.

Quote for the day: 'Dogs don't bite children, especially heelers.' Julia thought that one would have been good for The Senile Times.

S 33° 38' 09.3", E 146° 58' 46.7"    767 ft    0.0 km
Total: 7279.0 km
**Low point:** The weather — it's November! It's supposed to be better than this.
**High point:** $4 a head all-you-can-eat brekky buffet at the club.

Once I had got into the more populated areas I sent my rifle home. If I needed to euthanase a horse I am sure I could have found someone around with a weapon of some sort, and I was a bit nervous carrying it around for all to see. I still carried the leather scabbard, though, which was useful for dropping long skinny things in, and was also a bit of a deterrent for the Ivans of the world. If anyone asked what sort of gun I was carrying, Julia used to say it was an air rifle that I got on mail order out of *The Senile Times*.

Locusts were building up and the poor old horses were sick of them. As we walked, a cloud of insects in front of us would rise to head height and collide with us. Gum hated them and would walk with his head cocked to one side. I am not sure why because it only served to increase the surface he exposed to their flight path. Julia suggested we shoot the pests down with our air rifle.

I started reading *Pride and Prejudice* aloud at camp. One night we decided that for a full 24 hours we would speak only in the style of Jane Austen. Of course I was hopeless and finally just resorted to minimal talk with grunts and gestures, more like the language of the Neanderthal. Julia, on the other hand, had found her true calling and I spent the whole day either laughing or having no idea what she was saying, or both. A couple of people stopped for a chat that day but they didn't hang around long and seemed to look a little confused for some reason.

'Where are you heading to?' Far yonder from whence we came.

'So, did you have fun?' Indeed I did not. A scheme of which every part promises delight can never be successful and the general disappointment is only warded off by the defence of some little peculiar vexation.

'Are you going to write a book?' If I was so fortunate as to be able to display such penmanship, I should have great pleasure, I am sure, in obliging for I consider literature an innocent diversion.

'Have you discovered the answer to life, the universe and everything?' Good heavens, in vain I have struggled. Our importance, our respectability in the world must be affected by the wild volatility, the assurance and disdain of all restraint which mark our impulse.

'Would you do it again?' We are charmingly grouped and appear to uncommon advantage; however, the picturesque would be spoilt by admitting a further outing.

'What are you going to do when you get back?' My charges give me little trouble and are a very great favourite with many acquaintances. They shall be received with good grace to retirement.

'Will you be able to go back to work?' In matters of great weight, I may suffer from the want of money. I fear I must resume my office.

One night we camped at the Aramak silos. Aramak (which is its stage name) is a tiny little 'town' that consists of basically just grain silos on a railway line and about fifteen houses. It was pretty good because we had plenty of food, water on tap and shelter overhead. Julia went off knocking on doors looking for a beer and came back about two hours later and announced: 'This place is as rough as hessian undies!' Apparently, Aramak was where they found a baby that had cockroaches in its nappy which had to be surgically removed! Also, a guy was stabbed 28 times by five people, had his penis cut off and shoved in his mouth, then tied to the railway tracks at the very silos we were camped at (I'm sure that story hasn't been exaggerated over time!). The train stopped in time but Julia said she thought he died anyway. There had been a murder in one of the houses and another harboured a huge marijuana crop. The fellow that told Julia this, and gave her a few stubbies, then rounded the conversation off by revealing to her that he had a few rifles but no gun licence. It was a scary, feral town and the banjo music was deafening. We didn't get much sleep and spent all night waiting for an angry, penis-less spirit to come visiting. However, we conceded that would have been better than if one of the locals dropped by.

We struck a fair bit of rain and wind and I think Julia was a little stunned at the rain paranoia I had developed. I remember one night, sleeping in the wild wind with the doona tucked tight under my arms but that didn't stop it from raising off my body and flapping about like a flag. I am sure if I'd let go I would never have seen it again. In the end I had to zip my swag right up to stop me losing my bedding.

We stopped at Narrandera for a few days' rest. Dad and Penni drove up with Ambrose in the float so we had a riding horse each. Luxury! Julia had developed some really nasty blisters on the underside of her toes (very strange) but never complained, so I was glad she didn't have to walk any more. It was strange when Dad and Penni 'popped in'. I was still on my ride and I was used to being a long way from home. It struck me just how close we were – only a few hundred kilometres to go.

On our last day in Narrandera I fell over on the bitumen and gouged a great hole in my left knee. It's dangerous to walk down the street in the dark while texting! Bloody gutter, it suddenly appeared out of nowhere. Julia lost the plot completely and laughed hysterically for the entire five minutes I was rolling on the road swearing in excruciating pain. I had to wear a bandage on my knee for the rest of the trip and to this day I still have an ugly scar. I tell people I got it as I was wrestling a pack of wild dingoes on the Canning. Sounds much more impressive than 'I had a fall when I didn't see the gutter'. For about a week I couldn't bend my knee so had to get on Ambrose on the off side.

It was a really strange feeling, riding closer and closer to home. I was travelling through country I knew quite well and if I could describe it in one word I would have to say it was an anticlimax. The last couple of years, or even the last four years, had been leading up to this one day: riding through the gates at Brigadoon. One of the things I had been looking forward to was riding to the Conargo pub. I had all these wild ideas about riding into the pub and ordering a beer from the back of a horse, but as reality struck we walked into the tiny town, tired and gritty and smelly and windblown and keen to feed and water the horses, so we ended up walking straight past the pub and setting up camp. When we were a little more clean and motivated we walked across the road for a feed and water ourselves.

### Day 451, 7 December: Conargo

*I am so over this bloody wind! The horses got a belly full last night so that was good, but I didn't get much sleep. It was so windy I thought we were going to wake up buried in sand. Was windy all day but good now — I think it is quite sheltered here. We were going to ride into the Conargo pub with the Morundah pub sticker ( a rival pub further north) on Bart's butt as well as plastic pistols on our hips ... well, it was funny at the time when we bought them in the $2 shop at Narrandera. We seemed to lose motivation (as well as coming to our senses) and didn't bother. The horses are camped at the saleyards and we are in the sports ground next door.*

*I nearly died today (nothing like being a bit dramatic). I was walking and leading Ambrose while blowing my nose and all of a sudden a snake rose up and struck at me. It was so quick I am not even sure what it was — a brown snake maybe? Anyway, as it passed between my legs it was at a height above my socks (I was wearing shorts so had bare skin exposed, eeek!). I did that ridiculous snake yell I am so good at, accompanied with my Fred Flintstone shuffle. He was angry and active and didn't appreciate our presence at all and disappeared through Ambrose's front legs and into the grass.*

*We went across the road to the Conargo pub and got the 'Pauline experience'. We were having a quiet drink outside the pub and Pauline, a regular, came and introduced herself. Julia summed her up as 'rough as hessian undies with the language of a wheelie bin'. But she was certainly entertaining. The Conargo pub itself was a bit disappointing (decor and thus atmosphere was a bit ordinary) but the toilets and showers were great — an old woolshed building decked out in timber and gal. Julia and I were tempted to go out there and drink, to soak up the atmosphere.*

*Pen drove out and stayed for a few drinks then drove home. She too got the Pauline experience — she said it was a real treat! It is really weird being so close that Pen can just 'pop out' for a drink. Only three days to go. It's all a bit flat really.*

*S 35° 18' 15.7", E 145° 10' 55.5"    337 ft    27.0 km
Total: 7626.1 km*

**Low point:** *Nearly being bitten by a snake. And the bloody wind!*
**High point:** *Pen coming out to meet us.*

Trina met us the morning we left Deniliquin and she rode the last two days home on Gum. Julia rode Argee and Dick took a lot of the gear home so Bart didn't have to carry too much. I actually rode Ambrose the rest of the way but it didn't seem to matter anymore. Gum and I were still walking home together, even if I wasn't actually on his back. On the way out we went through the Kentucky Chuck drive-through to get breakfast but, although they were there roasting their little chooks in preparation for the day, they weren't open yet. We were very disappointed. They looked very confused and a little nervous, peering out the drive-through window at us as Ambrose was spinning in circles. I don't think she appreciates fast food.

On the last couple of days I think God decided to give us a farewell gift in the form of hot northerly winds, a dust storm, a thunderstorm and, you guessed it, rain. It didn't matter any more. I was over it. It could have rained 6 inches. I didn't care. I think I was cured of my ombrophobia.

On the 454th day on the road we walked through the Brigadoon gates to be met by some family and neighbours who had sandwiches and champagne in the garden while they were waiting for us. We were a little later than they anticipated so I think they had started the celebrations before we got there. It was quite surreal. All I could think was that it was over and now I would have to go back to living a normal life like everybody else. No longer would my needs consist only of the basics of food, water and shelter. No longer would the weather, seasons and terrain rule my world. No longer would I have that same relationship with my kids that you can only get by working all day, every day with them. I didn't really know how I felt about all this. I was a bit lost and had a sudden urge to retreat from the waiting crowd and take the kids out to the paddock and set up camp.

People crowded around us with glasses in hand, all chatting away and asking questions.

'So, did you have fun?' It was the holiday of a lifetime.

'Are you going to write a book?' Absolutely not. Never. What a horrific thought! No-one would be interested and I am not interested either. God! Fancy writing a book about this! I'd rather give birth to a chair.

'What are you going to do when you get back?' What I did before I left, I suppose. Oh, and pay off my new debts.

'Will you be able to go back to work?' I'll have to. No choice there, just bite the bullet. It won't be harder work than the last couple of years, that's for sure.

'Would you do it again?' Nope … never … nada … nil … no way. But Gum and I still have to do the Nullarbor.

'Have you discovered the answer to life, the universe and everything?' Well, nothing I didn't know already. Just stop chasing for the answer and live your life, that's it I suppose. Just live.

We unsaddled the kids for the last time then joined the festivities in the garden.

# Epilogue: Where are they now?

**Furphy** is still at Brigadoon following Dad's every step with an obsession that makes Imelda Marcos's shoe collection look insignificant. The operation for surgical detachment is booked for later in the year.

**Willow** semi-retired to the pony club circuit of Hughenden, where she is popular due to her rotating ears and tiny little steps.

**Argee** now lives at the Restdown Winery retreat with grapes on tap and Don and Jo attending to his every need in return for the odd bit of cattle work. He aspires to having a vintage named after him by 2015 and hopes to go to France to tour the vineyards.

**Pam** is currently terrorising tourists at Kings Canyon, carrying passengers on joy rides, much to her disgust. She is honing her haughty look to perfection. She is appalled at being exiled into semi-retirement and hopes one day she will be re-enlisted to do real work in the desert.

**Gypsy** has joined a string of seventeen pack camels in the Simpson Desert and is positioned in the centre so she doesn't have to worry about what is in front or behind her. She is surprised that she actually misses that strange little furry, white camel without a hump that she and Pam travelled with for a while and wonders if she will ever see him in another passing string.

**Tumbleweed** made it back down south, bringing the well-rested Piglet, and was sold on eBay for $3750. The proud owner drove her back up to north New South Wales but before they got there he was fined over $2000 for driving without registration or licence (I told him he should get a temporary registration). He had to have it towed to the nearest town, where somehow the motor blew up and had to be replaced for another $4000.

**Piglet** returned to Jen Moncur in Gippsland and is enjoying an illustrious career in endurance under her stage name of Elphine. Endurance enables her to fulfil her lifelong dream of passing everyone in sight and getting 'there' real fast, wherever 'there' is.

**Gillie** is still crazy, still a monster and still pointy. She is living the life of luxury with Gumby, Bart and Ambrose. Her favourite time of day is when she goes for a 30-kilometre run on a quiet road with me driving behind in the ute. She hopes one day to get back out on the road with the rest of the crew and start exploring the world again.

**Ambrose**, despite her age, refuses to retire and is still umpiring Bart and Gumby within an inch of their lives.

**Bart** retired to the paddock, never to be sold again. His pretty features would tempt anyone to buy then ride him which would invariably lead to tears and the dog meat yards yet again. He is currently seeing a hypnotherapist to address his butt issues.

**Gumby** is on the speaking circuit, doing guest appearances at pony clubs where he talks on chiropractic (and spends his time being draped in a horse spine) and packing (where he is fed hot dogs, Samboy chips and Fizz Wizz by the kids who practise putting pack saddles and gear on and off). He is currently reviewing a few movie deals from Hollywood and his autobiography, *My Life as a Camel*, will be released next June. He enjoys the quiet life back at home when he is not touring, living with Bart, Ambrose and Gillie.

RIP **Quinnie**, **Tank** and **Derek**.

# Glossary

Borrow pit – (Usually pronounced 'burra pit'.) An area where material (usually soil) has been dug up and 'borrowed' to put in another area. Often dirt roads have a borrow pit either side of them where the grader has taken soil to build the road up.

Britchin – Bart's least favourite bit of horse gear. It is a strap that goes from one side of the saddle, around the back of the horse, and attaches to the other side of the saddle. It helps to stabilise the pack and stops the saddle slipping forward. Is used in packing as well as on carriage horses, but not usually on ridden horses

Bungarra – An Aboriginal name for sand goanna. Non-Aboriginal West Australians commonly use it as a generic term for any goanna

Campdrafting – An Australian sport that involves riding a horse and cutting a single beast out of a mob, making him change directions a few times to show you are in control, then directing him go around an obstacle course. It is derived from the traditional method of drafting cattle without yards on outback properties.

Crupper – A strap that goes from the back of the saddle to around the horse's tail and stops the saddle slipping forward. Used on pack horses and on ridden horses when riding in hilly country

Donga – A term used to describe accommodation quarters or office that is usually a relocatable structure. Common in the northern areas of Australia. They can get bloody hot in summer.

Easy boots – Used instead of steel shoes to protect the horses foot from rocky country. They are made of a plastic/rubber compound and can be buggars to put on and remove, especially on a frosty morning when your fingers are frozen.

Farrier – A tradesman who trims and puts shoes on horse's feet and are often seen arguing with demanding horse owners.

Fetlock – The part of the horse's leg above the pastern that allows for flexion and extension of the lower part of the limb. For the non-horse people, it is the knobbly bit above the hoof.

Flea-bitten grey – A grey horse is usually born black, bay or chestnut and becomes grey with age. Some show a pattern of dark 'freckles' or flecks over their body as they age, lending them the name of flea-bitten grey.

Four horse gooseneck – An extended float that can carry four (or any number depending upon its setup) horses, often with limited living quarters at the front, with a towing hitch that attaches to the centre of the ute tray, rather than being towed behind on a tow ball.

Fourteen hands high – A 'hand' is a unit used in the measurement of the height of a horse and supposed to be the breadth of a human hand. It is standardised to four inches. A horse that is fourteen hands is 56 inches from the ground to the highest point of the wither. In other words, Gumby is not very big at all!

Gal – Refers to corrugated galvanised iron which was commonly used in the development of countries such as Australia from the 1840s. In rural Australia a sheet of gal can been seen to be used for just about any structure imaginable such as water tanks, windmill fans and sheep yards.

Green pick – Fresh green shoots of grass coming up through the ground, usually occurring after the first rain of the season

Grand Prix Dressage Horse – A horse that competes at the highest standard in dressage.

Hoochie – A flat, waterproof, rip-proof, light sheet used as a shelter or ground sheet at camp. Because of its simplicity it can be arranged in an infinite number of ways to suit each different campsite. Every time I set it up, it was a unique artistic masterpiece.

Inch – The old measurement of rain that is still used in rural circles. One inch is 2.54 centimetres.

Neck rein – A method of steering a horse while riding one handed. The reins touch one side of the neck and the horse turns away from the pressure. Poor old Gum never got the hang of it.

No mouth/hard mouth – A description of a horse that is not very responsive to their rider when being asked to slow down, stop or turn via the reins/bit.

Nose line – A string that goes from the camel's nose peg to the lead rope and is set to engage when the camel is reluctant to walk. If there is too much pressure on it, it acts as a weak point and breaks. For some reason Gypsy loved her nose line being attached and she would settle right down and even become quite affectionate.

Nose peg – A wooden or plastic peg placed through the nare (nostril) of the camel. It can then be attached to a nose line when the camel is being uncooperative, for finer control.

Packing – The action of travelling with pack animals.

Pannikin – A small metal cup or pan. In Australia it is usually an enamel mug used for a cup of tea.

Pastern - The part of the horse's leg just above the hoof.

Plant – Machinery, equipment and appliances used in the workplace. A drover's plant often refers to his horses, wagons, gear and dogs he travels with.

Point – The most common use of rain measurement with rural people. They resist the more modern metric measurements, I think, because it sounds like they are getting more rain in the imperial; 25 mm does not sound nearly as good as 100 points! (4 points = 1 mm, 100 points = 1 inch).

Polocrosse – An Australian sport that involves six players mounted on horses on a small field, riding like suicidal maniacs, with bamboo sticks with a net on the end, trying to take possession of a ball the size of a soft ball. It is loved by rider, horse and spectator alike.

Pony – A horse which is less than about 14 hands and 2 inches high is called a pony.

Purlin – A horizontal structural member in a roof that supports a load and usually supported themselves by the rafters

Quilty endurance ride – The Tom Quilty Gold Cup is a 100 mile (now 160 km) endurance ride originally sponsored by a man called Tom Quilty which is probably the ultimate endurance competition in Australia. They ride what would take me five days in less than 24 hours. That's the advantage of having a back up crew I suppose.

RM boots (or RMs) – The most comfortable pair of elastic-sided riding boots that ever existed. RM Williams started to make them by hand in the 1930s to help pay the expenses incurred by his sickly son.

Rut – Seasonal sexual activity of a male camel (over the winter months in Australia). Just imagine hundreds of kilos of sex-crazed, urine-drenched, drooling bull camel that will do anything to get to a woman. Don't get in the way.

Sacral – Referring to the sacrum, a section of the fused spine that joins to the pelvis.

Showing – Something I never really understood. At the risk of losing half my clients, I shall try to describe it. Showing is the horse sport where you feed your horse to the eyeballs until it is obese, decorate it to make it look very pretty and then ride in slow circles to be picked out for a ribbon by a biased judge. (This is just my opinion!)

Standardbred – A breed of horse especially chosen for its speed at the trot or pace gaits towing a sulky. They are often totally uncoordinated at the canter, usually rendering them very uncomfortable to ride.

Stifle – The joint in the back leg of a horse that is adjacent to the lower flank. A lot of people don't realise it is same joint in the body as our knee.

Stockhorse – The Australian Stockhorse is a breed of horse especially chosen for its versatility to do activities from working stock to polocrosse to endurance and showing. A stockhorse may also mean, in general, a horse used to work stock such as cattle and sheep.

Tail tie – A rope tied into the tail of a horse. It has a breakable strip of rubber and a clip at the end that hooks onto the bridle of the horse behind. This enables the horses to be lead by each other in one long string, and the rider only needs to worry about leading the first horse.

Tent pegging – A sport developed from cavalry exercises that involves various weapons and 3-inch wooden pegs hammered into the ground. It requires a person on horseback to lean over and pick up the pegs usually at a flat gallop. It is thought to be developed from the military strategy of galloping through an enemy's camp, pulling out the tent pegs with a sword or bayonet, causing them to collapse.

Thoroughbred – A breed of horse especially chosen for its speed at the gallop. They are generally regarded for their athleticism and good work ethic and are popular in many disciplines ranging from eventing to polocrosse to dressage to pony club.

Veterinary chiropractic – Chiropractic treatment of animals.

Working dog – Usually refers to a dog that works stock such as sheep or cattle either in the yards or out in the large paddocks mustering. It is often said that a good working dog is better, cheaper, easier and works harder than any stockman. The most common ones in Australia are Kelpies and Blue Heelers but I have heard of one man with a team of Boxer dogs that worked cattle.

# Acknowledgements

One can't achieve something like riding around Australia without the support of others. Yes, I rode on my own (mostly) but so many people seemed to be there in spirit, whether I invited them or not. Various friends and family members helped with the gear, horses, camels, transport and advice which made my ride possible and I am forever in their debt. I have to severely limit myself here in my acknowledgements and therefore am not doing justice to people's generosity. I am sincerely grateful for everybody's help and support. So, here goes ...

Sue jumped on board right at the start and helped me convert a silly childhood dream into a real possibility and then a reality. Jen entrusted me with her kids, Elphine (better known as Piglet) and Furphy. Trevor gave me great packing advice and James was my 'Camel Advice Hotline'. Kathy sewed up a storm with my pack bags and other gear, and Tia and Scott set up a great web site. Robyn entrusted me with her lovely Argee; Don and Jo helped me get back on the road, walking again (literally and figuratively), and Ken and Shirley delivered me essential fresh supplies and helped me transport my kids. Andrew Harper generously gave his time and expertise, as well as lending me the Pam and Gypsy team.

Cindy Barber pushed me, kicking and screaming, into writing this book (so if there are any complaints ... blame her!). Fred proofread this 'ugly monster' and was not too damning of my appalling literary skills. Julia Goudie saved my sanity and got me back on the road when I was ready to give up and crawl under the nearest rock; I have never laughed so much or had the privilege of working beside such a hard worker. There are so many other people that helped me; Mick and Laura Jarmaine, Rae and David at 'The Stables', Anissa and Ed, Helen and Jan, Peter Goudie, Big John, Jim from Granite Peak Station, Wal, Darrall Clifford ... the list goes on.

My family rose above and beyond the call of duty and I am quite sure when my brothers-in-law Tim and Dick said 'I do' they didn't realise they were committing themselves to driving across the country with their crazy sister-in-law and various animals. I am also sure that the duties of my niece, Gabby, did not include riding and working with horses when you really aren't that keen on them. Bronte diligently ploughed through my initial manuscript and Harry was my IT man. My sisters visited me and my kids, and gave me huge support from home; Sam and Tonia arrived up on the Barkly Stock Route just in the nick of time to help pick up the windblown shreds of my sanity, and Pen and Trina delivered my kids all around the country. Mum organised and posted my vital supplies to various towns everywhere, and Dad and Uncle Don turned up to rescue me and my kids in the heat and desperation of the Canning Stock Route.

I am no good with words so feel very inadequate when trying to express what Trina did for me. She never seemed to doubt I could do it (or never showed it anyway), was a huge support for me when my horses died and always propped me up when I was stumbling. How can the words 'thank you' possibly express my gratitude?

I know Mum and Dad were a bit stunned when I first announced my plans for riding around Australia. I really do appreciate the way they jumped on the crazy wagon and rode it for the whole trip. Without the knowledge that I had a family behind me all the way, I don't think I could have even embarked on such a ridiculous adventure.

**_I'll have a great big 'T', thanks Glen_**